T0280856

Android on x86

An Introduction to Optimizing for
Intel® Architecture

Iggy Krajci
Darren Cummings

Apress
open

Android on x86: An Introduction to Optimizing for Intel® Architecture

Iggy Krajci and Darren Cummings

Copyright © 2013 by Apress Media, LLC, all rights reserved

ApressOpen Rights: You have the right to copy, use and distribute this Work in its entirety, electronically without modification, for non-commercial purposes only. However, you have the additional right to use or alter any source code in this Work for any commercial or non-commercial purpose which must be accompanied by the licenses in (2) and (3) below to distribute the source code for instances of greater than 5 lines of code. Licenses (1), (2) and (3) below and the intervening text must be provided in any use of the text of the Work and fully describes the license granted herein to the Work.

(1) **License for Distribution of the Work**: This Work is copyrighted by Apress Media, LLC, all rights reserved. Use of this Work other than as provided for in this license is prohibited. By exercising any of the rights herein, you are accepting the terms of this license. You have the non-exclusive right to copy, use and distribute this English language Work in its entirety, electronically without modification except for those modifications necessary for formatting on specific devices, for all non-commercial purposes, in all media and formats known now or hereafter. While the advice and information in this Work are believed to be true and accurate at the date of publication, neither the authors nor the editors nor the publisher can accept any legal responsibility for any errors or omissions that may be made. The publisher makes no warranty, express or implied, with respect to the material contained herein.

If your distribution is solely Apress source code or uses Apress source code intact, the following licenses (2) and (3) must accompany the source code. If your use is an adaptation of the source code provided by Apress in this Work, then you must use only license (3).

(2) **License for Direct Reproduction of Apress Source Code**: This source code, from *Android on x86, ISBN 978-1-4302-6130-8* is copyrighted by Apress Media, LLC, all rights reserved. Any direct reproduction of this Apress source code is permitted but must contain this license. The following license must be provided for any use of the source code from this product of greater than 5 lines wherein the code is adapted or altered from its original Apress form. This Apress code is presented AS IS and Apress makes no claims to, representations or warrantees as to the function, usability, accuracy or usefulness of this code.

(3) **License for Distribution of Adaptation of Apress Source Code**: Portions of the source code provided are used or adapted from *Android on x86, ISBN 978-1-4302-6130-8* copyright Apress Media LLC. Any use or reuse of this Apress source code must contain this License. This Apress code is made available at Apress.com/9781430261308 as is and Apress makes no claims to, representations or warrantees as to the function, usability, accuracy or usefulness of this code.

ISBN-13 (pbk): 978-1-4302-6130-8

ISBN-13 (electronic): 978-1-4302-6131-5

Trademarked names, logos, and images may appear in this book. Rather than use a trademark symbol with every occurrence of a trademarked name, logo, or image we use the names, logos, and images only in an editorial fashion and to the benefit of the trademark owner, with no intention of infringement of the trademark.

The use in this publication of trade names, trademarks, service marks, and similar terms, even if they are not identified as such, is not to be taken as an expression of opinion as to whether or not they are subject to proprietary rights.

While the advice and information in this book are believed to be true and accurate at the date of publication, neither the authors nor the editors nor the publisher can accept any legal responsibility for any errors or omissions that may be made. The publisher makes no warranty, express or implied, with respect to the material contained herein.

President and Publisher: Paul Manning
Lead Editors: Jeffrey Pepper (Apress); Stuart Douglas (Intel)
Contributing Editor: Sarah Yost (Intel)
Coordinating Editor: Mark Powers
Cover Designer: Anna Ishchenko

Distributed to the book trade worldwide by Springer Science+Business Media New York, 233 Spring Street, 6th Floor, New York, NY 10013. Phone 1-800-SPRINGER, fax (201) 348-4505, e-mail orders-ny@springer-sbm.com, or visit www.springeronline.com.

For information on translations, please e-mail rights@apress.com, or visit www.apress.com.

About ApressOpen

What Is ApressOpen?

- ApressOpen is an open access book program that publishes high-quality technical and business information.

- ApressOpen eBooks are available for global, free, noncommercial use.

- ApressOpen eBooks are available in PDF, ePub, and Mobi formats.

- The user friendly ApressOpen free eBook license is presented on the copyright page of this book.

I'd like to dedicate this book to my mother Julie. I can never thank you enough for making me into the man that I am today. Thank you.

—Iggy

I dedicate this book to my SAIFE team - you guys are awesome!

—Darren

Contents at a Glance

Contents

About the Authors

Iggy Krajci earned his Bachelor of Science degree in computer science from the University of Advancing Technology in Tempe, Arizona. He currently is employed as a software engineer at Go Daddy in North Scottsdale, AZ, where he works on Java development. Previously, Krajci worked with SAIFE Inc. on the Android platform and its incorporation in the x86 ecosystem. In his free time, Krajci supports the open source and information technology communities by attending related conferences and releasing open source projects.

Darren Cummings is the CEO and founder of Cummings Engineering and SAIFE® Inc., with a mission to seamlessly and pervasively protect and connect the world's data, bringing security to any device, across any network, for any mission. His companies leverage their Secure Agile Interoperable Framework for the Enterprise (SAIFE) security-as-a-service to provide holistic solutions for secure communications, software and systems architecture, defense projects, secure wireless, and real-time embedded systems. Cummings holds undergraduate degrees in electrical engineering and math from Iowa State University and a Master's degree in software engineering from Walden University. Before founding SAIFE Inc., Cummings served in senior systems and software engineering roles with ViaSat, General Dynamics and the Motorola Government Group where he gained substantial telecommunications and real-time embedded project experience.

Acknowledgments

I would like to thank Sarah Yost, Jeffrey Pepper, and Javier Leija for their help with this book! I'd also like to thank Sarah's team at SAIFE Inc.: Jen Haldaman, Tayler "Pickles" Nichols, and John Curtis.

—Iggy

Thank you to my team at SAIFE Inc. Your support during the writing process has been invaluable - this book would not be a reality without you! Many thanks to Sarah Yost, for being the most dedicated editor, champion, and author-wrangler ever.

We would both like to acknowledge the Intel® Industry Education division for assisting with content architecture for this book project. Some material was provided by Intel and is used with permission. We would like to thank Ryan Cohen, Stephen Farmer, Eng Kean Lee, Robert Mueller, Dmitry Shkurko, Tao Wang, Keng Lai Yap, and Li Yuming in particular for their contributions!

—Darren

Introduction

We wrote *Android on x86: an Introduction to Optimizing for Intel® Architecture* to provide a one-stop, detailed resource for the topic's best practices and procedures. The book encompasses the installation issues, hardware optimization issues, software requirements, programming tasks, and performance optimizations that emerge when you consider programming for x86-based Android devices. Having worked on related projects ourselves, we committed to collecting our experience and information into one book which could be used as a guide through any project's specific requirements. We dove into fine-tuned optimizations, native code adjustments, hardware acceleration, and advanced profiling of multimedia applications.

The book is not dedicated solely to code, although you'll find plenty of code samples and case studies inside. Instead, we've filled *Android on x86* with the information you need in order to take advantage of the x86 architectures. We will guide you through installing the Android Software Development Kit for Intel Architectures, help you understand the differences and similarities between the processors available for commercial Android devices, teach you to create and port applications, debug existing x86 applications, offer solutions for NDK and C++ optimizations, and introduce the Intel Hardware Accelerated Execution Manager. The information we've pulled together provides the most useful help for getting your development job done quickly and well.

Why Android on x86?

In 2011, we experienced a paradigm shift in how we communicate. Smart device sales outpaced personal computer sales for the first time. This changing of the guard emerged from three sources:

- Our increasing professional and social need for open, constant communication

- The lower cost and compelling new features of smartphones and tablets

- The increased ease of use and availability of mobile apps

In the next few years, mobile access to the Internet is likely to exceed access via laptops and desktops; the hardware we use to communicate may change, but our passion for connectivity anytime, anywhere is sure to continue.

Holding more than 80% of the market share for smartphone shipments worldwide, Google's Android operating system has proven to be the leader of this mobile revolution. The key reasons for the success of Android are its open platform and flexible partnerships. The wealth of open-source resources available for Android developers spurs the creation of more apps, giving consumers more choices. In addition, the open platform supports a competitive and diverse hardware environment.

As the market for high-performing mobile devices widens, Google has teamed up with Intel to envision the next frontier for Android: getting the OS to run on devices with Intel architectures inside. The journey towards Android on Intel architectures began unofficially in 2009, when a group of developers started the open source Android-x86 initiative in order to port Android onto devices running on Intel x86 processors. Soon after, with the official Android on Intel architecture project, Intel started contributing code and resources to the Android Open Source Project (AOSP). In 2012, the first Android smartphones featuring Intel processors were released to market worldwide; by late 2013, Android smartphones and tablets with unprecedented processing power were entering United States' markets. Most recently, the two groups committed to getting Android to run on 64-bit devices, including netbooks, laptops, and traditional desktop PCs, meaning that in 2014, Android will break into a market historically dominated by Microsoft Windows and Apple OSX. Android will bring its enormous, thriving community of application developers forward to a wide range of devices and hardware architectures.

The collaboration brings a number of benefits from both groups. Intel's x86 architecture comes with 35 years of well-documented processing excellence, a mature developer ecosystem, and a sophisticated set of development tools. In terms of performance, Intel's latest chips strike a balance between high performance and low power consumption that is ideal for smartphones, tablets, and netbooks. Native x86 emulator support is a key feature of the latest Android SDK versions, and Intel is dedicated to providing developers with a host of tools for optimizing Android application performance for their chips.

By expanding onto both 32-bit and 64-bit architectures, the Android landscape is opening wide. More Android-equipped mobile devices with Intel processors are hitting shelves and our fingertips every day, and the upcoming addition of Intel-powered netbooks and laptops will shape the environment into something amazing. A new Android experience will take shape, one that remains diverse and becomes optimized for larger screens, robust multi-windowing, and ever-faster processor speeds. It's an exciting time, and we hope that developers will seize this new opportunity to expand Android's horizons.

Who Is This Book For?

This book is aimed at two general categories of people: developers and those interested in choosing Android x86 as a platform for their applications. With this in mind, the beginning chapters focus on much more high-level, nontechnical questions, so that people from all technical backgrounds can make informed choices. The later chapters focus heavily on the developers' side of the world, starting with a basic foundation of microprocessor architectures and Android development environments and then building to very advanced, performance-focused content. Our goal is to reach the entire spectrum of people who are interested in Android on x86, and to do our best at getting you the answers you need.

We really hope you enjoy the book. We certainly have enjoyed exploring this topic, and look forward to seeing what will happen in this rapidly-expanding field in the upcoming years. We would also like to note that while we may know a thing or two about Android, we recognize that we are certainly not the most knowledgeable about everything. Feel free to challenge any information that you find in this book – we encourage you to use outside resources and really involve yourself in the communities that surround this technology!

CHAPTER 1

■ ■ ■

History and Evolution of the Android OS

I'm going to destroy Android, because it's a stolen product. I'm willing to go thermonuclear war on this.

—Steve Jobs, Apple Inc.

Android, Inc. started with a clear mission by its creators. According to Andy Rubin, one of Android's founders, Android Inc. was to develop "smarter mobile devices that are more aware of its owner's location and preferences." Rubin further stated, "If people are smart, that information starts getting aggregated into consumer products." The year was 2003 and the location was Palo Alto, California. This was the year Android was born.

While Android, Inc. started operations secretly, today the entire world knows about Android. It is no secret that Android is an operating system (OS) for modern day smartphones, tablets, and soon-to-be laptops, but what exactly does that mean? What did Android used to look like? How has it gotten where it is today? All of these questions and more will be answered in this brief chapter.

Origins

Android first appeared on the technology radar in 2005 when Google, the multibillion-dollar technology company, purchased Android, Inc. At the time, not much was known about Android and what Google intended on doing with it. Information was sparse until 2007, when Google announced the world's first truly open platform for mobile devices.

The First Distribution of Android

On November 5, 2007, a press release from the Open Handset Alliance set the stage for the future of the Android platform. The alliance stated some of the goals of Android as, "fostering innovation on mobile devices and giving consumers a far better user experience than much of what is available on today's mobile platforms."

1

At that time, more than 2 billion mobile phones were used worldwide, compared to the 4.6 billion used as of 2010. However, there was no coordination of platforms between the various companies that provided mobile devices. With the introduction of Android, a single operating system removed the need for reimplementation of phone applications and middleware. The companies creating new devices could now focus much more intently on the hardware and underlying components.

But these companies weren't the only ones who benefited from the launch of Android; software developers could now release applications to multiple devices with very few changes to the underlying code base. This allowed developers to spend more time working on the applications these phones were running and create the rich and impressive applications that we are all used to. This was in part due to the open source philosophy behind Android, and the Apache license, which is the license used on most of the Android source code.

Open Source Apache License

The Apache License is just one of many different licenses that exist in the open source community. While there are differences in all of these licenses, they all facilitate the same open source mindset that is best summed up as follows:

> *"Free software" is a matter of liberty, not price. To understand the concept, you should think of "free" as in "free speech," not as in "free beer."*

> —Richard M. Stallman

The Apache License specifically grants freedom to use the software for any purpose, as well as the ability to distribute, modify, or distribute modified versions. The Apache License is also permissive, meaning that modified versions do not have to succumb to the Apache License. For more information about the Apache License, go to `http://www.apache.org/licenses/LICENSE-2.0`.

What Is Android?

So what exactly is Android? Android OS is the open source technology stack that runs on over 400 million devices worldwide. This technology stack consists of various components that allow developers and device manufacturers to work independently. This can be broken into five primary pieces—applications, application frameworks, native libraries, Android runtime, and the Linux kernel—as shown in Figure 1-1.

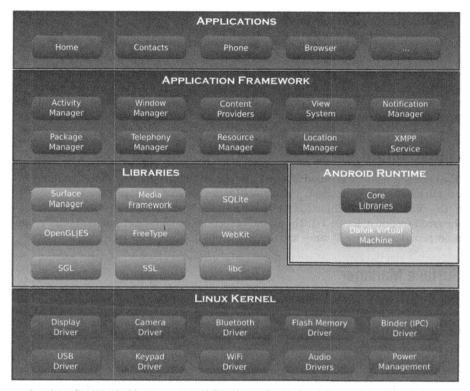

Android OS (Wikipedia) http://en.wikipedia.org/wiki/File:Android-System-Architecture.svg

Figure 1-1. *The Android System Architecture*

Applications

The applications exist at the highest level. These are the tools that everyone who uses Android is most familiar with. Android comes with various robust applications that support everyday phone needs, such as messaging, e-mail, Internet browsing, and various third-party applications. These applications are primarily written in the Java programming language. In a recent legal case with Oracle, Google's Android chief Andy Rubin explained why he chose Java as the language of use for developers. Rubin's primary points were that Java had a well-known brand name and that Java is taught in almost all universities worldwide.

These applications are distributed through various means, most commonly from the Google Play Store (formerly Android Marketplace); however, the Android OS also supports installation of applications over a USB connection and from an SD card.

3

Application Frameworks

Android provides developers the ability and tools to create extensive, interactive, rich graphical applications to users, and is targeted to deploy these applications to the Google Play Store. Developers have access to the same APIs that are used inside of core applications, as well as access to almost all existing Java libraries. For the development process of Android applications, consult **Chapter 6: Installing the Android SDK for Intel Application Development.**

Native Libraries

The next level is where the road diverges. The native libraries and the Android runtime exist in roughly the same space. The native libraries are compiled and preinstalled C/C++ binaries that the Android system depends on. These include all of the libraries in the green section of Figure 1-1. The following sections contain descriptions of some of the more prominent native libraries and their functions inside of Android.

Surface Manager

This is often referred to as Android's Window Manager. Surface Manager is used for composing what any individual screen will look like. It also does some more subtle things that help Android run smoothly, such as off-screen buffering and transitions.

SQLite

This is a database used to persist information across sessions of an Android device. On Android, the SQLite database is stored inside of the device's internal memory so SD cards can be interchanged without losing device-specific information.

WebKit

WebKit allows for HTML to be rendered and displayed to Android very quickly and efficiently. This is the default browser engine in the Android system and is available to system and third-party applications.

OpenGL/ES

The OpenGL engine processes graphics in Android. OpenGL can render both 2D and 3D objects on Android. This also supports hardware acceleration on devices with dedicated graphic chips.

Android Runtime

Inside of the Android runtime are two primary components: the core Java libraries that Android provides, and the Dalvik virtual machine. The Dalvik virtual machine is Google's implementation of Java that is optimized to be used on mobile devices. The more specific differences within Dalvik are very technical and aren't covered in this book.

Linux Kernel

The last of the layers is the Linux kernel. Android was initially based on the Linux 2.6 kernel, with some optimizations for mobile use. Current versions of Android are based on the Linux 3.1 kernel. The Linux kernel provides access as close to the hardware as possible. As a result, drivers are written in the kernel space to operate as fast and as efficiently as possible. These include things like controlling the internal radios, turning on the stereo and camera, dealing with power and battery charging, and operating the physical keyboard or buttons on the device. The Linux kernel, like Android, is an open source project and is used widely, particularly on servers in enterprise environments.

The Open Handset Alliance

In November 2007, the Open Handset Alliance (OHA) was established by 34 founding members dedicated to development of open mobile standards, including Google, mobile device manufacturers, application developers, embedded systems developers, and commercialization companies. The goal of this alliance as described in the web site is as follows:

> *The Open Handset Alliance™, a group of 84 technology and mobile companies who have come together to accelerate innovation in mobile and offer consumers a richer, less expensive, and better mobile experience.*

As it stands today, OHA has 84 firms who are developing and working on the consortium's main and only project to date, Android. Thanks to the services and products offered by members of the OHA, devices and related services are produced at higher quality for a lower price.

Android Open Source Project

After the purchase of Android, Inc., the Android Open Source Project (AOSP) was created and has since been led by Google. The AOSP is in charge of the development and maintenance of the Android software stack. As stated by Google, the goal of the project is as follows:

> *The goal of the Android Open Source Project is to create a successful real-world product that improves the mobile experience for end users.*

Android is designed and maintained with backward capability in mind. This means that new devices can run applications developed all the way back to Android's Cupcake (1.5). Official support for the Android SDK only goes back to Cupcake (1.5), so applications written for pre-Cupcake devices aren't guaranteed to run on the latest Android devices.

Through the course of the AOSP, there have been many different versions of Android released for mobile devices. When new Android versions are released, mobile device owners are allowed to choose whether to upgrade their OS. With every iteration of Android, a new SDK is made available to developers and various new features are added to supported devices. Software developers need to stay mindful of the legacy features from previous versions when developing new applications.

Astro (1.0)

Astro is where Android started, released as a beta in November 2007, and released to the public in September of 2008 on the HTC Dream. Astro showed off various core features of the Android OS and included many of the apps that Android users now know and love. These include Android Market, a web browser, e-mail/Gmail, Google Maps, Messaging, Media Player, YouTube, and various others.

Cupcake (1.5)

Cupcake, released April 30, 2009, was the next major version of Android to hit the commercial markets. Cupcake was based on the Linux kernel 2.6.27 and included many new features to users and developers. The major changes were support for virtual keyboards, support for widgets on the home screen, animations added in various places, and auto-pairing and stereo support for Bluetooth-capable devices. On a humorous side note, from Cupcake and onward all Android versions to date have been named after desserts.

Donut (1.6)

On September 15, 2009, Google released Android version 1.6, named Donut. With Donut came an updated Linux kernel from 2.6.27 to 2.6.29, as well as some new features and supported devices. Major features included voice and text search of contacts/web/bookmarks, support for WVGA screens, and improvements to camera functionality and speed. Donut was the last version of Android in the 1.x series to be released.

Éclair (2.0/2.1)

Éclair was released October 26, 2009, which continued to be built on the Linux kernel version 2.6.29. With SDK version 2.0 came many new features and capabilities for both developers and consumers. Large changes were made to the way that Android looked and felt on capable devices, including significant speed improvements in many different applications. The premier device for Android 2.0 was Motorola's Droid on Verizon Wireless.

On December 3, 2009, Google updated Android to version 2.0.1 in efforts to fix some small bugs and update the API for developers. It wasn't until January 12, 2010 that Android was moved to version 2.1. Similar to the update in December, version 2.1 primarily included updates to the underlying API and bug fixes.

Froyo (2.2.x)

On May 20, 2010, the Android SDK version 2.2 (Froyo) was released with Linux kernel 2.6.32. Google's Nexus One was the first device on the market to show off Froyo and its new capabilities. Very significant features were added to Froyo, including Adobe Flash support, Android Cloud to Device Messaging, Wi-Fi hotspot functionality, and significant performance optimizations. It's important to note that the Android SDK recommends choosing Froyo as your base development version to hit the largest current user base of Android users.

Three subsequent updates were released for the Android 2.2 SDK: 2.2.1 on January 18, 2011, 2.2.2 on January 22, and 2.2.3 on November 21. These updates were primarily bug fixes and security updates to Android.

Gingerbread (2.3.x)

Gingerbread was released on the December 6, 2010 and was based on the Linux kernel 2.6.35. Similar to the Froyo release, Google's Nexus S was introduced to show off Gingerbread. Features of Gingerbread include support for WXGA and other extra-large screen sizes, improvements to the virtual keyboard, support for more internal sensors (namely gyroscopes and barometers), support for multiple and front-facing cameras, and the ability to read Near Field Communication (NFC) tags.

Five updates were released to Gingerbread, 2.3.3–7, from February to September of 2011. With these updates came various features, security updates, and bug fixes. One of the most significant features introduced was Open Accessory support, which lets a compatible device function as an USB peripheral to compatible software platforms.

Honeycomb (3.x)

In February of 2011, Honeycomb, the first tablet-only Android version, was released on the Motorola Xoom. Because Honeycomb was created specifically for tablet devices, Android was tweaked to allow for a more enjoyable experience with larger screen real estate. This included a redesign of the onscreen keyboard, a system bar to allow for quick access to notifications and navigation, multiple browser tabs to allow for easier use of the web, and support for multi-core processors.

Honeycomb has had six updates, two of which were major, through its current life cycle. The first update was Android SDK version 3.1 on May 10, 2011, and it namely added support for USB accessories such as keyboards, joysticks, and other human interface devices (HIDs). The second major SDK update was 3.2 on July 15, 2011. The most significant feature of 3.2 was compatibility display mode for Android applications that were not designed for tablets. The last four updates to Honeycomb have been minor improvements, bug fixes, and security updates.

Ice Cream Sandwich (4.0.x)

Ice Cream Sandwich (ICS) was released on October 19, 2011 and was based on the Linux kernel 3.0.1. Samsung's Galaxy Nexus was the device released with ICS as it hit public markets. ICS was packed with a multitude of features and improvements to the Android user interface (UI). Some features include a customizable launcher, a tabbed web browser, facial recognition to unlock the device, a built-in photo editor, hardware acceleration of the UI, and software buttons originally introduced in 3.x (Honeycomb). It is important to note that ICS merged version 3.x (Honeycomb) and 2.3.x (Gingerbread) into a single OS supporting both phones and tablets.

Four minor updates have since been released for ICS devices from November of 2011 to March of 2012. These updates focused on stability improvements, camera performance, and bug fixes.

Jelly Bean (4.1.x)

Jelly Bean was released on July 9, 2012 and is based on the Linux kernel 3.1.10. Asus' Nexus 7 tablet device was the flagship user of Jelly Bean. Jelly Bean released a number of improvements and performance upgrades to the UI and audio within Android. Version 4.2, released on November 13, 2012 and based on Linux kernel 3.4.0, added accessibility improvements. Version 4.3 was released on July 24, 2013, and added OpenGL ES 3.0 support for better game graphics, security enhancements, and upgraded digital rights management APIs. Other features of the Jelly Bean versions include customizable keyboard layouts, expandable notifications, application-specific notification filtering, and multichannel audio.

KitKat (4.4.x)

The last version of Android as of this writing, KitKat, was released on September 3, 2013. Its features included performance optimizations for devices with less RAM, expanded accessibility APIs, wireless printing capability, and a new experimental runtime virtual machine, called ART, which may come to replace Dalvik. KitKat debuted on Google's own Nexus 5 smartphone on October 31. 2013.

Overview

With all of these versions of Android, the features and changes to the OS have led to a rich and user-centered experience. The average user, who knows little to nothing about the technical aspects of the device, can operate the device like it is second nature. Now that you have acquired more insight into the underlying systems and architectures that make this possible, the only thing left to ask is, what's next?

■ ■ ■

CHAPTER 2

The Mobile Device and Operating System Landscape

50 billion connected devices by 2020.

—Ericsson, 2010

Networked computers. Connected devices. Mobile devices. Machine-to-machine (M2M). On-the-Go (OTG). Portable computing. Smart services. The list goes on and on. The terminology used to describe machines that send data to other machines seems to change every day. With all of these different types of devices that are seemingly similar, it's easy to confuse them.

Android is certainly not the only operating system used on devices in today's markets. Various mobile operating systems have existed, and many are still in competition with Android. Although the focus of this book is on the Android market, an understanding of the competition—iOS, Windows Phone, and so on—is important for any successful business venture and is therefore the focus of this chapter. This is best put into words by the famous Chinese general and strategist Sun Tzu, in his *The Art of War:* "If you know the enemy and know yourself, you need not fear the results of a hundred battles."

Competition in the Mobile Space

The Android operating system is a very popular choice among consumers in the current commercial market. Over 250 million Android devices are in use today. But Android is not the only choice, nor was it the first mobile operating system implemented. There are several additional mobile operating systems, including iOS from Apple, MeeGo from Intel and Nokia, Windows Phone from Microsoft, and so on. There are many differences in the implementation of these operating systems and many diverse reasons that these platforms are used. This section provides a light overview of these other mobile operating systems, by discussing their strengths and weaknesses.

iOS

Developed and distributed by Apple, Inc., iOS was originally released in 2007 on the original iPhone and iPod Touch. Next to Android, iOS is currently the closest competitor in market share for the mobile OS space. As of May 2012, Android held 50.9 percent of subscribers as opposed to the iOS platform at 31.9 percent. It is important to note that iOS was originally called iPhone OS, based on its primary launch device, the iPhone.

Overview

Unlike Android, iOS has been a closed source since its inception and has been released on a limited number of platforms. Each new version of iOS includes new iOS devices developed and manufactured primarily by Apple. iOS is based loosely on OS X, Apple's desktop operating system, which in turn is partially based on the UNIX operating system. (OSX and Linux, and therefore iOS and Android, share a common developmental ancestor in BSD Unix, an open-source UNIX operating system variant developed and released by the University of California, Berkeley).

Applications

iOS comes with various system applications such as basic phone operations, a web browser (Safari), a media player, and an e-mail client. iOS is also capable of running a wide array of third-party applications created by developers using Apple's iOS Software Development Kit (SDK). Applications have access to all of the devices peripherals, which typically include various cameras, accelerometers to detect device movement, a microphone, onboard graphics chips for hardware acceleration, and a touch screen.

There are some significant differences in the supply of third-party applications for the Android OS. In order to develop applications for iOS devices, you are required to purchase a developer's license for the SDK. Applications for iOS devices are typically written in Objective-C and typically developed in Xcode, a development environment for OS X platforms. Furthermore, applications created using the SDK are screened and validated by Apple before being sold on iOS's market. This allows Apple to stop developers from releasing applications that could potentially hurt its user base, such as malware or information stealers.

There have been situations where Apple stopped valid applications from being released. In one case, a third-party application used the device's volume buttons as an alternative to pressing the onscreen button to take a photo with the camera. After realizing this, Apple removed the application from the App Store, claiming that this feature was a "violation of Apple's policies." The third-party company removed this feature, and Apple eventually released an update to its onboard camera that included this feature.

Platforms

Devices that run iOS are developed and sold through Apple, and for this reason there is very little variation. Although this may seem limiting, the lack of diversity of hardware enables applications to be standardized. For example, since there are only a few possible screen

10

sizes and graphics hardware, application developers only have to deal with a few different situations. iOS is featured on three main platforms—iPhone, iPad, and iPod Touch.

- **iPhone**—The iPhone is Apple's version of a smartphone, originally released in January of 2007. Each new version of the iPhone includes incremental updates to the iOS as well as new major features. The iPhone features a pocket-sized device, a multitouch screen, a camera in the back (and on the front in newer versions), and a microphone for audio.

- **iPad**—Released in April of 2010, the iPad is a tablet computer created and sold by Apple. It's about the size of a standard magazine. The iPad features a much larger screen than the iPhone, as well as some upgraded hardware. Each generation of the iPad has added significant hardware upgrades as well as new features. The iPad runs the same applications as the iPhone and the iPod Touch; however, applications can be created specifically for the iPad when desired.

- **iPod Touch**—Similar to the iPhone in almost every way, the first generation of iPod Touch hit consumers' fingers in September of 2007. The primary difference between the iPod Touch and the iPhone is the lack of cellular communications on the iPod Touch. Most applications created for the iPhone run on the iPod Touch with little to no code modifications on the developer's side. The iPod Touch offers an option to play with the iOS without having to pay the subscription fee of iPhone's cellular plan, or the added cost of the iPad.

BlackBerry

Sometimes referred to as the original smartphone, the BlackBerry was introduced in 2003. BlackBerry as of Q3 2013 held three percent of the mobile smartphone market share. The original BlackBerry featured a small color screen, a full QWERTY keyboard, a trackball, and a camera. Similar to Apple's practice, BlackBerry devices are developed and manufactured in-house by Research in Motion (RIM), which was renamed BlackBerry in early 2013. The original marketing goal of BlackBerry was to create devices for the average businessperson. This focus included the ability to check e-mails, access the Internet, and set up meetings easily and efficiently.

Windows Phone

Developed by Microsoft as the successor to Windows Mobile, Windows Phone is the fourth major competitor in the mobile operating system space. Windows Phones hit the consumer market in November of 2010, and unlike Windows Mobile, were aimed away from the enterprise markets. As of Q3 2013, Windows Phone and Windows Mobile held two percent of the mobile market share. Windows Phone has a much different layout than the traditional smartphone user interface. Microsoft has placed a lot of focus on ease of use, and connectivity with existing Windows services, such as Windows Live.

Symbian

Previously called Symbian OS, Symbian was developed by Accenture, one of the largest consulting and technology services firms in the world, for Nokia. As of May 2012, Symbian has dropped to 1.1 percent, from a massive 47 percent in February of 2009. Symbian features include various applications, multitouch screen, Wi-Fi, Bluetooth, and multitasking capabilities.

MeeGo

In February of 2010, Intel and Nokia at Mobile World Congress announced their latest adventure, MeeGo. MeeGo is a Linux-based, open source operating system targeted at a wide range of mobile devices. MeeGo was designed to run on lower performance devices such as netbooks, tablets, in-vehicle infotainment devices, smart TVs, and various other embedded systems. MeeGo featured a user interface very similar to Android with an assortment of applications. In September of 2011, the MeeGo project was canceled and the Intel team brought their experience and skills to Tizen, a new joint project between Intel and Samsung.

Before Android

It may seem like an eternity since Android-enabled devices have been out in the world and in our pockets. There was, however, extensive footwork and several predecessors that lead to the creation and innovation that is Android. Although there was nothing quite like Android prior to its existence, there are obvious inspirations for its common and sought-after features.

Smartphone History

In the days before Open Handset Alliance mobile devices, the software that ran on them was developed specifically for every new phone. Some of the decisions that were made for the Android OS trace back to the phones of the early 21st Century.

Simon Personal Communicator

Many credit IBM and BellSouth's Simon Personal Communicator (1994) with being the first smartphone. Simon combined many of the features of personal digital assistants (PDAs) with the features of existing cellular devices. In addition to being able to do cellular communication, Simon had a touch screen and various applications such as a calendar, games, a notepad, a calculator, and a touch-screen keyboard. Simon jump-started the smartphone market during a computer trade show in Las Vegas where the Simon prototype unit received notable interest. The Simon prototype was so popular it was featured on the front page of *USA Today*'s Money section the day after the trade show.

Nokia 9000 (Nokia Communicator)

Similar in many ways to Simon, the Nokia 9000 introduced in 1996 continued the vision and direction of the smartphone. The Nokia 9000 featured a twofold approach—it looked like a bulky phone when closed, and revealed a full QWERTY keyboard and a larger horizontal screen when opened. Like Simon, the Nokia 9000 featured various applications that allowed for functionality beyond a regular cellular device.

Kyocera 6035

Released five years later in 2001, the Kyocera 6035 looked much more like the modern-day smartphone. When closed, the Kyocera had physical buttons for use as a dial pad. When opened, it had a much larger vertical screen that contained various applications and tools. The Kyocera featured Palm OS, which enabled e-mail and web browsing.

BlackBerry 5810

The first BlackBerry phone released by Research In Motion (RIM) was the BlackBerry 5810 (2002). It featured a look that has stayed with BlackBerry to this day. Optimized for e-mail and business use, the BlackBerry 5810 was marketed toward business professionals. Features included a large touch screen, a full QWERTY keyboard, and an internal antenna.

The Mobile Market: Success and Failure

In any developing market, new ideas and innovations can generate significant interest or turn consumers off entirely. The mobile space is no exception. Although many mobile devices have sold very well, just as many have lost significant amounts of money. This section highlights some of the more recent successful and unsuccessful mobile devices to hit commercial markets.

Motorola i1

The Motorola i1, released in June of 2010, is an example of a less-than-successful mobile device. Although it was released on Boost Mobile with no contract necessary, the i1 only managed to run Android OS v1.5 (Cupcake) and could handle only 2G data speeds. In comparison to Motorola's other devices of 2010, namely the Droid X, the i1 sold poorly.

Droid X

Released in July of 2010, the Droid X is far from a failure. The Droid X features Android OS v2.1-2.3, a 4.3-inch multitouch screen, and 8GB of internal flash memory. With the imminent release of the iPhone 4, Motorola took an aggressive marketing campaign with the Droid X, announcing the device exactly one day before the iPhone 4 hit stores. It appears to have paid off, because the Droid X sold out online and in many retail locations.

BlackBerry Torch

The BlackBerry Torch, which featured BlackBerry OS 6, was described by Research In Motion's (RIM's) CEO Jim Balsillie as "a quantum leap over anything that's out there." However, the Torch sold a mere 150,000 units in the first three days of its launch. In comparison, the Apple iPhone 3G and 3GS both sold over a million units. The Torch is a prime example of a good product in a market of very good products. Although 150,000 units is a sizable number, it meant that the BlackBerry could not sustain its market share.

iPhone

One of the most successful devices of all time, selling millions of units on almost every release, Apple's iPhone device is a prime example of market success. Focusing on ease of use and presentation, the iPhone offers a different mobile experience. Apple's marketing focus for the iPhone can be described as simple, using Apple's logo as a means of capturing past iPod fans.

The Mobile Market: Trends

Although no guarantee can be made for the future, visible trends can help predict where the market will go next. The mobile space is no exception to these trends; in fact, in some cases they are even more easily recognizable. The connection between mobile devices and their users is an evolving situation that is creating a world of new possibilities. This "cyber fiber" allows users to be connected to the world around them at all times.

Location

Most modern devices have some sort of GPS or other method of locating where you are in the world. Many of the more popular applications have utilized this feature to encourage users to use their devices on the go. Whether you are checking the current temperature, tagging your location in a Facebook update, or trying to find your way back home, location services are being used more and more frequently.

With the release of iOS 5, Apple introduced location to its core operating system. For example, when you pass by a certain location, your mobile device can remind you that you need to pick up groceries. The appeal of this feature is obvious—instead of having to think of a specific time, you can now be reminded the next time you pass a drugstore that you need to pick up more aspirin. Building location features into applications is a current hot button for developers in all areas of smartphone development.

Current Mobile Uses

With Android, and all of the other operating systems, users have what feels like unlimited options for what to do with their mobile devices. But how are consumers using their devices, and how much time do they spend on them?

According to a Pew Internet & American Life study in May of 2013, 56 percent of all American adults are now smartphone users. The two most common uses of mobile phones are browsing the Web and searching for specific information, both of which account for a solid majority of all time spent on the device. Facebook and YouTube hold a very significant amount of this traffic, with Facebook having over 800 million mobile users as of 2013.

Of all smartphone owners, about 59 percent spend more than 30 minutes every day using web applications and utilities on their smartphones. However, the percentage of people actually communicating over phone calls and texting during a 30-minute period each day is much lower, at 32 percent. As our phones' applications have gotten richer, there has been a shift from old forms of communication like phone calls to newer social messaging formats such as Facebook, Twitter, and MySpace.

Commerce

Since mobile devices can do practically anything a laptop or home computer can do, it was only a matter of time until mobile devices were used directly for commerce. Whether it's buying new products from Amazon, purchasing applications from an App Store, or buying tickets for the game on Sunday, mobile devices have become a way to purchase goods and services on the go.

The mobile commerce market is in its infancy. Experts believe that the amount we spend from our phones will increase from just under a billion U.S. dollars to well over 99 billion by 2015.

Overview

The "cyber fiber" that is connecting modern society is very evident. Our mobile devices let us connect with the world at any time and in any place. The applications and operating systems that let us access this rich environment so easily act as the glue holding our world together. The next chapter discusses in detail how Android devices interact with existing technologies and what kinds of interfaces developers can use.

■ ■ ■

CHAPTER 3

Beyond the Mobile App—A Technology Foundation

In this business, by the time you realize you're in trouble, it's too late to save yourself. Unless you're running scared all the time, you're gone.

—Bill Gates

Mobile devices are connected and involved in so much more of our life than just simple communications. Connected devices are all around us: Wi-Fi photo frames, Bluetooth receivers in automobiles, and even wireless headphones. These devices allow us to stay up-to-date and engaged with all of our surroundings in a way that has never been seen before. Mobile phones allow us to interact with the world in a whole new way.

Connected Devices

As predicted by Kirk Skaugen, Corporate Vice President of Intel, over 15 billion devices will be connected to the Internet in the coming years. The Internet currently supports more than 4 billion connected devices, allowing for practically nonstop communication.

The low prices of computer chips that power these connections have enabled a wave of connected devices. Devices that previously did not have wireless functionality now do, and that has changed how we interact with them. For example, modern televisions include wireless chips that allow them to receive streamed television and movies directly over the Internet.

Home Computing

It may feel like old news, but home computing is still a very legitimate and lucrative business. In a study conducted by U.S. Energy Information Administration, just fewer than 30 million Americans do not have a home computer of some kind. Compared to the 80 million Americans who have one or more personal computers, the United States is more connected than ever before.

Applications on personal computers have come a long way since the creation and induction of smartphones into the marketplace. The ability to use and control your home computer from your smartphone, and vice versa, has taken off. You can view your desktop on the go, sync files and contacts from your phone to your laptop, use your phone as a remote control, or stream videos from your phone directly to your television.

Automotive

Modern cars are loaded with tons of new technologies. You can watch television in the back seats, stream music over Bluetooth, or make a hands-free call to anyone in the world.

Smartphones have added even more functionality to the vehicles that we rely on daily. The ability to make a hands-free call over Bluetooth is often included in modern smartphones. This capability allows you to communicate with others while you are on the road—legally. GPS is another application inside of vehicles that is being used on smartphones. You no longer need a separate GPS device to map your route, which has significantly hurt the standalone GPS device market. Porting all of the functionality of these devices directly onto a smartphone adds convenience and ease of use. In addition, you can stream music to your vehicle's speaker over the auxiliary port, find the cheapest gas in the city that you are passing through, and find things to do that are happening right now.

Applications that interact directly with automobiles are just starting to take off. As mobile phones get more powerful and vehicles are released with more technological interfaces, new smartphone applications will be created for this purpose.

Digital Entertainment

A new age of digital entertainment is upon us. The connected nature of the modern world has created new possibilities and uses for entertainment devices and services. There are now multiple ways to stream television, movies, and music over the Internet, whenever you want. The entertainment industry embraces and encourages these services, often offering on-demand content for a subscription fee.

With the addition of these capabilities, smartphone application developers created new uses for mobile phones. You can use your mobile phone as a television remote, as a media center that plays movies from the HDMI port on select devices, or as a portable media player that streams music from the radio.

Special Requirements

The public side of the market is not the only place that smartphones are used. There are many military and private-sector uses for modern communication devices. Whether they are specially built hardened devices, extra-long range capabilities, or top-secret level communications, there are many special requirements for these types of devices.

Ruggedization

Sometimes also called *hardening*, *ruggedization* involves altering a device so that it can be used in more intense conditions than regular users might encounter. Used often in military applications, these devices might be needed underwater, in sandstorms, or in rain, or might need to survive impact after falling from great distances. Technical specifications document exactly what these devices must be able to handle in order to be licensed for military applications.

Ingress Protection Rating

The Ingress Protection (IP) Rating Code is a standard that classifies the degree of protection against outside forces. The IP Code standard specifies that each classification contain two characters representing its degree of physical and liquid protection. If there is no protection, an X is placed in that spot.

The first digit is its protection against solid particles and objects. The highest rating that you can get on the first character is a 6. Scoring a 6 means that the device has complete protection against damage from contact, as well as no ingress to dust. The second character describes the protection against liquids, specifically water. The highest water rating is an 8, specifying that the device can be fully submersed beyond one meter for any length of time without sustaining internal damage.

IP Codes are just one of the various standards for classifying protection. Inside of the United States there also exists the National Electrical Manufacturers Association (NEMA), which publishes protection ratings. Outside the United States, there are extensions of the IP Code specification, as well as entirely new systems. For example, the German standard called IP69K rates high-pressure and high-temperature situations.

Medical

The medical world has its own list of requirements. The information and use of medical data must be confidential. In the United States, patient-doctor confidentiality is taken very seriously and these devices must be protected. At select hospitals across the country, Android tablets operate with and contain sensitive information. A patient's electronic medical record (EMR) contains the patient's entire medical history, which is sensitive information.

To protect these devices, information is encrypted and locked. Password authentication is required to use the device, as well as possible secondary forms of authentication to ensure identity. These devices also feature screens and designs to make the lives of medical professionals easier. This often means large, easy-to-read screens, with applications specifically catered to medical situations.

Virtualized

Hardware is expensive and creating virtual platforms on a single hardware device has become a common practice. This saves money and resources, because you can replace virtual instances at any time without touching the hardware. Virtual instances also let you interface with systems without needing any sort of specific hardware. For example, virtual Android devices that run on the Android Emulator allow users to interact with it as if the application were deployed on the actual device.

Secure Communications

Keeping military communications secure has always been a challenge. Sending and receiving secure communications in the field is a very difficult problem. The ability to talk securely is a powerful advantage over opposing forces. The difficulty of secure communication is a multipart problem with few answers. You must establish a method of encrypting, decrypting, and transmitting your communications with as little delay as possible. In addition, you must offer some means for determining who to trust and who not to trust.

Because of all of these complications, the hardware and software used in the military is often years behind consumer-grade products. On Android devices, companies have been working to develop secure communications that will be used on the battlefield, as well as in government buildings.

Type 1

The National Security Agency (NSA) has certified a Type 1 device, or system, for use with secure information. Type 1 certification is a rigorous process that involves extensive testing and formal analysis. Some of the areas of analysis include cryptographic security, tamper resistance, manufacturing, and emissions testing.

Federal Information Processing Standard

A Federal Information Processing Standard (FIPS) certification grants software and computer systems access to use sensitive and highly classified information. There are different classifications of FIPS that deal with different standards. For example, FIPS 46-3 is the code for the United States Data Encryption Standard (DES), whereas FIPS 197 deals with the Advanced Encryption Standard (AES).

The Cyber Fiber of Our Connected World

The modern world has become very dependent on constant connectivity, and it's easy to forget just how many forms of connection exist. These methods of connection all have different benefits and restrictions. It is important to have a solid technical understanding of how these methods operate, in order to find the correct match for your business's needs.

Cellular Networks

Cellular networks are incredibly technical and complicated systems; even small networks require specialized hardware and software. Cellular networks transfer data from point to point through the use of cellular towers. There are two major communication protocols of cellular networks—Global System for Mobile Communications (GSM) and Code Division Multiple Access (CDMA). These protocols allow multiple types of data to be streamed from one device to another. Their data includes voice calls, Short Message Service (SMS), and Multimedia Messaging Service (MMS). The Open Mobile Alliance (OMA) standardized the technical details and specifications for many of the protocols and services provided on cellular networks.

Open Mobile Alliance

The Open Mobile Alliance was formed in June of 2002 and acts as a standards body for the mobile phone industry. The OMA is responsible for the maintenance and creation of many standards within the mobile space, and works with various standards bodies. Some of the more notable are the 3rd Generation Partnership Project (3GPP), the 3rd Generation Partnership Project 2 (3GPP2), the Internet Engineering Task Force (IETF), and the World Wide Web Consortium (W3C).

Wireless Communications

Wireless communications transfer data between two or more endpoints that have no physical connection. The distance of this connection can be as short as a few inches or as far as hundreds of thousands of miles. Many forms of wireless communication exist, the most popular of which are Wi-Fi, Bluetooth, and radio frequency (RF). Each method has distinct benefits and issues.

Wi-Fi

Wi-Fi is available on almost every electronic communication device produced today; it allows for data connections from a Wireless Access Point (WAP). Wi-Fi networks have ranges of between 120 feet (36 meters) and 300 feet (91 meters), depending on the environment. The two major types of Wi-Fi in common use are 802.11b and 802.11g. Most Android devices support Wi-Fi that connects to the Internet and to local networks. When using Wi-Fi on Android devices, any cellular data connection will be suspended until connectivity is lost or until Wi-Fi is disabled. Using Wi-Fi on an Android device generally means a much faster connection speed with less latency.

Bluetooth

Bluetooth is similar to Wi-Fi, but is a newer wireless technology created in 1994 by the telecommunications vendor Ericsson. It's good for transferring data over short distances with high levels of security. Bluetooth devices operate primarily by pairing, focusing on one-to-one communication. Security is increased by requiring physical intervention during the pairing process to ensure that the user has access to both sides of the device. Bluetooth supports direct data transfer, and because of the short range and the higher data speeds, typical Bluetooth devices act as interfaces or controllers to existing systems. These systems include headsets, keyboards, mice, and mobile devices.

Most modern Android devices are Bluetooth-enabled, with Bluetooth 2.0 or greater support. These Android devices can stream music, chat from phone to phone, and even create Internet hotspots using Bluetooth. When using Bluetooth, Android allows your enabled device to act as either a server or a client.

Mobile Interfaces

The way we communicate with our mobile devices has changed over the years as new technologies have been integrated into smartphones. Instead of just a simple physical dial pad with some sort of display, modern phones contain multitouch screens, vibration motors, LED notification lights, sophisticated noise detection, speakers, accelerometers, and physical buttons. Android developers provide these technologies using the Android SDK.

Touch Screens

Full-color touch screens are a newer, popular technology that has taken over the smartphone market. The best touch screens used in mobile devices support high resolution, multiple touches, and non-scratch covers. There are two primary types of touch screen currently used in the mobile space—capacitive and resistive.

Capacitive

The capacitive touch screen is composed of an insulator, typically glass, which is coated in a conductive material. When a finger touches the surface, the electronic field is distorted, and the capacitance is measured to find the location of the press. As a result of this technology, the screen is quite accurate and requires only the slightest touch. The most notable downside to capacitive screens is the requirement for some sort of electronically conductive material to operate the screen. This means that styluses must be conductively enabled in order to work (and so must your gloves)!

Resistive

Resistive touch screens, as the name implies, have two flexible sheets covered in a resistive material. One of the sheets has sensors running horizontally and the other sheet has sensors running vertically. When the screens make contact, the exact point is located based on which lines crossed. Any object can operate resistive touch screens; however, the amount of force required is much greater and precision is less accurate than with capacitive touch screens.

Apple Inc. has chosen to use only capacitive touch screens for all of its products that employ touch screens. Within the Android device market space, device manufacturers have been split on their choices between capacitive and resistive.

Vibration Motors

The touch screen is only one of many methods for interacting with a mobile device. Almost all modern smartphones have some sort of vibrating motor. The vibrating motor consists of a smaller electric motor with a weight purposely attached in an unbalanced fashion. When the motor attempts to spin, the off-balanced nature of the weight causes the device to shake and vibrate. In Android, developers have full access to the motor and can at any time turn it on and off.

LED Lights

Modern smartphones contain one or more lights that can be used as a secondary means of notification. On the Droid 2 for example, the light is illuminated green after an unread text message is received and blue for changes to the radio status. The light color and status can be modified at will by any Android developer.

Accelerometer

Many modern smartphones include onboard-embedded accelerometers. An *accelerometer* is an electronic chip that measures acceleration in one or many directions. The Android OS uses the built-in accelerometer as a means of detecting screen orientation. Third-party developers have expanded on this technology by developing applications that use the measurements as a form of input.

Tilt Sensor

Similar in many ways to the accelerometer, the tilt sensor is an embedded device contained in some modern smartphones. A tilt sensor is used in the Android OS as an alternative to an accelerometer to determine the device's current orientation.

Hardware Buttons

In addition to the touch screen, many phones have physical buttons that allow for quicker access to tasks like adjusting the volume, putting the phone to sleep, returning to the home screen, and using the camera. When an Android application has the focus of the device, these buttons can generally be reprogrammed to act as input for the specified application. For example, inside of many media applications, the volume buttons change to adjust the volume of the media controller instead of the phone's ring volume.

Overview

Android devices are much more than just communication and entertainment devices. They are used in many different ways, such as interaction with standard personal computers, control of our vehicles, interlacement with digital entertainment systems, and much more. The potential extends beyond the general consumer market. To accommodate all the possible situations that these devices can be used in, there are special requirements that you must address. Devices can be hardened to work in underwater and extreme duty environments, encrypted and protected for use in sensitive areas, virtualized for testing and development, and even secured for use by military forces. This is all possible because of the cyber fiber that allows devices to remain connected at all times. It's this very cyber fiber that has created the rich and ever-changing digital world of the modern age. We can interact with our devices through various mediums. The high-resolution touch screen provides responsive and accurate control; the vibration motors can inform us about new events; and the built-in sensors can detect real-time changes in device orientation. All of these interfaces, and more, are available for Android developers to use in any and every way possible.

■ ■ ■

CHAPTER 4

Android Development— Business Overview and Considerations

Data is a precious thing and will last longer than the systems themselves.

—Tim Berners-Lee

The Android Industry has its own requirements for entry. It's helpful to have a full understanding of these requirements and specifications when you're deciding whether to pursue a business venture. As discussed in previous chapters, the Android OS is already the industry leader for mobile devices, and its market share is growing with each passing year. With the introduction of x86 to the Android software stack, applications written for x86 systems are now supported, which expands the market even further.

The Android Market Share

According to International Data Corporation (IDC), Android's second quarter 2013 sales have reached 187 million units shipped. The previous record–100 million units sold–was broken by Android in 2012. These numbers bring Android up to 79 percent market share of smartphone operating systems. Compared to last year's 136 million units, Android has grown by over 74 percent. Much of Android's growth can be counted from Samsung's success in the last quarter, with over 39 percent of the smartphone manufacturing market share. IDC's senior analyst Kevin Restivo had this to say about Android's success:

> *The share decline of smartphone operating systems not named iOS since Android's introduction isn't a coincidence. The smartphone operating system isn't an isolated product, it's a crucial part of a larger technology ecosystem. Google has a thriving, multifaceted product portfolio. Many of its competitors, with weaker tie-ins to the mobile OS, do not. This factor and others have led to loss of share for competitors with few exceptions.*

The future of Android's market share is a much more debated topic. Some industry experts have made claims that this is the peak of Android's dominance. Experts have suggested that with the release of new iPhone models, and new iOS updates, Apple may steal the market share back from Google over the coming years. Others claim that this is just the start, best stated by John Koetsier:

> *Android is a train that has left the station, and it is stopping for no one. The number of Android phones sold in this quarter alone is greater than the total number of smartphones of all kinds sold in the entire year of 2007.*

It is hard to say what the future of the smartphone operating system market looks like. No one can say for sure, but how does success in market share translate of profits? With Android being a free and open source platform, how is Google making money from it?

How Android Makes Money

Google is a giant successful company; there is no denying it. But how does Google make money from the Android project? Apple charges not only for their operating system, but also for upgrades and applications. Google's strategy is in line with their primary company revenue streams, *advertisement.*

Google has various avenues for collecting money from Android and its software stack. To start with, Google collects money from Android through advertising in the browser, and in its Google Play store. This advertising avenue may seem small; however, this is where the majority of Google's money is made. Google also takes royalties from applications on Google Play, and charges for adding content to the Google Play store.

The industry leader makes billions of dollars in revenue each year from advertising on Google sites, and on networked "partner" sites through AdSense. In Q3 of 2012, Google's total advertising revenue was over 14 billion dollars. Larry Page, Google's CEO, put Google's mobile business on an 8 billion dollar run rate. This has grown by almost three times the amount since last year's 2.5 billion dollar run rate. Page did not further break down what sections this revenue was coming from; he only commented on the growth saying, "users paying for content and apps in Google Play." Google's SVP and CFO Patrick Pichette commented on the growth saying, "clearly we don't break down the categories. Ads continue to be the bulk of the 8 billion—the vast majority of it."

Why Android Is Successful

What is it exactly that makes Android so successful and commercially viable? Some experts claim that it's the powerful financial companies that sit behind its products; others claim that it's the backing of the open source community and the free sharing mindset; and yet others claim it's the features and the extensive development capabilities. It is hard to find a single reason, but much easier to point out the areas of success.

Free

Android has always been, and will always be, free. This enables massive bonuses for all parties involved. Manufacturers can build hardware with confidence that the Android stack will be free, developers can write applications without needing to worry about complex platform costs, and researchers can find flaws and improve the underlying systems without needing to purchase licenses and agreements.

Open Source

The open source community is a gigantic collection of developers and likeminded individuals who believe that sharing information can lead to stronger and better products. Android is a child of this community, and has been open sourced thanks to Google. This allows programmers from all over the world to contribute and extend the software that they use every day.

Customization

The Android software stack allows you to personalize your device to the point that you feel comfortable. You can change the colors, the way your phone responds to notifications, remove and add applications, and even change the way you secure your device. This level of customization allows users to enjoy and utilize the device to its fullest potential.

Application Base

The Google Play store has over 1 million Android applications available at various prices. These applications can use the device in any way a developer can imagine. In comparison to iOS's App Store, the Google Play store consists of predominantly free applications. This is a primary reason the Apple App Store generates higher revenue. With this in mind, the Google Play store outpaced the Apple App Store for number of apps downloaded in the second quarter of 2013. Developers can earn revenue from advertising inside of the applications, which allows consumers to use the applications free of cost.

Hardware Choices

Unlike the other mobile operating system choices, Android has the largest selection of devices to choose from. There are over 3,900 Android devices that exist in the market right now. Consumers can find a device that has all of the features that they need. These choices also cover all of the major cellular service providers in the United States, and European countries, providing greater outreach.

Device Price

Android devices offer various price points for users. Consumers can choose how much they want to pay for an Android device based on the features that are important to them. Some third-party cellular service providers offer Android devices on pay-as-you-go plans.

For much higher prices and service contract packages, the latest and greatest Android devices are available. The more money you spend, the greater the hardware and features your device will contain.

Legacy and Future Platform Support

Android has been commercially available for five years, and has produced a multitude of software versions and hardware platforms. With the robustness of the platform, Android must make choices about how to deal with past versions, as well as future revisions. Backward compatibility is a problem that all large platforms face.

Legacy Support

Android, from version 1.5 and upward, is packaged onto hardware platforms, and exists in commercial markets. Software for Android is fully backward compatible. This means that applications built for version 1.5 can be used to their full extent on version 4.2 devices. This alleviates some concerns that developers have about losing market share in new devices. It is important to note, however, that this compatibility does not utilize the new features of Android. For the best quality and functionality, applications should be rewritten for new versions.

Android also has some interesting hardware requirements. In order to gain Google's Android stamp of approval, manufacturers must meet certain qualifications like having a cellular radio, GPS capabilities, and Wi-Fi chips. However, many of the things users take for granted are not mandated or regulated. This list includes screen size, screen resolution, internal storage size, GPU speed, and even processor specifications. This provides manufacturers the freedom to create high-powered devices, cheap consumer friendly devices, and anything in between.

Future Support

Google's strategy for Android's future releases is catered toward backward compatibility and engaging the largest market share. New versions of Android will have mechanisms for running applications developed years before. It is important to note that new applications cannot run on old systems. If you use the Android Software Development Kit version 4.1 to develop an application, that application cannot run on a 2.3 Android device. However, an application that is written for a 2.3 Android device will run without modification on a 4.1 device.

Why x86 and Android Are Right for You

Android and the x86 family is a business with low barriers to entry and significant probability of success. These low entry requirements give even the smallest companies the opportunity to be successful, mainly because startup costs are minimal. The question is not whether Android and x86 are right for you, but rather what steps you need to take to be successful.

Cross Compatibility

The x86 architecture offers a diverse network of systems deployed in many industries. From cash registers, to televisions, to mobile devices, and even major utility control systems, x86 platforms are everywhere. Few industries in the world exist that don't have the x86 architecture incorporated in some manner. With the combination of the Android platform, the outreach is even larger.

Applications written for Android will run on all Android devices that are the same version, regardless of the underlying processor. This means that applications written and tested on ARM Android devices require little to no effort to be used to their full capabilities on Intel x86 Android devices. The exception to this is applications that use Android's NDK. However, with a simple recompile, the application should be up and running. For more information about software migration, refer to **Chapter 7: Creating and Porting NDK-based Android Applications.**

Barrier to Entry

Economically speaking, to use Joe S. Bain's classic definition, "a *barrier to entry* is an advantage of established sellers in an industry over potential entrant sellers, which is reflected in the extent to which established sellers can persistently raise their prices above competitive levels without attracting new firms to enter the industry."

Barrier to entry is the reason why many companies can aggressively dominate certain industries. For example, the oil industry has an incredibly high barrier to entry. The cost of starting a successful oil company is outrageously high, since you are required to have so many resources and tools to compete with the existing leaders.

The Android industry has a very low barrier to entry. The costs and requirements to create a successful business in the Android space are much lower than most other technical industries. The largest challenges involve finding a product idea and building a development team. With a strong idea and a foundational team, success is only a matter of development and marketing. Indeed the costs are low enough that even individuals can succeed in this marketplace.

Security of Android

Security, when it comes to software systems, is often of much deeper concern to the provider than the customer. A good security system can be explained in depth, without being compromised. Android is one of these systems. The security that surrounds the platform and its components is well documented and researched. For more information and technical details about the system, consult *Android on x86 Security Guide.*

Application Security

With the introduction of an application market, Android's security model has grown incredibly complex. Android must secure its own applications and also provide some level of security for third-party applications. Its security system must be simple enough that the average user can understand the applications, and it must allow the users to decide whether or not to use them.

Android's solution to the problem was to use *permissions*. In order to access certain functions of a device, you must register for the related permission. For example, to use data or Wi-Fi services in the application, you must register to use the Internet permission. When the application is displayed to the users, the different permissions are displayed as well. If an application attempts to use a feature without registering for the permission, the application simply crashes.

Another major section of application security is the separation of information between applications. If an application can freely interact with other applications on the phone, malicious things can occur. There are various situations when users need applications to be able to send messages to each other. Android's inner-application messaging system uses the concept of *intents* to relay information across the operating system.

An intent is simply a free-form message produced by an application and handed to Android. These messages can have various types of data, and come in two primary flavors. An *implicit intent* is a message that exists for any application that can access it. For example, on many Android applications, when you click a link, a window appears, letting you choose from all several applications that can view the site. In the background, the application fired an implicit intent that was then relayed to all available applications. *Explicit intents*, on the other hand, are directed at one very specific application. This intent can be seen and handled only by the application for which it was crafted.

Third-party applications also operate as separate users on the underlying operating system. This means that third-party applications cannot access files and resources that another application owns. The exception to this is with system applications. System applications can access all sections of the device that are required for operation.

Platform Security

The security surrounding the phone and its onboard features is a widely discussed topic. Android provides many different security features to help secure users and their data. Some of these features include screen locks, text and e-mail encryption, multiple types of passwords, and extra password prompts when you access certain sections of the device. These features verify authenticated users.

Third-party applications have also been created to aid this effort. Applications exist that can help you find your device if it is stolen, remove data from your phone, lock the device remotely, and add even more customization for the way you authenticate with the device.

Licensing

In the software development industry, licensing fees are very common. From library licensing costs, to platform licensing costs, and even device licensing costs, there are plenty of situations where you'll need to spend a little money to develop and sell products. Since Android is an open source and developer-friendly community, it aims to keep these costs low.

Android Licensing Cost

There is none. Android is open sourced under the Apache 2.0 license, which permits commercial usage, modification, and distribution absolutely free of any cost. This means that anyone can play with the Android operating system's source code, and create a whole new product out of it.

Application Licensing Cost

Creating applications for Android is a slightly more involved process. The development suite and software development kit are free to anyone who wants to download them. With these tools you can build, test, and deploy to development devices, any Android application from the source. Releasing your Android application is a different story.

Android devices can install third-party applications via USB and from the SD card, provided the option is enabled, but these mediums are not very convenient for consumers. Enter the Google Play Store, an Android application market where developers can quickly and easily upload and update applications for the entire Android population to see and purchase.

The process of selling applications in the Google Play Store is straight-forward. The first step is setting up a Google account. This gives you access to the Android development site, where you can manage your applications. Once you create your account, Google requires a one-time $25 fee to distribute applications inside of the Google Play market. You can then upload and configure your applications to distribute in the market.

Now that you have an application you want to distribute, how do you earn money, and what does that look like? To collect money from your Android application sales, you need a Google Checkout Merchant Account. Purchases of your application in the Google Play store will contribute to the your Google Wallet, which can be transferred to USD using various methods. Google does take a percentage of all your profits, based on many factors such as application sales and rate of sales.

Physical Development Costs

When you're starting off in the software business, it is important to remember that there are physical requirements for the virtual product you'll create. Unlike in traditional engineering, the thing that is being sold won't necessarily have a physical component. To create and fully test an Android application, there are a couple of physical platforms that are required.

Software Development Systems

Developers use software development systems to write the code that will run on the Android devices. The Android Software Development Kit (SDK) can run on Windows, Linux, and Mac, so choosing an operating system is up to the developer. When it comes to hardware choices, there are a couple of things to consider.

The Android SDK is a relatively large application, especially after it downloads the files needed to run the different versions of Android. Getting a hard drive large enough to hold all of the required tools and files is a must, but hard drive speed is also a serious concern. With the price of solid state hard drives dropping, it's worth considering one for development. A solid state hard drive operates at read and write speeds often more than double the speeds of a traditional hard drive. This translates to significant time savings—the system will boot faster, Integrated Development Environments (IDEs) will operate more quickly, and the applications will run faster.

If you plan to run the Android Emulator on a laptop, it is also worth investing in a significant amount of RAM for the laptop. Anywhere from 4GB and higher should be sufficient. If you have less than 2GB, you will have problems. With more memory on the system, more applications can be run at the same time.

Finally, you need a processor powerful enough to run the SDK and the required development tools. The choice is up to your development team; however, the newer the better. Something with multiple cores is always a plus.

Android Testing Systems

The Android Emulator is capable of nearly all the functionality provided by physical Android devices. Even so, it's paramount that testing occur on true hardware. The real hardware system will respond exactly as customers can expect, so testing on true hardware allows for a much more natural experience.

A single Android device will not be enough. It is important to test on multiple devices of the same Android version as your target version. If the application is being developed for a previous version of Android, it is imperative to test on devices that have newer versions as well. The greater variety of devices you use to test software and confirm usability, the more bugs and problems you'll identify pre-launch. Finding and fixing problems before a customer deals with them will help establish your product.

Overview

Android and x86 are a powerful combination. With a low barrier to entry, a strong security backing, low licensing costs, and an easy mechanism to deploy applications, Android is an easy and profitable industry to get involved with. Thanks to Android's success and Google's profits, the Android stack is something that has an ever-growing backing. Android and x86 are the right choice for development. With careful consideration for the development team and the product, a viable strategy, and successful management, there is much money to be made from the Android ecosystem.

CHAPTER 5

The Intel Mobile Processor

If GM had kept up with technology like the computer industry has, we would all be driving $25 cars that got 1,000 MPG.

—Bill Gates

Intel is the original microprocessor designer: the first commercially available microprocessor was the Intel 4004 in 1971. Intel processors currently dominate the high-performance market, capturing almost all modern high-end servers. Intel's Pentium line of processors were ubiquitous in personal computing during the 1990s, and their Core i-series are the most popular central processing units for laptops and ultrabooks today. In addition, Intel has entered the mobile marketplace with mobile specific microprocessor products competitive with ARM Ltd., the market leader in the mobile space. Combined with the robustness and flexibility of the Android OS, the power and compatibility of the x86 series of processors is bringing a competitive new device family to the mobile market.

Intel's x86 Line

x86 forms the base architecture of an enormous family of Intel processors, ranging from the earliest Intel 8086 to the Pentium line, the i-series, recent virtualization hypervisor-equipped server processors, low-power Atom and Haswell microprocessors designed for mobile and embedded use, and the tiny Quark system-on-chip aimed at wearable computing. Originally, the 8086 architecture was designed for embedded systems. But Intel's early implementations of the 8086 architectures were wildly successful and led to a long line of revisions and upgrades adding power and rich features.

The x86 architecture is a Complex Instruction Set Computing (CISC) system, built with more complex instructions facilitating ease of use and simpler implementations. ARM, Intel's main competitor for mobile processors, is a Reduced Instruction Set Computing (RISC) system, without these features. For example, in a RISC system it might take three to four instructions to load a given value into memory, whereas in a CISC system there is one single instruction specifically written to do this. The x86 architecture is also register-to-memory based, meaning instructions can affect both registers and memory.

History

Intel is one of the oldest semiconductor manufacturing companies in the world, and is known for building innovative and functional technologies in the computer hardware and related industries. The company was started by Bob Noyce and Gordon Moore in 1968. Venture Capitalist Arthur Rock solidified this company with an initial investment of $10,000 and a later contribution of $2.5 million, resulting in his position as chairman.

Intel released their first two products in 1969: the 3101 Schottky bipolar random access memory, and the 1101, the world's first metal oxide semiconductor (MOS). As mentioned, the first Intel processor was released in 1971, and it was called the 4004.

In 1978, Intel first released the 8086 series of processor architectures that would change the world. Only five years after that, Intel could officially call itself a billion dollar company. Intel is the largest semiconductor company in the world, and per the 2012 year-end reports, holds a market share of 15.7% and a revenue of 47.5 billion dollars. The original x86 architecture has split, diversified, added new specifications, and been reshaped into smaller form factors, continuing to be used in products around the world. The incorporation of Android on x86 is just another step forward for Intel.

Because the x86 architecture has been used in so many technologies, from servers to personal computers, mobile phones, laptops, and tablets, compiling a complete list of its devices would be prohibitively difficult. Its wide use has resulted in the creation of tools, applications, frameworks, and libraries specific to x86 platforms for developer use.

It all started in 1978 with the Intel 8086, originally built as an experimental 16-bit extension to the Intel 8080 8-bit microprocessor. The 8086 was the processor that drove the "IBM PC" and all of its clones. The term x86 was derived from the successors to the 8086, all of which ended in "86." In 1985, Intel continued the x86 architecture with the Intel 80386, the first 32-bit processor. It wasn't until 2005, with the release of the Pentium 4, that x86 64-bit processors hit the market.

Intel's latest home computing processor series based on x86 architectures is nicknamed the Intel Core i-series. This series supports 64-bit operations and is focused on performance and speed. All of the processors support hyperthreading and have multiple cores, which allow for concurrent processing. Running parallel to the personal computing Core i-series of microprocessors is the x86-based Atom series for mobile devices.

Strengths and Weaknesses

As industry leaders in the semiconductor market, Intel processors have distinct advantages. First and foremost, Intel processors have the highest performance of any other processors. This performance consists of both processor speed and the number of cores and virtual cores. The x86 architecture also grants developers access to the largest collection of software available. The last major advantage is the scalability of high-end systems that use Intel CPUs; the addition of processors gives direct performance improvements.

Table 5-1 highlights some of the differences of the Intel Atom processor family, which implement the x86 instruction set. The Intel Atom processor family consists of many different varieties for each platform type, including tablets, smartphones, netbooks, and other mobile consumer electronics, and Table 5-1 represents comparable high-end models for each.

Table 5-1. *Intel Atom Processor Family Comparison*

Name (Code Name)	System Type	Processor Speed	Cores (Threads)
Intel Atom Z2480 (Medfield)	Mobile	2GHz	1 (2)
Intel Atom D2700 (Cedarview)	Desktop	2.13GHz	2 (4)
Intel Atom C2750 (Avoton)	Server	2.40GHz	8 (8)

Note *These are the top-of-the-line Atom processors for each system type.*

There are situations where the x86 family is not the right choice of microprocessor. The Intel family is physically much larger than other brands of CPUs, taking more than an inch of space in the Core series. Up until the Intel Atom series, the power consumption of Intel's processors was too demanding for embedded devices; however, leading Atom processors compete with ARM for battery life. Lastly, Intel processors cost significant amounts and there are systems in which a 4-core 3GHz processor is overkill. In these situations using an ARM or some other lower performance CPU may be desirable.

Business Model

In its home computing efforts, Intel has continued to produce powerful and energy-efficient processors for laptops, ultrabooks, and desktop platforms. The closest competitor is the Semiconductor company Advanced Micro Devices, Inc. There was a point in 2006 when the desktop market was close to being split between AMD and Intel, but that is no longer the case. As of November 2012, Intel CPU's hold roughly 71% of the market, to AMD's 28%.

As laptops and tablets grew in popularity, Intel released the Atom series of processors. The atom processor balances heat and power with performance aimed specifically at items that will run on batteries for extended periods. The Atom series can be found in over 100 million devices, and is now expanding to the mobile market place.

Clash of the Mobile Titans: ARM versus Intel

ARM entered the microprocessor market in 1983, and emerged as a strong competitor in certain areas. Intel and their x86-based processors have managed to capture a majority of the desktop and home computing market. ARM on the other hand is the current leader in the mobile and embedded device market. This next section discusses in detail the properties of each company's processors, including its benefits and weaknesses.

ARM

If you look at per-unit sales, ARM is the current mobile-arena winner. With over 30 billion units in the current market, and 16 million sold per day, ARM is generating revenues of well over 900 million dollars a year. ARM's history, business strategies, and future plans are all relevant to the reason for ARM's success.

History

The ARM story begins at the British personal computer company Acorn. The original Acorn RISC machine was developed between the years of 1984 and 1985. In 1982, prior to ARM, the British Broadcasting Company (BBC) signed with Acorn to develop a home computer that would be later known as the BBC microcomputer. The *BBC micro* was wildly successful, and lead to the growth of Acorn as a small company with a handful of employees, to a medium-sized business with hundreds of employees.

Around the end of the BBC micro era, Acorn began looking for the next processor to carry their new personal computer forward. Acorn tried a variety of 16- and 32-bit processors, including the 65C816 used in the Apple IIGS, but couldn't find one with the performance that Acorn needed. Acorn's solution to this problem was simply to develop a new processor, the ARM1.

Despite its incredible power and performance, the ARM1 wasn't largely used until the release of Archimedes, the first true ARM-based platform. Archimedes was a desktop computer, released in mid-1987, which primarily was used in schools and other educational environments. Even with the mild success and response from consumers, the ARM team pushed forward and created the ARMv3, focusing on increasing performance to compete with Intel and Motorola workstations.

In 1990, the Acorn RISC machine became the Advanced RISC Machine, and Advanced RISC Machines Ltd was created. With help of founding partners Apple, Acorn, and VLSI Technology, the company was founded for the sole purpose of continuing development of the ARM processor. From this foundation came the birth of the ARMv6, released to licensees in October of 2002. The ARMv6 architecture is used widely in embedded and mobile devices today, along with its more recent relatives, ARMv7 and ARMv8.

Strengths and Weaknesses

ARM processors have some very attractive qualities. To start, they are incredibly small. In fact the most modern ARM11 family of processors is under $2mm^2$. Because of the small form factor, the heat generated from use is generally low enough to avoid any sort of heat sink or cooling system. Even as small as it is, ARM chips can contain many core system components inside of a single piece of silicon. These components include CPUs, GPUs, and DSPs. The last major advantage is the minimal amount of power consumed relative to competitors; some reports claim as much as a 66% savings. The less power used, the longer batteries last and the cheaper the electricity bill.

Table 5-2 showcases some of the more popular ARM processors currently used in the mobile market. This table is only a sample of the many options that ARM provides for mobile devices, but comparison with Table 5-1 demonstrates the significant differences from the Intel processor family. The comparable ARM mobile processors offer significantly less processor speeds, even at the high-end of the spectrum with the A15.

Table 5-2. ARM Cortex-A Series Comparison

Name (Architecture)	System Type	Processor Speed	Cores
A15 (ARMv7)	Mobile	1-2.5GHz	1-4 + clustering*
A7 (ARMv7)	Mobile	.8-1.5GHz	1-4
A5 (ARMv7)	Mobile	.3-.8GHz	1-4

Note *The A15 supports up to four clusters of processors with 1-4 cores each.*

For all of the strengths that ARM chips have, there are plenty of weaknesses. To start with, ARM chips lack the serious performance required for any sort of heavy processing situations. The ARM processors are also inherently less scalable, especially in comparison to modern Intel CPUs. Software for ARM needs to be specifically created for the architecture; luckily, some of the more common tools and utilities already exist for ARM.

Business Model

An analysis of ARM's corporate decisions can help reveal their focus in the processor market. It is obvious the primary values that are held—RISC architecture, high performance, low power consumption, and low price point. These differentiations set ARM up perfectly for the mobile market, and are the key reasons that ARM processors are almost exclusively used in smartphones.

ARM processors however are not sold or manufactured by ARM Ltd. Instead, the processor architecture is licensed to interested parties. ARM Ltd. offers a variety of terms, and varying costs. With all its licensees, ARM provides in-depth documentation, a complete software development toolset, and the right-to-sell manufactured silicon with the licensed CPU.

This business model has done well for the company; in the second quarter of 2013, ARM reports categorized 51% of their income from royalties, with 39% from licensing. The report went on to detail the number of units for both royalties and licenses. The average cost of royalties per unit was roughly $.07 cents, with over 2.6 billion units. On the other hand, there were 25 new licenses signed that quarter, averaging about $1.84 million dollars per license.

Future

The latest processor that ARM has publically released is the ARM7, with various modified implementations. The ARM7 is used widely in the modern smartphone market. There have been rumors in corporate waters that ARM will be pursuing additional directions with its processors.

With the release of Windows 8 for x86, Microsoft has created a version of Windows called Windows RT for ARM processors. Windows RT was written almost entirely from scratch, and has managed to eliminate many, but not all, of the bottlenecks of modern backward-compatible Windows versions. Tests have concluded that RT applications are running as much as 20% faster than the same applications on competing Intel chips.

Experts have also projected ARM's entry into the server and datacenter markets. With support from ARM-based Linux server operating systems, this is becoming more of a reality. The ability to run performance systems on ARM conceivably means lower power costs. This has yet to be seen in the current performance of high-end ARM systems versus the performance of high-end Intel systems.

Intel's Atom Line of Microprocessors

Atom processors are featured in devices that are used on the go. Typical devices include small laptops, netbooks, tablet computers, televisions, and new smartphones. The Atom balances performance and power usage to enable much longer battery life for the device.

With over 100 million Atom CPUs shipped, the outreach of the Atom is apparent. As with all Intel processors, the Atom is a member of the Intel Architecture (IA) family. The distinct and cross portability of the IA family allows for quick and effortless transitions between processors.

Intel Atom Evolution

The Intel Atom is the successor of the Intel A100 and A110, low-power processors primarily used in notebook computers. The A100 and A110 were code-named Stealey and originally built at the size of 90nm. Tables 5-3 and 5-4 highlight some of the iterations of Atom, for tablets and for smartphones, from the processor family's infancy in April of 2008 through its modern releases.

Table 5-3. *Intel Atom Smartphone Processors*

Code Name	GPU* Speed	Processor Speed	Cores (Size)	Release
Silverthorne	200MHz	800MHz – 2.13GHz	1 (45nm)	April 2008
Lincroft	400MHz	800MHz – 1.9GHz	1 (45nm)	May 2010
Penwell	400MHz	1.2GHz – 2.0GHz	1-2 (32nm)	2012

Note **GPU stands for Graphics Processing Unit, the hardware responsible for producing graphics for a given device.*

Table 5-4. *Intel Atom Tablet Processors*

Code Name	GPU* Speed	Processor Speed	Cores (Size)	Release
Lincroft	400MHz	1.2GHz – 1.5GHz	1 (45nm)	May 2010
Cloverview	300MHz – 533MHz	1.2GHz – 2.0GHz	2 (32nm)	2012
Bay Trail-T	311MHz – 688MHz	1.33GHz – 2.41	4 (22nm)	2013*

Note **Bay-Trail T devices are expected in the first half of 2014.*

At first glance, the processors listed in Table 5-3 only seem to be getting marginally better, but in order to truly understand what's going on, you need to take into account all of the variables. The Penwell is the forerunner for processors that Intel produces for smartphones today, with a size of only 32nm, multi-core support, and top-of-the-line operating frequency with embedded GPU support. It is the obvious choice from Intel for modern device manufacturers.

In comparison to the existing processors in Table 5-3, the tablet processors listed in Table 5-4 are much more capable. These tablet processors support even more cores, and have faster GPU speeds, which help accommodate much larger and often high-resolution display components.

Intel Atom Security

With technology in this modern day and age, security is always a concern. The Intel Atom processor offers support for many security features. These include Secure Boot, Intel Platform Trust Technology, hardware-enhanced encryption, and operating system-level key storage. Secure Boot is part of the current Unified Extensible Firmware Interface (UEFI) specifications, and is best described in Intel's own words:

> When enabled and fully configured, Secure Boot helps a computer resist attacks and infection from malware. Secure Boot detects tampering with boot loaders, key operating system files, and unauthorized option ROMs, by validating their digital signatures. Detections are blocked from running before they can attack or infect the system.

The Intel Platform Trust Technology, or PTT for short, is a virtual smartcard reader on tablets that allows for certificate-based authentication through the CPU.

Intel Atom Features

The Intel Atom processor supports a significant amount of the features that exist in other Intel processors. Energy efficiency is a new idea in the Intel world, and the Atom brings this to the forefront. The Atom processor can be custom-tailored to bring the correct balance of incredibly low power with varying performance scalability options. Performance-wise, the Atom supports both Intel Hyper-Threading and Intel Burst Technology to help deal with required performance and power efficiency. The last major feature that Intel promotes with the Atom is the concept of mobility, supporting NFC, advanced camera imaging, 3G, and 4G LTE.

Android and the Atom

The Atom processor is the current x86 processor of choice for Android platforms. The Atom Android team brings a wardrobe packed with top-of-the-line features. This includes 3D graphics with full 1080p HD support for multiple formats, screen sharing and device pairing, optimized web page rendering, and simple cross computability. Android SDK applications are supported out-of-the-box on Atom Android platforms. Android NDK applications require only a recompile, in most cases, to be fully supported. More information about the compatibility and conversion process can be found the following section titled **Application Compatibility** and in **Chapter 7: Creating and Porting NDK-Based Android Applications**.

Inside the Medfield System-on-Chip

Intel's Medfield platform is intended for smartphones and tablets running the Android operating system. One model of Medfield, the Intel Atom Z2610 System-on-Chip (SOC), will be discussed in greater detail shortly (in Figure 5-1). As stated earlier, Intel has recently started producing standalone mobile processors, including one codenamed Penwell. Although the Penwell processor contains some of the same segments as the Medfield SoC, namely Saltwell-family microprocessor architectures, Penwell is a standalone processor primarily targeted at smartphones as opposed to Medfield's multiple-part and higher-performance system targeting both smartphones and tablets.

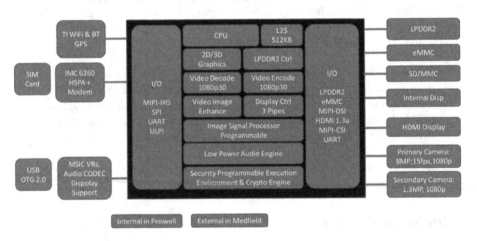

Figure 5-1. *Medfield Block Diagram*

This Medfield model, the Z2610, is physically divided into two complexes, the North Complex and the South Complex. The North Complex consists of a Saltwell-family single-core processor, a 32-bit dual channel LPDDR2 memory controller, a 3D graphics core, video decode and encode engines, a 2D display controller that is capable of supporting up to three displays, and an image processor for camera input. The South Complex consists of all the necessary I/O interfaces to complete a smartphone design, such as a security engine, a storage controller supporting SD/eMMC storage cards, a USB OTG controller, a 3G modem, Complimentary Wireless Solution (CWS) interfaces, SPI, and UART. See Figure 5-1.

Zooming In on the Saltwell CPU Architecture

The Saltwell CPU architecture is fairly simple. The idea of the design is to create a processor with a balance between optimized performance and efficient power consumption. The processor uses in-order architecture, which is different from most of the other processors in the market, which instead use out of order execution. The processor has a 64-KB L1 cache and a 512-KB L2 cache. This processor supports Intel Burst Performance technology, which lets the processor dynamically increase the CPU speed. There are three frequency modes in Saltwell: Low Frequency Mode (LFM) runs at 600MHz, High Frequency Mode (HFM) runs at 900MHz, and Burst Frequency Mode (BFM) runs at 1.6GHz. Among the power optimization features, Saltwell has an ultra-low power smart L2 cache that keeps data while the CPU is in C6 states, in order to lower the latency during the resumption of C states. In addition, Saltwell has separate power planes and clock inputs for the core and the rest of the SoC, which makes power and clock gating easily configurable through Intel Smart Idle Technology (Intel SIT). This technology enables the CPU to be switched off completely while the SoC is still in the ON state (S0 state).

Architecture Differences between Intel's Saltwell and ARM's Cortex A15

As listed in the book, *Break Away with Intel Atom Processors: A Guide to Architecture Migration,*[1] the Intel Atom architecture is very different from the ARM architecture in every way. Table 5-5 shows a list of high-level differences between Saltwell and ARM Cortex architecture.

Table 5-5. *High-Level Differences Between Saltwell and ARM (Cortex A15)*

Feature	Saltwell	ARM Cortex
Technology	32nm	28nm
Architecture	In-order	Out-of-order
Integer pipelines	16	15
L1 cache	64KB	Configurable up 64KB
L2 cache	512KB	Max 4MB
Instruction set	IA32, Intel Streaming SIMD Extensions, Intel Supplemental Streaming SIMD Extensions 3	ARM, Thumb
Multi core/thread support	Single core with Intel Hyper-Threading Technology	Multi-core
Security technology	Intel Smart & Secure Technology (Intel S&ST)	TrustZone* Technology

---

[1]Matassa, Lori and Max Domeika, *Break Away with Intel® Atom™ Processors: A Guide to Architecture Migration.* Intel Press, 2010.

Architecture

As mentioned, Saltwell has an architecture similar to other processors in the Intel Atom series. It uses an in-order execution design. With an in-order processor, all the instructions are executed according to the order they are fetched, whereas out-of-order processors are capable of executing multiple instructions simultaneously and reordering them later in the pipeline. ARM processors use out-of-order architecture, which has the advantage of executing instructions with minimal latency. However, this increases the complexity of the core design. The elimination of the reordering logic is one of the power reduction initiatives of the Intel Atom processor.

Integer Pipelines

There are six phases in Intel Atom pipelines; the details are listed in Table 5-6.

Table 5-6. *Intel Atom Instruction Phases and Pipeline Stages*

Phase	Pipeline Stages
Instruction fetch	3
Instruction decode	3
Instruction issue	3
Data access	3
Execute	1
Write back	3

This instruction architecture results in a total of 16 integer pipelines in the Intel Atom processor, and three extra stages are required to execute floating point instructions. The latest ARM processor has 15 integer pipelines. The lengthy pipeline in the ARM processor trades energy over performance. Saltwell can decode up to two instructions per clock cycle while the latest ARM processor is a triple issue superscalar architecture.

Instruction Sets

ARM instruction sets are always 32-bit and aligned on a four-byte boundary, whereas IA32 instruction sets vary in size and do not require any alignment. Another difference between ARM instructions and IA32 instructions is how the instruction is executed. For ARM, all the instructions are conditionally executed to reduce branch overhead and mis-prediction during branching. There are condition flags that each instruction needs to fulfill in order to take effect, otherwise the instruction will act as NOP and get discarded. There are conditional instructions as well in Intel architecture; these are called conditional MOV instructions. Other instructions in IA32 are not conditionally executed.

Multi-Core/Thread Support

As mentioned previously, Saltwell supports Intel Hyper-Threading Technology (Intel HT Technology), where tasks are completed by using shared resources. The details of the technology are discussed further in the next section. ARM multi-core architecture has unique resources to perform its tasks on each core. The coherency of the cores is handled by AMBA 4 AXI, a compatible slave interface that is directly interfaced to the core.

Security Technology

There is a security subsystem in Medfield called Intel Smart & Secure Technology (Intel S&ST). It is a complete hardware and software security architecture. This subsystem is compliant with industry standards, supporting AES, DES, 3DES, RSA, ECC, SHA-1/2, and DRM. It also supports 1,000 bits of OTP and enables SecureBoot. The implementation in the ARM processor for a security system is different. There is no separate controller for the security subsystem as Intel implemented. The ARM processor uses TrustZone technology, where resources in the system such as processor and memory are divided into two worlds: the *normal world* and the *secure world*. There are three motivations for this Trust Zone architecture:

- To provide a security framework that allows designers to customize the functions needed depending on the use cases.

- To save silicon area and power where there will be no need to have a dedicated processor for secured tasks.

- To prevent intrusion during debug to security-sensitive tasks in the *secure world* or non-security-sensitive tasks in the *normal world*, by providing a single debug component.

Intel Hyper-Threading Technology

Intel Hyper-Threading Technology (Intel HT Technology) enables software to have a view of multiple logical processors in a physical processor package. The Saltwell CPU architecture uses Intel Hyper-Threading Technology as a boost to its performance. Having a second thread in a single in-order architecture processor enables Saltwell to execute multiple instructions within a clock cycle sharing the execution resources among the two threads, giving a 50% performance improvement compared to a single thread processor, as shown in Figure 5-2.

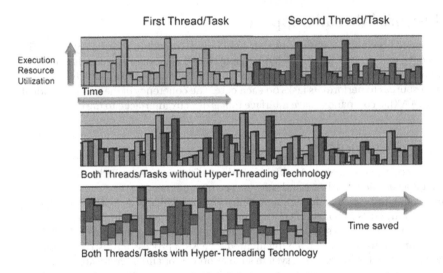

Figure 5-2. *Benefits of the Intel Hyper-Threading Technology*

In Intel HT technology, the processor has duplicates of the architecture state that consists of general purpose registers, control registers, the advanced programmable interrupt controller (APIC) registers, and some machine state registers. The duplication of architecture states is the reason software can view a single core processor as two logical processors. Caches, execution units, branch predictors, control logic, and buses are shared between the two threads. This created a concern where there might be resource contention and workload imbalance between the threads. However, most of the current development kits such as Dalvik and JavaScript already have the capability to support multi-threaded environments, giving developers an easy way to generate applications that utilize the advantage of Intel HT technology. Applications developers on Android can also utilize the Intel VTune performance tool to analyze the workload and perform resource tuning on their applications.

Application Compatibility: Native Development Kit and Binary Translator

Android has been ported to x86 and all further releases will be available in both the x86 and ARM architectures. It is not an issue to run the OS on an Intel Atom platform. However, in some cases, existing Android applications may need to be recompiled with or without source code modification.

It is believed that roughly 75–80% (commonly cited numbers) of Android applications in the Google Play Store run on top of the Dalvik VM and use the Android Framework (see Figure 5-3). The vast majority of Dalvik VM applications written in the Java language using the Android Software Development Kit (SDK) are processor agnostic. They run "as-is" on Intel Atom platforms transparently without requiring porting efforts. For the subset of applications that include C and C++ code, developers need to recompile their code using the latest Android Native Development Kit (NDK).

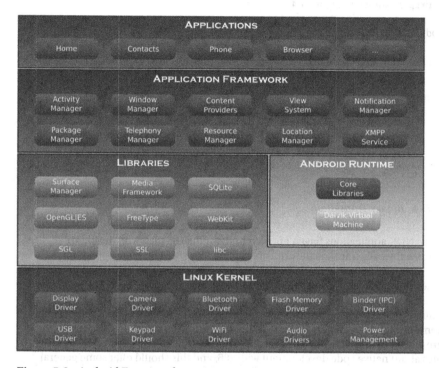

Figure 5-3. Android Framework

In most cases, NDK application developers simply need to recompile the project, which supports x86 (x86), ARMv5 (armeabi), and ARMv7 (armeabi-v7a). Compiling for x86 (by GCC with compiler flags `-march=i686 -msse3 -mstackrealign -mfpmath=sse`) will generate code that is tailored exactly to the Intel Atom CPU feature sets. Only applications that use an ARM vendor's specific feature will require source code to be rewritten and then recompiled.

The resulting APK application package may comprise three versions of machine code for x86, ARMv5, and ARMv7. Upon installation, only the appropriate version of code is unpacked and installed onto the target platform.

The rest of the applications are either Dalvik VM applications that use Java Native Interface (JNI) libraries built for ARM, or Native Development Kit (NDK) applications that haven't been compiled for x86. These applications cannot run without alteration on the Intel Atom platform due to the calls to native libraries (especially ARM-specific native libraries).

Intel and Google have worked together to ensure native application execution on Intel Atom platform "as-is" without porting efforts. Intel provides Binary Translation (BT) that translates ARM code to x86 code on-the-fly during execution, as shown in Figure 5-4.

This translation mitigates the inconvenience of JNI libraries and NDK applications that have not yet been ported to x86. It allows the device to expose itself as supporting two applications binary interfaces (ABIs): x86 and ARMv5. This could be observed from the **build.prop**, as shown in Figure 5-4.

```
ro.product.cpu.abi=x86
...
ro.product.cpu.abi2=armeabi
```

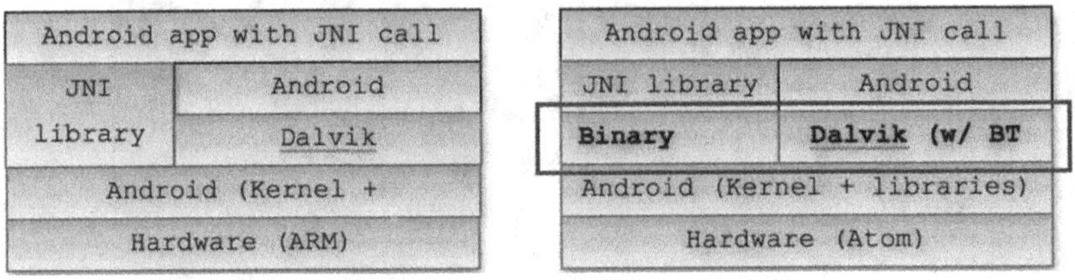

Android app with JNI call	
JNI library	Android
	Dalvik
Android (Kernel +	
Hardware (ARM)	

Android app with JNI call	
JNI library	Android
Binary	Dalvik (w/ BT
Android (Kernel + libraries)	
Hardware (Atom)	

Figure 5-4. Binary Translation

If the NDK applications haven't been rebuilt for the x86 platform, the binary translator will locally translate the armeabi version into x86. The same applies for Dalvik VM applications that request ARM-based JNI libraries. The translation process is optimized and completely transparent to the end users.

The combination of all of these efforts should result in approximately 90% of applications in the Google Play working right away. The other 10% of applications may take some additional configuration and setup to be fully functional. In **Chapter 7: Creating and Porting NDK-Based Android Applications**, we will cover some more specifics about native code development with x86, and this should offer some general suggestions to help with any applications that fit into this bucket.

Overview

This chapter covered a brief history of both Intel and ARM from a company and a processor standpoint. You looked at some specific processors from Intel and Arm and read about what each brings to the table. After a brief overview of each company, we spent some time talking about the Intel Atom processor and which features and specifics exist with the modern versions. Finally we jumped into a technical discussion about Intel Atom's Medfield architecture, which is being featured in the newest x86 phones and tablets. We have discussed how the Integer pipeline flows, which security systems are in place, and even how the Intel Hyper-Threading optimizes performance. Binary translation was discussed at length, with an explanation of how NDK-based applications have to be prepared to later be ported to the Intel platform.

■ ■ ■

CHAPTER 6

Installing the Android SDK for Intel Application Development

How could this Y2K be a problem in a country where we have Intel and Microsoft?

—Al Gore

This chapter covers the information necessary to get started developing an Android application on an Intel Architecture processor. The first step is installing the software development kit (SDK) and setting up the appropriate environments for developing applications running on Intel Architecture-based Android devices. The SDK includes tools and platform components for developers to develop, build, test, debug, and optimize their Android applications, and manage the Android platform component installation. The SDK also provides easy ways to integrate with the build and development environments, for examples, with Eclipse or Apache Ant.

Preparing for the SDK Installation

This next section is dedicated to setting up a development environment available so that you can start producing Android applications on Intel platforms. If you already have an Android development environment setup, you can skip this section.

Supported Operating Systems

The following operating systems are supported:

- Windows XP (32-bit), Vista (32- or 64-bit), Windows 7 (32- or 64-bit), and Windows 8 (32- or 64-bit)

- Mac OS X (32- or 64-bit)

- Linux (Ubuntu, Fedora); GNU C library (**glibc**) 2.7 or later is required

- On Ubuntu Linux, version 8.04 or later is required

- On Fedora, target versions are F-12 and higher

- 64-bit distributions must be capable of running 32-bit applications

Hardware Requirements

The Android SDK requires disk storage for all of the components that you choose to install. Additional disk space is required to run the emulator, for example, to create SD cards for the Android Virtual Devices (AVDs).

Installing the JDK

At minimum, Java JDK 5 or JDK 6 is required by the SDK. JDK 7 is also supported. JRE (Java Runtime Environment) alone is not sufficient. If your system does not have JDK 5, 6, or 7 installed, you can download JDK SE 7 from http://www.oracle.com/technetwork/java/javase/downloads/index.html and install it on your system.

Installing Eclipse

Using the SDK with Eclipse to develop Android applications is highly recommended. You can go to http://www.eclipse.org/downloads/ to download or update Eclipse. We suggest using the following Eclipse setups to develop Android applications for Intel Architecture:

- Eclipse 3.5 (Galileo) or greater

- Eclipse Classic (versions 3.5.1 and higher)

- Android Development Tools plug-in (recommended)

Installing Apache Ant (Optional)

Developing Android applications using an integrated development environment such as Eclipse is highly recommended. But as an alternative, you can use Apache Ant to work with the SDK to build Android applications. You can visit http://ant.apache.org/ to download the binary distributions and install Ant. To work with the SDK, Ant 1.8 or later is required.

Downloading the SDK Starter Package and Adding SDK Components

You can download the SDK starter package at http://developer.android.com/sdk/index.html. The SDK starter package does not include the platform-specific components you need to develop Android applications. It only provides the core SDK tools for you to download the rest of the platform components.

After installing the SDK starter package, run the Android SDK and AVD Manager.

- On Windows, select Start ➤ All Programs ➤ Android SDK Tools ➤ SDK Manager

- On Linux, run **your-android-sdk-directory/tools/android**

In the left panel of the Android SDK and AVD Manager dialog box, select Available packages, and in the right panel, click and expand the Android Repository node and select the packages to install, as shown in Figure 6-1.

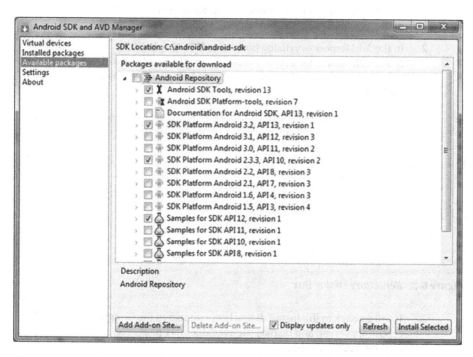

Figure 6-1. *Installing the Android SDK and AVD Manager in Linux*

■ **Note**   You may see an error message displayed if you attempt to download from behind a firewall. If this occurs, try again from outside the firewall. If you still see an error message, close the SDK Manager, then right-click it in the Start menu and select Run as Administrator. These two steps will resolve most error messages you'll see when attempting to download.

Setting Up Eclipse to work with the SDK

If you use the Eclipse IDE to develop software, we highly recommend you install and set up the Android Development Tool (ADT) plug-in.

Installing the ADT Plug-in for Eclipse

To install the ADT plug-in for Eclipse, follow these steps:

1. Start Eclipse, select Help ➤ Install New Software in the Install dialog box, and click the Add button.

2. In the Add Repository dialog box, enter **ADT Plugin** in the Name field and enter https://dl-ssl.google.com/android/eclipse/ in the Location fields, as shown in Figure 6-2. Then click OK.

Figure 6-2. *Repository Dialog Box*

3. It will go back to the Install dialog box, connect to the Google repository server, and display the available ADT packages, as shown in Figure 6-3.

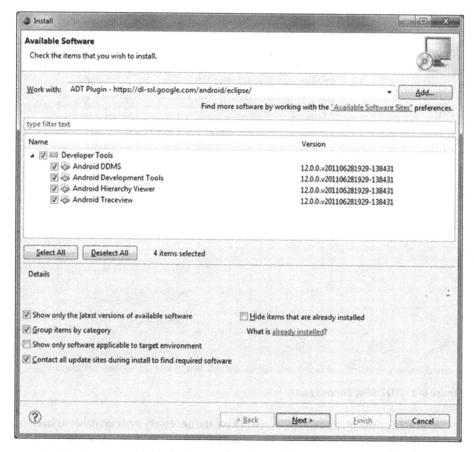

Figure 6-3. ADT Package List

4. Select Next, accept the license agreement, and then select Finish.

5. Restart Eclipse.

Configuring the ADT Plug-in

To configure the ADT plug-in, follow these steps:

1. Start Eclipse and select Windows ➤ Preferences.

2. In the Preferences dialog box, select Android from the left panel. On the right panel, use the Browse button to navigate to your Android SDK installation directory and click Apply. A list of SDK targets you have installed will show up, as shown in Figure 6-4. At this point, click OK.

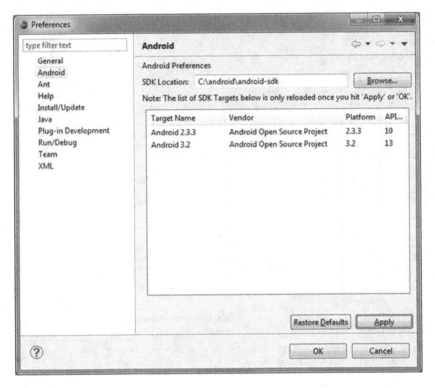

Figure 6-4. *ADT SDK Targets List*

After going through these steps, you will have the necessary tools available to start Android development. You now have everything you need to write your first app, but it would probably be best to also install the Intel Architecture (x86) emulator at this time, so that you can test your app as soon as it is ready. This next section takes you through the Intel Architecture (x86) emulator install. We discuss building an emulator image with AOSP sources, and emulating the resulting system images for x86.

The Android Developer Tools are updated regularly to include the latest APIs. When building an emulator image, the tools to build the most up-to-date Android version are at your fingertips. If you choose to download pre-built emulator system images, your choices will be a few months out of date. For this chapter, we use case studies emulating Android 2.3, codenamed Gingerbread and covering API levels 9 and 10, and Android 4.0, codenamed Ice Cream Sandwich and covering API levels 14 and 15. Gingerbread was the first Android release available on platforms other than ARM and its new features emerged directly from the Android open source project's efforts, which were discussed in **Chapter 1: History and Evolution of the Android OS**.

Overview of Android Virtual Device Emulation

Android runs on a variety of form factor devices with different screen sizes, hardware capabilities, and features. A typical device has a multitude of software (Android API) and hardware capabilities like sensors, GPS, camera, SD card, and a multitouch screen with specific dimensions.

The emulator is quite flexible and configurable with different software and hardware configuration options. Developers can customize the emulator using the emulator configuration called Android Virtual Device (AVD). AVD is basically a set of configuration files that specify different Android software and device hardware capabilities. The Android emulator uses these AVD configurations to configure and start the appropriate Android virtual image on the emulator.

As documented on the Android web site (see http://developer.android.com/guide/developing/devices/index.html), a typical AVD configuration has:

- A hardware profile that specifies all the device capabilities (such as cameras and sensors).

- A *system image*, which is used by the emulator for this AVD (designating which API level to target, such as 10 for Gingerbread or 19 for KitKat).

- A *data image* that acts as the dedicated storage space for user's data, settings, and SD card.

- Other options including emulator skin, the screen dimensions, and SD card size.

Developers are encouraged to target different API levels, screen sizes, and hardware capabilities (such as camera, sensors, and multitouch). The AVD configuration can be used to customize the emulator as needed. Developers can create as many AVDs as desired, each one targeting a different Intel architecture–based Android device. For example, a developer can create an Intel architecture–based Gingerbread AVD with a built-in skin like WVGA800, or a custom one that manually specifies the screen resolution.

The Android SDK has supported Intel architecture–based Android emulation since version r12. The SDK integrates this support into all developer tools, including the eclipse ADT plug-in. Figure 6-5 is a sample screenshot of the Android emulator for x86 running Gingerbread. The model number is highlighted, and shows Full Android on x86 emulator.

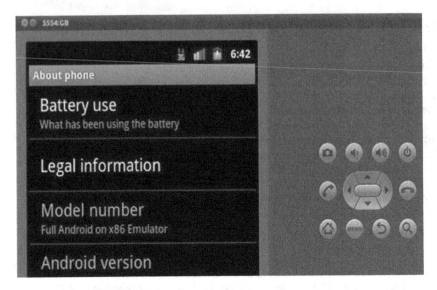

Figure 6-5. *Android Emulator*

For detailed instructions on how to use the emulator, refer to the following Android documentation: `http://developer.android.com/tools/devices/emulator.html`.

Which Emulator Should You Use

At the time of this writing, emulator images are available for Intel architecture (x86) for Android 2.3.7 (Gingerbread), Android 4.0.4 (Ice Cream Sandwich), and Android 4.3 (Jelly Bean). You can find the most recent image at `http://software.intel.com/en-us/articles/android-43-jelly-bean-x86-emulator-system-image`.

Although there are many advantages to developing for the latest Android operating system release, many developers prefer to target Android 2.x or Android 4.x, as a majority of Android phones run Android 4.x or higher. This percentage will change over time, so it is strongly suggested that you keep market conditions in mind when determining your target operating system.

For more Gingerbread-specific operating system information, the following article may prove useful: `http://blogs.computerworld.com/17479/android_gingerbread_faq`.

For Ice Cream Sandwich information, use this article: `http://www.computerworld.com/s/article/9230152/Android_4.0_The_ultimate_guide_plus_cheat_sheet_`.

Why Use the Emulator

First of all, it's free. The Android SDK and its third-party add-ons cost absolutely nothing and allow developers to emulate devices that they do not own and may not have access to. This is important, as not all phones acquire the latest Android OS versions via over-the-air (OTA) updates, and it may not be feasible for developers to purchase every device that is expected to support their software package(s).

- *Development and testing.* Developers can use the SDK to create several Android Virtual Device (AVD) configurations for development and testing purposes. Each AVD can have varying screen dimensions, SD card sizes, or even versions of the Android SDK (which is useful for testing backward compatibility with prior Android builds).

- *Playing with a new build.* The emulator allows developers to just have fun with a new build of Android and learn more about it.

Let's now walk through the steps required to build and run an emulator image on an x86 build. For simplicity's sake, this section focuses on the Gingerbread emulator, although most of this content applies to the Ice Cream Sandwich emulator as well.

Building an Emulator Image

The first step is to follow the setup instructions listed here: `http://source.android.com/source/initializing.html`.

Google has made Gingerbread documentation available at `http://source.android.com/source/downloading.html`.

Currently, the default repo initialization instructions are only for getting the latest master branch or a specific branch, such as when using the command **android-2.3.7_r1**. The repo and branch instructions for building Gingerbread x86 emulator images were not given.

Use the branch labeled **gingerbread** to download the latest Android source branch, as shown in Listing 6-1. This branch has the required build files and modules to build the x86 SDK emulator images.

Listing 6-1. Set Up the Repository

```
$ repo init -u
https://android.googlesource.com/platform/manifest -b gingerbread
$ repo sync
```

Initialize the build environment, as shown in Listing 6-2.

Listing 6-2. Build Environment Initialization

```
$ source build/envsetup.sh
including device/htc/passion/vendorsetup.sh
including device/samsung/crespo4g/vendorsetup.sh
including device/samsung/crespo/vendorsetup.sh
```

Use the **lunch** command to configure the build for building the x86 SDK, as shown in Listing 6-3. This will build the emulator images for x86, along with other SDK modules.

Listing 6-3. Lunch Command

```
$ lunch sdk_x86-eng
=======================================================
PLATFORM_VERSION_CODENAME=REL
PLATFORM_VERSION=2.3.7
TARGET_PRODUCT=sdk_x86
TARGET_BUILD_VARIANT=eng
TARGET_SIMULATOR=false
TARGET_BUILD_TYPE=release
TARGET_BUILD_APPS=
TARGET_ARCH=x86
TARGET_ARCH_VARIANT=x86_atom
HOST_ARCH=x86
HOST_OS=linux
HOST_BUILD_TYPE=release
BUILD_ID=GINGERBREAD
=======================================================
```

Finally, issue the **make sdk** command in order to kick off the build, as shown in Listing 6-4.

Listing 6-4. Make SDK

```
$ make sdk
=======================================================
PLATFORM_VERSION_CODENAME=REL
PLATFORM_VERSION=2.3.7
TARGET_PRODUCT=sdk_x86
TARGET_BUILD_VARIANT=eng
TARGET_SIMULATOR=false
TARGET_BUILD_TYPE=release
TARGET_BUILD_APPS=
TARGET_ARCH=x86
TARGET_ARCH_VARIANT=x86_atom
HOST_ARCH=x86
HOST_OS=linux
HOST_BUILD_TYPE=release
BUILD_ID=GINGERBREAD
=======================================================
```

Additionally, you can specify the number of parallel jobs for **make** using the **-j** parameter, to speed up the build process. (It is recommended that you use a value that is at least greater than or equal to the total number of CPUs in the system.)

The build will create three images, including the QEMU Android kernel **image:t system.img** (Android), **userdata.img**, and **ramdisk.img**.

When the build completes, the images will be in the **build** folder **$ANDROID_BUILD_TOP/out/target/product/generic_x86/**, as shown in Figure 6-6.

```
$ ls $ANDROID_BUILD_TOP/out/target/product/generic_x86/ -Altr

total 261476
-rw-r--r--  1 user user      4129 2011-10-31 20:16 clean_steps.mk
-rw-r--r--  1 user user       406 2011-10-31 20:16 previous_build_config.mk
drwxr-xr-x  2 user user      4096 2011-10-31 20:20 sdk
drwxr-xr-x  3 user user      4096 2011-10-31 20:20 data
drwxr-xr-x  2 user user      4096 2011-10-31 20:24 grub
drwxr-xr-x  4 user user      4096 2011-10-31 20:24 symbols
drwxr-xr-x  8 user user      4096 2011-10-31 20:24 root
-rw-r--r--  1 user user    212904 2011-10-31 20:24 ramdisk.img
drwxr-xr-x  3 user user      4096 2011-10-31 20:25 dex_bootjars
drwxr-xr-x 12 user user      4096 2011-10-31 20:27 system
-rw-------  1 user user   4587264 2011-10-31 20:27 userdata.img
-rw-------  1 user user 131539584 2011-10-31 20:28 system.img
drwxr-xr-x 13 user user      4096 2011-10-31 20:28 obj
-rw-r--r--  1 user user 131362140 2011-10-31 20:28 sdk_x86-symbols-eng.user.zip
```

Figure 6-6. *Image Location*

The Android kernel image for QEMU (**kernel-qemu**) comes with Android Sources. It is located under the prebuilt folder (**$ANDROID_BUILD_TOP/prebuilt/android-x86/kernel**), as shown in Figure 6-7.

```
$ ls $ANDROID_BUILD_TOP/prebuilt/android-x86/kernel -Altr

total 86332
-rw-r--r-- 1 user user    15872 2011-10-27 21:31 LINUX_KERNEL_COPYING
-rw-r--r-- 1 user user      589 2011-10-28 03:01 README
-rw-r--r-- 1 user user  2471824 2011-10-28 03:01 kernel-qemu
-rw-r--r-- 1 user user  2512912 2011-10-28 03:01 kernel-vbox
-rwxr-xr-x 1 user user  5930056 2011-10-28 03:01 vmlinux-qemu
-rwxr-xr-x 1 user user 77463163 2011-10-28 03:01 vmlinux-vbox
```

Figure 6-7. *Kernel Image*

You now have all the image files required for running an x86 Android Gingerbread image on the Android x86 emulator. You need to set up the image files with the SDK, which is covered in next section.

Setting Up the SDK to Use x86 Emulator Images

The Android SDK tools (Android and the AVD manager) expect the x86 emulator images to be present in the default SDK folders for platform images, which is **/platforms/android-10/images**.

The images that follow assume the **$ANDROID_SDK_TOP** environment variable is set to the location of the Android SDK installation folder.

As in Figure 6-8, Android-10 comes with emulator images for ARM by default. In order to set up the x86 emulator images in the SDK, you need to create an **x86** folder and copy the images you build into that folder. You can also move the ARM images to their own folder, as shown in Listing 6-5.

```
$ cd $ANDROID_SDK_TOP/platforms/android-10/images/
$ls -l
```

```
total 97012
-rw-r--r-- 1 user user  4112064 2011-11-01 09:56 userdata.img
-rw-r--r-- 1 user user   146641 2011-11-01 09:56 ramdisk.img
-rwxr-xr-x 1 user user  1466272 2011-11-01 09:56 kernel-qemu
-rw-r--r-- 1 user user 93282816 2011-11-01 09:56 system.img
-rw-r--r-- 1 user user   322846 2011-11-01 09:56 NOTICE.txt
```

Figure 6-8. *Image Location*

Listing 6-5. ARM Folder

```
$ mkdir arm
$ mv *.img kernel-qemu arm/
```

Listing 6-6 shows instructions for the x86 folder.

Listing 6-6. x86 Instructions

```
$ mkdir x86

$ cp $ANDROID_BUILD_TOP/out/target/product/generic_x86/*img x86/
$ cp $ANDROID_BUILD_TOP/prebuilt/android-x86/kernel/kernel-qemu x86/

$ cp NOTICE.txt arm/
$ cp NOTICE.txt x86/
```

The final images folder of the Android-10 platform is shown in Figure 6-9.

```
$ ls -l *
```

```
arm:
total 97012
-rwxr-xr-x 1 user user  1466272 2011-11-01 09:56 kernel-qemu
-rw-r--r-- 1 user user   322846 2011-11-01 10:03 NOTICE.txt
-rw-r--r-- 1 user user   146641 2011-11-01 09:56 ramdisk.img
-rw-r--r-- 1 user user 93282816 2011-11-01 09:56 system.img
-rw-r--r-- 1 user user  4112064 2011-11-01 09:56 userdata.img

x86:
total 135880
-rwxr-xr-x 1 user user    2471824 2011-11-01 10:11 kernel-qemu
-rw-r--r-- 1 user user     322846 2011-11-01 10:03 NOTICE.txt
-rwxr-xr-x 1 user user     212904 2011-11-01 10:10 ramdisk.img
-rwxr-xr-x 1 user user 131539584 2011-11-01 10:10 system.img
-rwxr-xr-x 1 user user   4587264 2011-11-01 10:10 userdata.img
```

Figure 6-9. *Final Images Folder*

Before using the Gingerbread Intel architecture images with the x86 emulator, you must create an AVD configuration that specifies the required software and hardware customizations. More detailed information about AVDs can be found next, and in the Intel Software Network article titled "Android Virtual Device Emulation for Intel Architecture" (http://software.intel.com/en-us/articles/android-virtual-device-emulation-for-intel-architecture).

At this point, your emulator and x86 image are ready to use. Note that the emulator performance will see drastic improvements if you use Intel Hardware Acceleration Execution Manager (Intel HAXM) with this system image—without it, performance may vary. (Intel HAXM requires an Intel processor with Intel VT-x support. For more information about Intel HAXM, see **Chapter 11: Using Intel® Hardware Accelerated Execution Manager to Speed-up Android on x86 Emulation**.

It is now time to use the Gingerbread x86 emulator to emulate an x86 image.

Open the Android tool or bring up the AVD creation tool directly from Eclipse.

Figures 6-10 and 6-11 show the creation of an AVD for Gingerbread with an Intel Atom (x86) CPU.

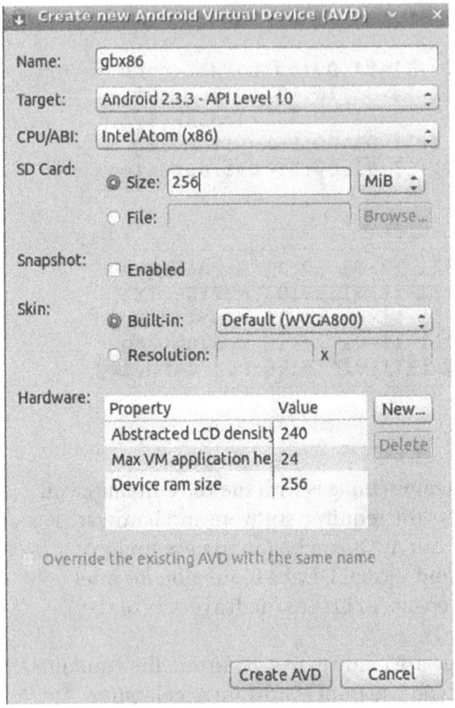

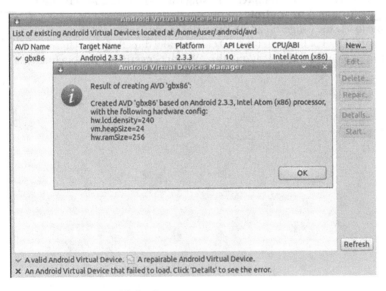

Figure 6-10. *New AVD Creation*

Figure 6-11. *Success Dialog Box*

Test the x86 Gingerbread AVD by selecting the AVD and clicking on Start, as shown in Figure 6-12.

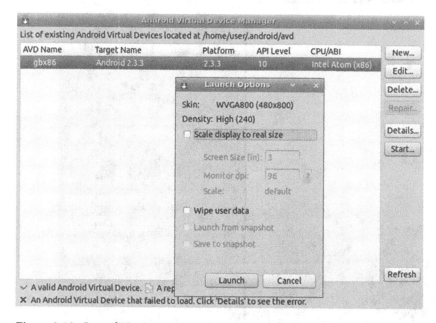

Figure 6-12. *Launch Options*

Figure 6-13 shows the home screen of the Gingerbread for Intel Atom (x86) on emulator x86.

Figure 6-13. *Home Screen*

It is recommended that you use the x86 emulator with Intel VT hardware acceleration. On Linux, you can do this using the Linux KVM. Ubuntu has further documentation on how to configure and use it at https://help.ubuntu.com/community/KVM.

Listing 6-7. KVM

```
$ emulator-x86 –avd gbx86 –qemu –m 512 -enable-kvm
```

With KVM, shown in Listing 6-7 (**-enable-kvm**), users will likely notice performance boosts during the Android boot, along with quicker emulator responsiveness.

Key Gingerbread Features

This next section highlights a few of the key features that Gingerbread supports. These features are also supported in the latest release of Android, with full plans to have continued support.

Battery Usage Stats

In About Phone, as seen in Figure 6-14 there is a Battery Use section. Battery stats will vary based on the emulation device and build. In the case where the developer can **telnet** into the emulated device, some simple commands can be used to mock battery drain. Take a look at one such example at http://android-er.blogspot.com/2010/09/how-to-set-battery-status-of-android.html.

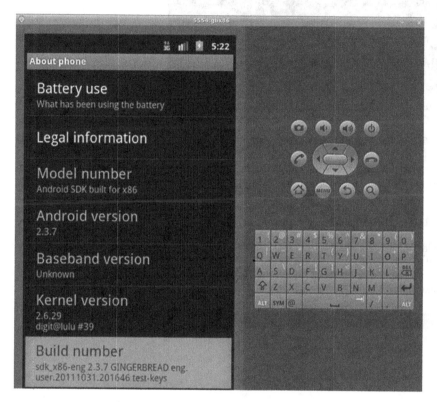

Figure 6-14. *About Phone View*

Task Manager

From Settings ➤ Applications ➤ Running Services, choose the Running tab. It shows what's currently running, as you can see in Figure 6-15.

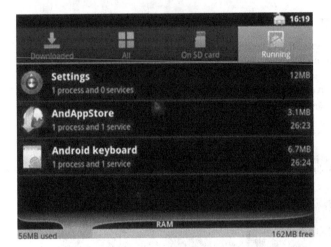

Figure 6-15. *The Task Manager's Running Tab*

For example, the developer can close the Settings process by clicking on the item and selecting Stop.

Cut and Paste Text

Opening the Messaging application and choosing New Message allows you to type a message as if you're sending an SMS. By clicking in the text field and typing on the host keyboard, characters appear seamlessly on the Android screen. After typing **Hello 2.3.5!**, the screen looks like Figure 6-16.

Figure 6-16. *Messaging Fun*

If you dragged the mouse into the text field where **Hello 2.3.5!** is found and then held down the mouse button (or touchpad button) for about two seconds, a tooltip menu appears to Edit Text. If you choose Select All and then repeat the mouse operation, you can cut the text. After cutting the text, you can repeat the mouse operation again to paste the text elsewhere.

Ice Cream Sandwich Emulation

The x86 Android 4.0.4 emulator system image enables you to run an emulation of Android Ice Cream Sandwich on your development machine. In combination with the Android SDK, you can test your Android applications on a virtual Android device based on Intel architecture (x86).

In order to install the emulator system image, you can use the Android SDK Manager (recommended method), or you can download the binary ZIP file and unzip and copy the included directory into the **add-ons** directory of your Android SDK installation. (Note that this method does not allow for automatic updates of the add-on.)

The following section provides a guide for ICS image installation.

Prerequisites

The Android x86 emulator image requires the Android SDK to be installed. For instructions on installing and configuring the Android SDK, refer to the Android developer website (see http://developer.android.com/sdk/).

■ **Note** The x86 emulator image for Android can be accelerated using Intel Hardware Accelerated Execution Manager (Intel HAXM). For more information, refer to **Chapter 11: Using Intel® Hardware Accelerated Execution Manager to Speed-up Android on x86 Emulation.**

Downloading Through the Android SDK Manager

1. Start the Android SDK Manager.

2. Under Android 4.0.4 (some screenshots may refer to older versions), select Intel x86 Atom System Image, as shown in Figure 6-17.

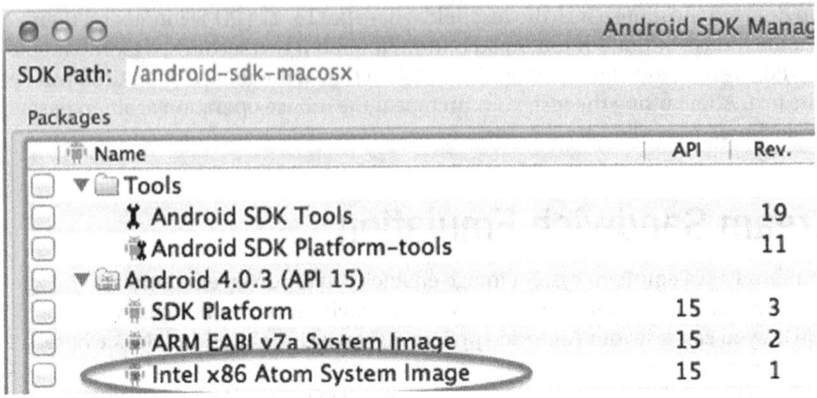

Figure 6-17. Intel x86 Atom System Image

3. Once it's selected, click the Install Package button.

4. Review the Intel Corporation license agreement. If you accept the terms, select Accept and click Install.

5. The SDK Manager will download and extract the system image to the appropriate location within the Android SDK directory.

Using the System Image

1. Start the Android AVD Manager and create a new AVD, setting Target to Android 4.0.X, and CPU/ABI to Intel Atom (x86), as shown in Figure 6-18.

Figure 6-18. Setting the Target

■ **Note** If the Intel Atom (x86) CPU/ABI option is not available, make sure that the system image is installed correctly.

---

2. Click the Create AVD button.

3. The AVD has been successfully created and is now ready to use, as shown in Figure 6-19.

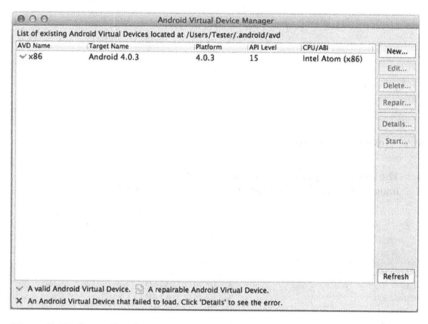

Figure 6-19. Image Ready

Downloading Manually

1. Go to http://www.intel.com/software/android.

2. Download the Intel x86 Atom System Image (found under the Tools and Downloads tab).

3. Navigate to the directory containing the Android SDK, as shown in Figure 6-20.

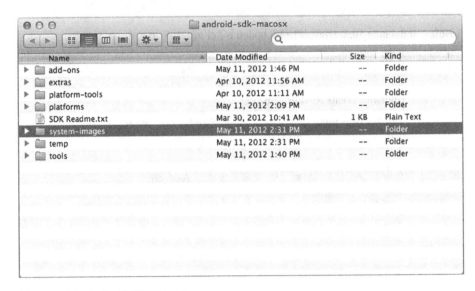

Figure 6-20. *Android SDK Directory*

4. The **system-images** directory contains Android's system images, separated by architecture, as shown in Figure 6-21.

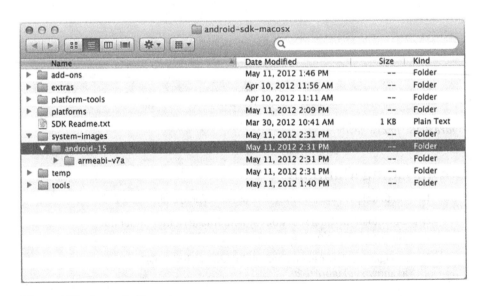

Figure 6-21. *Separated Images*

5. Expand **android-15** (this directory contains API level 15 system images), as shown in Figure 6-22.

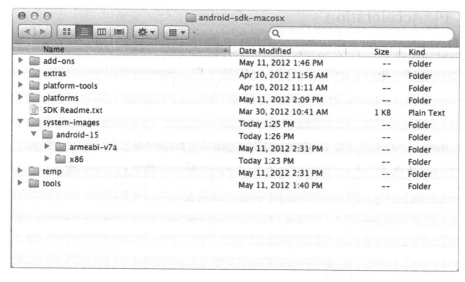

Figure 6-22. *API Level 15*

6. Extract the **x86** directory contained in the downloaded system image archive directly into the **android-15** directory.

7. The directory structure should now look like Figure 6-23.

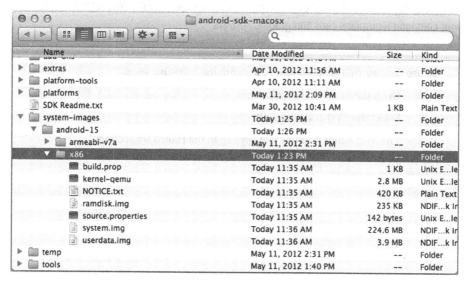

Figure 6-23. *Expected Directory Structure*

8. The system image is now installed and ready to be used.

CPU Acceleration

You can improve the performance of Intel Atom x86 Image for Android Ice Cream Sandwich using hardware-based virtualization with Intel VT-x technology. If your computer has an Intel processor with VT-x support, it is recommended that you use Intel HAXM with this system image. For more information about Intel HAXM, visit http://int-software.intel.com/en-us/android.

■ **Note**   Intel HAXM is for Windows and OS X operating systems only. For Linux hosts, you can use Kernel-based Virtual Machine (KVM) to accelerate emulation performance. For information on installing and configuring KVM on Ubuntu, refer to the following guide at https://help.ubuntu.com/community/KVM/Installation.

GPU Acceleration

The Intel Atom x86 image for Android Ice Cream Sandwich can make use of hardware GPU features to increase the performance of games, graphics-intensive programs, and user interface elements.

■ **Note**   The functionality and performance of GPU acceleration is highly dependent on your computer's graphics card and graphics drivers.

To use hardware GPU acceleration, perform the following steps:

1. Open the Android AVD Manager.

2. Select the AVD and click Edit.

3. The AVD editor window will appear. In the Hardware section, click New, as shown in Figure 6-24.

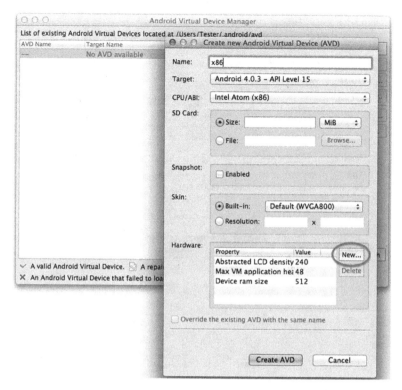

Figure 6-24. *Hardware Section*

4. In the Property drop-down box, select GPU Emulation, as shown in Figure 6-25.

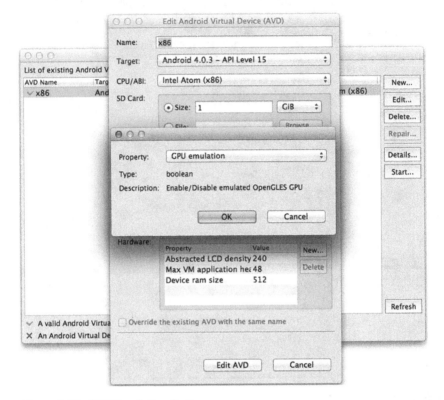

Figure 6-25. *GPU Emulation Option*

5. Click OK.

6. After the GPU Emulation property has been added, change the Value to Yes, as shown in Figure 6-26.

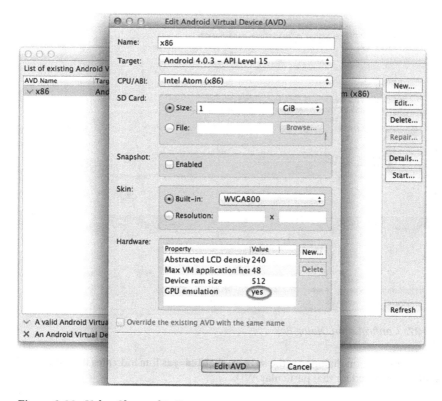

Figure 6-26. *Value Changed to Yes*

7. Click Edit AVD to save the AVD.

8. After the AVD has been modified, a dialog box will appear confirming the AVD settings, shown in Figure 6-27.

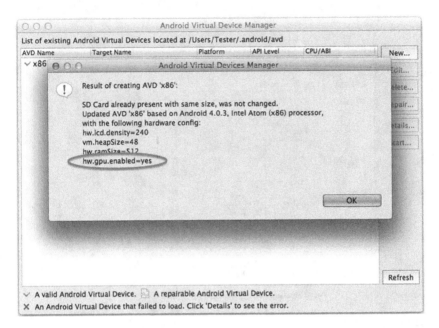

Figure 6-27. Confirmation Dialog Box

In the confirmation dialog box, the **hw.gpu.enabled=yes** line indicates that GPU acceleration is enabled for that particular AVD.

▨ **Note**   The GPU acceleration must be enabled on a per-AVD basis.

Overview

In this chapter, you set up a fully functioning Android development environment. You also installed the prerequisites for Android and the SDK. The chapter discussed the Android emulator in detail, and you created an x86 emulator for easy testing. You even created a fully functioning Android 4.0.4 (Ice Cream Sandwich) emulator on a virtual x86 platform, for testing the latest features of Android. In the next chapter, you will learn how to install and use the Android Native Development Kit in order to create and port applications for the Intel platform.

■ ■ ■

CHAPTER 7

Creating and Porting NDK-Based Android Applications

It has become appallingly obvious that our technology has exceeded our humanity.

—Albert Einstein

Android applications can incorporate native code using the Native Development Kit (NDK) toolset. It allows developers to reuse legacy code, program for low-level hardware, and differentiate their applications by taking advantage of features otherwise not optimal or possible.

This chapter provides an in-depth introduction on how to create NDK-based applications for the Intel architecture. It also covers the cases of porting existing NDK-based applications. It discusses in-depth the differences between the Intel compiler and the default NDK compiler, and explains how to take full advantage of the Intel NDK environment.

JNI and NDK Introduction
JNI Introduction

We know that Java applications do not run directly on the hardware, but actually run in a virtual machine. The source code of an application is not compiled to get the hardware instructions, but is instead compiled to get the interpretation of a virtual machine to execute code. For example, Android applications run in the Dalvik virtual machine; its compiled code is executable code for the Dalvik virtual machine in DEX format. This feature means that Java runs on the virtual machine and ensures its cross-platform capability: that is its "compile once, run anywhere" feature. This cross-platform capability of Java causes it to be less connected to and limits its interaction with the local machine's various internal components, making it difficult to use the local machine instructions to utilize the performance potential of the machine. It is difficult to take advantage of locally based instructions to run a huge existing software library, and thus functionality and performance are limited.

Is there a way to make Java code and native code software collaborate and share resources? The answer is yes—by using the Java Native Interface (JNI), which is an implementation method of a Java local operation. JNI is a Java platform defined as the Java standard to interact with the code on the local platform. (It is generally known as the *host platform*. But this chapter is for the mobile platform, and in order to distinguish it from the mobile cross-development host, we call it the *local platform*.) The so-called "interface" includes two directions—one is Java code to call native functions (methods), and the other is local application calls to the Java code. Relatively speaking, the former method is used more in Android application development. This chapter therefore focuses on the approach in which Java code calls the native functions.

The way Java calls native functions through JNI is to store the local method in the form of library files. For example, on a Windows platform, the files are in .DLL file format, and on a UNIX/Linux machine the files are in .SO file format. By an internal method of calling the local library file, Java can establish close contact with the local machine. This is called the *system-level approach* for various interfaces.

JNI usually has two usage scenarios: first, to be able to use legacy code (for example C/C++, Delphi, and other development tools); second, to more directly interact with the hardware for better performance. You will see some of this as you go through the chapter.

JNI general workflow is as follows: Java initiates calls so that the local function's side code (such as a function written in C/C++) runs. This time the object is passed over from the Java side, and run at a local function's completion. After finishing running a local function, the value of the result is returned to the Java code. Here JNI is an adapter, mapping the variables and functions (Java methods) between the Java language and the native compiled languages (such as C/C++). We know that Java and C/C++ are very different in function prototype definitions and variable types. In order to make the two match, JNI provides a jni.h file to complete the mapping between the two. This process is shown in Figure 7-1.

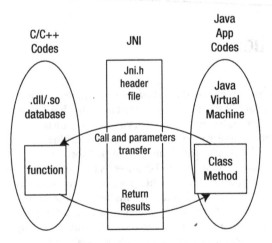

Figure 7-1. JNI General Workflow

The general framework of a C/C++ function call via a JNI and Java program (especially an Android application) is as follows:

1. The way of compiling native is declared in the Java class (C/C++ function).

2. The .java source code file containing the native method is compiled (build project in Android).

3. The javah command generates an .h file, which corresponds to the native method according to the .class files.

4. C/C++ methods are used to achieve the local method.

5. The recommended method for this step is first to copy the function prototypes into the .h file and then modify the function prototypes and add the function body. In this process, the following points should be noted:

   - The JNI function call must use the C function. If it is the C++ function, do not forget to add the extern C keyword.

   - The format of the method name should follow the following template: Java_package_class_method, namely the Java_package name classname and function method name.

6. The C or C++ file is compiled into a dynamic library (under Windows this is a .DLL file, under UNIX/Linux, it's a .SO file).

Use the System.loadLibrary() or System.load() method in the Java class to load the dynamic library generated.

These two functions are slightly different:

- System.loadLibrary(): Loads the default directory (for Windows, for example, this is \System32, jre\bin, and so on) under the local link library.

- System.load(): Depending on the local directory added to the cross-link library, you must use an absolute path.

In the first step, Java calls the native C/C++ function; the format is not the same for both C and C++. For example, for Java methods such as non-passing parameters and returning a String class, C and C++ code differs in the following ways:

C code:

```
Call function:(*env) -> <jni function> (env, <parameters>)
Return jstring:return (*env)->NewStringUTF(env, "XXX");
```

C++ code:

```
Call function:env -> <jni function> (<parameters>)
Return jstring:return env->NewStringUTF("XXX");
```

in which both Java String object NewStringUTF functions are generated by the C/C++ provided by the JNI.

Java Methods and Their Corresponding Relationship with the C Function Prototype Java

Recall that in order for Java programs to call a C/C++ function in the code framework, you use the javah command, which will generate the corresponding .h file for native methods according to the .class files. The .h file is generated in accordance with certain rules, so as to make the correct Java code find the corresponding C function to execute.

For example, for the following Java code for Android:

```
public class HelloJni extends Activity
```

```
1.  {
2.      public void onCreate(Bundle savedInstanceState)
3.      {
4.          TextView tv.setText(stringFromJNI() );   // Use C function Code
5.      }
6.      public native String  stringFromJNI();
7.  }
```

For the C function stringFromJNI() used in line 4, the function prototype in the .h file generated by javah is:

```
1.  JNIEXPORT jstring JNICALL Java_com_example_hellojni_HelloJni_
stringFromJNI
2.      (JNIEnv *, jobject);
```

In this regard, C source code files for the definition of the function code are roughly:

```
1.  /*
2.  ...
3.  Signature: ()Ljava/lang/String;
4.  */
5.  jstring Java_com_example_hellojni_HelloJni_stringFromJNI
    (JNIEnv* env,  jobject thiz )
6.  {
7.      ...
8.      return (*env)->NewStringUTF(env, "...");
9.  }
```

From this code you can see that the function name is quite long, but still very regular, in full accordance with the naming convention: java_package_class_method. The stringFromJNI() method in Hello.java corresponds to the Java_com_example_hellojni_HelloJni_stringFromJNI() method in C/C++.

Notice the comment for Signature: ()Ljava/lang/String;. The parentheses () of ()Ljava/lang/String; indicate that the function parameter is empty, which means, beside the two parameters JNIEnv * and jobject, there are no other parameter. JNIEnv * and jobject are two parameters that all JNI functions must have, respectively, for the jni environment and for the corresponding Java class (or object) itself. Ljava/lang/String; indicates that the function's return value is a Java String object.

Java and C Data Type Mapping

As mentioned, Java and C/C++ variable types are very different. JNI provides a mechanism to complete the mapping between Java and C/C++. The correspondence between the main types is shown in Table 7-1.

Table 7-1. *Java to C Type Mapping*

Java Type	Native Type	Description
boolean	jboolean	C/C++ 8-bit integer
byte	jbyte	C/C++ unsigned 8-bit integer
char	jchar	C/C+ unsigned 16-bit integer
short	jshort	C/C++ signed 16-bit integer
int	jint	C/C++ signed 32-bit integer
long	jlong	C/C++ unsigned 64-bit integer
float	jfloat	C/C++ 32-bit floating point
double	jdouble	C/C++ 64-bit floating point
void	void	N/A
Object	jobject	Any Java object, or does not correspond to an object of java type
Class	jclass	Class object
String	jstring	String objects
Object[]	jobjectArray	The array of any object
Boolean[]	jbooleanArray	Boolean array
byte[]	jbyteArray	Array of bits
char[]	jcharArray	Character array
short[]	jshortArray	Short integer array

(continued)

Table 7-1. (*continued*)

Java Type	Native Type	Description
int[]	jintArray	Integer array
long[]	jlongArray	Long integer array
float[]	jfloatArray	Floating point array
double[]	jdoubleArray	Double floating point array

■ **Note** The correspondence between Java types and the local (C/C++) type.

When a Java parameter is passed, the idea of using C code is as follows:

- Basic types can be used directly; for example, double and jdouble can be interoperable. Basic types are the types listed from the line boolean through void in Table 7-1. In such a type, if the user passes a boolean parameter into the method, there is a local method called jboolean corresponding to the boolean type. Similarly, if the local methods return a jint, then an int is returned in Java.

- Java object usage. An Object object has String objects and a generic object. The two objects are handled a little differently.

- The String object. The String object passed over by the Java program is the corresponding jstring type in the local method. The jstring type and char * in C are different. So if you just use it as a char *, an error will occur. Therefore, you need to convert jstring into a char * in C/C++ prior to use. Here we use the JNIEnv method for conversion.

- The Object object. Use the following code to get the object handler the class:

```
jclass objectClass = (env)->FindClass("com/ostrichmyself/jni/Structure");
```

Then use the following code to take required domain handler of the class:

```
jfieldID str = (env)->GetFieldID(objectClass,"nameString","Ljava/lang/String;");
jfieldID ival = (env)->GetFieldID(objectClass,"number","I");
```

Then use the following similar code to assign value to the incoming fields of the jobject object:

```
(env)->SetObjectField(theObjet,str,(env)->NewStringUTF("my name is D:"));
(env)->SetShortField(theObjet,ival,10);
```

- If there is no incoming object, then C code can use the following code to generate the new object:

  ```
  jobject myNewObjet = env->AllocObject(objectClass);
  ```

- Java array processing. For an array type, JNI provides some operable functions. For example, GetObjectArrayElement can take the incoming array and use NewObjectArray to create an array structure.

- The principle of resource release. Objects of C/C++ new or objects of malloc need to use the C/C++ to release memory.

- If the new object of the JNIEnv method is not used by Java, it must be released.

- To convert a string object from Java to get UTF by using GetStringUTFChars, you need to open the memory, and you must release the memory after you are finished using char *. The method to use is ReleaseStringUTFChars.

These are brief descriptions of type mapping when Java exchanges data with C/C++. For more information on Java and C/C++ data types, refer to related Java and JNI books, documentation, and examples.

NDK Introduction

From the previous description, you know that the Java code can visit local functions (such as C/C++) using JNI. To achieve this effect, you need development tools. There is a whole set of development tools based on the core Android SDK that you can use to cross-compile Java applications to applications that can run on the target Android device. Similarly, you need cross-development tools to compile the C/C++ code into applications that can run on an Android device. This tool is the Android Native Development Kit, or Android NDK.

Prior to the NDK, third-party applications on the Android platform were developed on a special Java-based Dalvik virtual machine. The native SDK allows developers to directly access the Android system resources and use traditional C or C++ programming languages to create applications. The application package file (.apk) can be directly embedded into the local library. In short, with the NDK, Android applications originally run on a Dalvik virtual machine can now use native code languages like C/C++ for program execution. This provides the following benefits:

- Performance improvement. It uses native code to develop the part of the program that requires high performance and directly accesses the CPU and hardware.

- The ability to reuse existing native code.

Of course, compared to the Dalvik virtual machine, using native SDK programming also has some disadvantages, such as added program complexity, difficulty in guaranteeing compatibility, the inability to access the Framework API, more difficult debugging, decreased flexibility, and so on. In addition, access to JNI incurs some additional performance overhead.

In short, NDK application development has its pros and cons. You need to use the NDK at your own discretion. The best strategy is to use the NDK to develop parts of the application for which native code will improve performance.

The NDK includes the following major components:

- Tools and a build file generate the native code libraries from C/C++. This includes a series of NDK commands, including `javah` (use the `.class` files to generate the corresponding `.h` files), `gcc` (to be described later), and other commands. It also includes the `ndk-build` executable scripts, and so on, which are covered in detail in the following sessions.

- A consistent local library will be embedded in the application package (application package files, that is, `.apk` files), which can be deployed in Android devices.

- Support for some native system header files and libraries for all future Android platforms.

The process framework of the NDK application development is shown in Figure 7-2. An Android application consists of three parts: Android application files, Java native library files, and dynamic libraries. These three parts are generated from different sources through the respective generation paths. For an ordinary Android application, the Android SDK generates Android applications files and Java native library files. The Android NDK generates the dynamic library files (the file with the .SO extension) using non-native code (typically C source code files). Finally the Android application files, Java library files, and native dynamic libraries are installed on the target machine, and complete collaborative applications run.

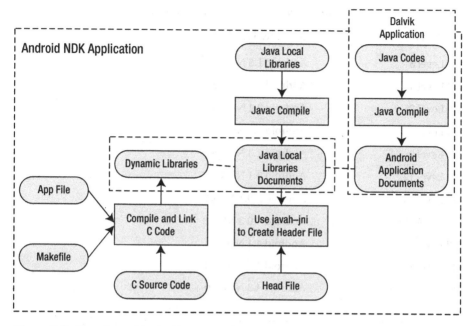

Figure 7-2. Flowchart of Android NDK Application Development

Applications projects developed by the NDK (referred to as NDK application projects) have components, as shown in Figure 7-3. In contrast to typical applications developed using the Android SDK, projects developed in the NDK add the Dalvik class code, manifest files, common resources, and also the JNI and a shared library generated by the NDK.

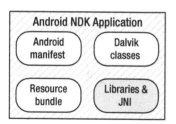

Figure 7-3. Application Components for an Android NDK Application

Android adds the NDK support in its key API version. Each version includes some new NDK features, simple C/C++, a compatible STL, hardware expansion, and so on. These features make Android more open and more powerful. The Android API and its corresponding relationship with the NDK are shown in Table 7-2.

Table 7-2. Relationship Between Main Android API and NDK Version

API Version	Supported NDK Version
API Level 3	Android 1.5 NDK 1
API Level 4	Android 1.6 NDK 2
API Level 7	Android 2.1 NDK 3
API Level 8	Android 2.2 NDK 4
API Level 9	Android 2.3 NDK 5
API Level 12	Android 3.1 NDK 6
API Level 14	Android 4.0.1 NDK 7
API Level 15	Android 4.0.3 NDK 8
API Level 16	Android 4.1 NDK 8b
API Level 16	Android 4.2 NDK 8d
API Level 18	Android 4.3 NDK 9b

■ **Tip**   Each piece of native code generated using the Android NDK is given a matching Application Binary Interface (ABI). The ABI precisely defines how the application and its code interact with the system at runtime. The ABI can be roughly understood as similar to an ISA (instruction set architecture) in computer architecture.

A typical ABI contains the following information:

- Machine code the CPU instruction set should use.

- A runtime memory access ranking.

- The format of executable binary files (dynamic libraries, programs, and so on) as well as what type of content is allowed and supported.

- Different conventions used in passing data between the application code and systems (for example, when the function call registers and/or how to use the stack, alignment restrictions, and so on).

- Alignment and size limits of enumerated types, structure fields, and arrays.

- The available list of function symbols for application machine code at runtime usually comes from a very specific set of libraries. Each supported ABI is identified by a unique name.

Android currently supports the following ABI types:

- *armeabi*–This is the ABI name for the ARM CPU, which supports at least the ARMv5TE instruction set.

- *armeabi-v7a*–This is another ABI name for ARM-based CPUs; it extends the armeabi CPU instruction set extensions, such as Thumb-2 instruction set extensions and floating-point processing unit directives for vector floating-point hardware.

- *x86*–This is ABI name generally known for the support of x86 or IA-32 instruction set of the CPU. More specifically, its target is often referred to in the following sessions as i686 or Pentium Pro instruction set. Intel Atom processors belong to this ABI type.

These types have different compatibility. X86 is incompatible with armeabi and armeabi-v7a. The armeabi-v7a machine is compatible with armeabi, which means the armeabi framework instruction set can run on an armeabi-v7a machine, but not necessarily the other way around, because some ARMv5 and ARMv6 machines do not support armeabi-v7a code. Therefore, when you build the application, users should be chosen carefully according to their corresponding ABI machine type.

NDK Installation

Here we use NDK Windows environment as an example to illustrate the NDK software installation. The Windows NDK includes the following modules:

- Cygwin runs Linux commands in the Windows command line.

- Android NDK package, including ndk-build and other key commands, is the core of the NDK software; it compiles C/C++ files into .SO shared library files.

- CDT (C/C++ Development Tooling, C/C++ development tools) is an Eclipse plug-in and can compile C/C++ files into .SO shared library in Eclipse. This means you can use it to ndk-build replace the command-line commands.

The CDT module is not required, but does enable development in the familiar Eclipse IDE. The Cygwin module must be installed in the Windows environment, but is not required in the Linux environment. Of course, the entire development environment needs to support the Java development environment. The following sections explain the installation steps for each module separately.

Android NDK Installation

This section describes how to install the Android NDK:

1. Visit the Android NDK official web site at http://developer.android.com/sdk/ndk/index.html and download the latest NDK package, as shown in Figure 7-4. In this case, you click on the file android-ndk-r8d-windows.zip and download the files to the local directory.

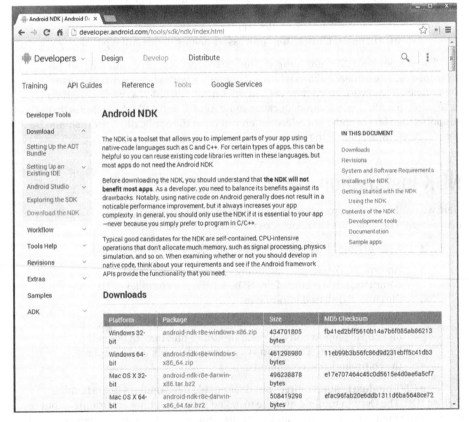

***Figure 7-4.** The NDK Package Download Page from the Android Official Web Site*

2. Install the Android NDK.

Android NDK installation is relatively simple. All you need to do is to extract the downloaded android-ndk-r4b-windows.zip to a specified directory. In this case, we install Android NDK in the directory D:\Android\android-ndk-r8d. You need to remember this location, as it is required for the following configuration to set up the environment.

Install Cygwin

This section describes how to install Cygwin:

1. Visit Cygwin's official web site (http://www.cygwin.com/). Download the Cygwin software, as shown in Figure 7-5. Go to the download page, and then click on the setup.exe file to download and install packages.

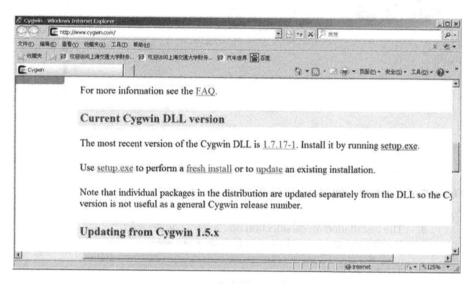

Figure 7-5. *Cygwin Download Page*

2. Double-click the downloaded setup.exe file to start the installation. The pop-up shown in Figure 7-6 appears.

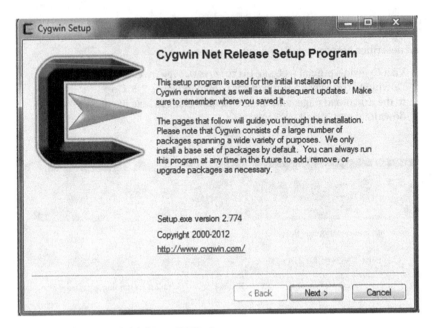

Figure 7-6. *Cygwin Initial Install Window*

3. The installation mode selection box is shown in Figure 7-7. In this example, select Install from Internet mode.

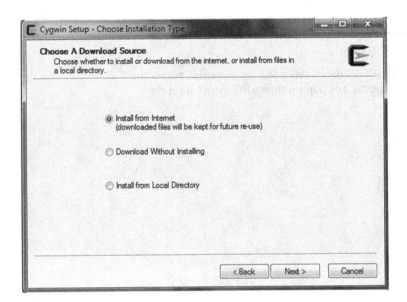

Figure 7-7. *Cygwin Install Mode Selection*

4. The display installation directory and user settings selection box is shown in Figure 7-8.

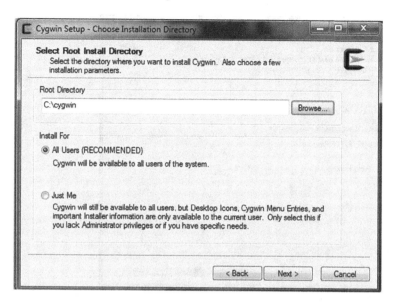

Figure 7-8. Installation Directory and User Settings Selection

5. You are next prompted to enter a temporary directory to store the downloaded files, as shown in Figure 7-9.

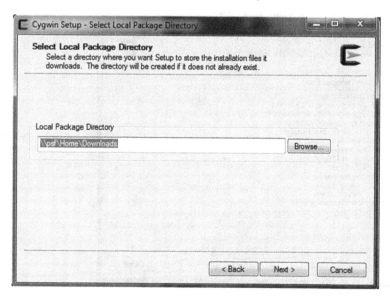

Figure 7-9. Cygwin Temporary Directory Setting for Downloaded Files

6. Next you are prompted to select an Internet connection type, as shown in Figure 7-10. For this example, select Direct Connection.

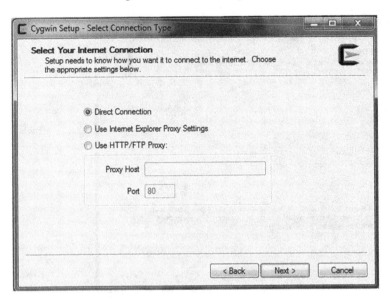

Figure 7-10. Cygwin Setup Internet Connection Type Selection

7. You are now prompted to select a download mirror site, as shown in Figure 7-11.

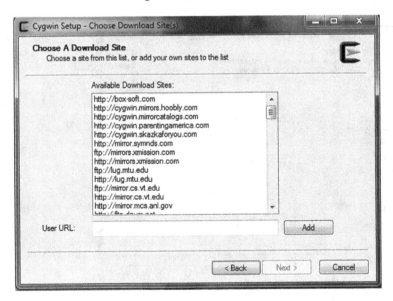

Figure 7-11. Cygwin Install: Prompt to Select Download Mirror Site

8. Start the download and install the basic parts, as shown in Figure 7-12(a). During the setup, a Setup alert will indicate that this is the first time you are installing Cygwin, as shown in Figure 7-12(b). Click OK to continue.

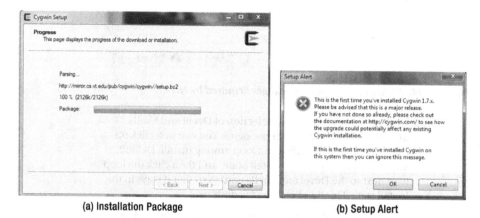

(a) Installation Package   (b) Setup Alert

Figure 7-12. *Cygwin Installation Package Download and Install*

9. Select the packages to install, as shown in Figure 7-13. The default is to install all of the packages.

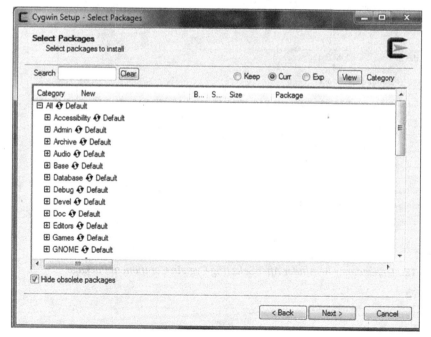

Figure 7-13. *Cygwin Packages Install Selection*

If you download all components, the total size is more than 3GB. This requires a very long time on normal broadband Internet speeds; it is actually not recommended to install all the components. You need to install the NDK Devel component and the Shells components, as shown in Figure 7-14.

Figure 7-14. Cygwin Components Packages Required by NDK

There are some tricks to the selection of Devel and Shells from the Install component packages. You can first click on the loop icon next to All; it will loop among Install, Default, and Uninstall. Set it to Uninstall State, and then click the loop icon next to the Devel and Shells entries so that it stays in the Install state. Finally, click Next to continue.

10. The contents of the selected components are displayed next, as shown in Figure 7-15.

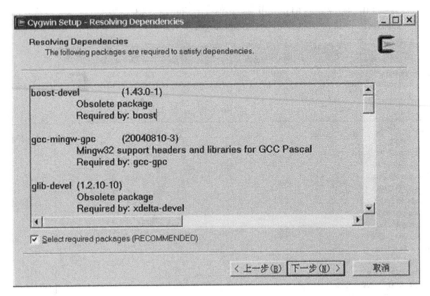

Figure 7-15. Dependency Reminder After Selecting Cygwin Component Package

11. Start to download and install the selected components, as shown in Figure 7-16.

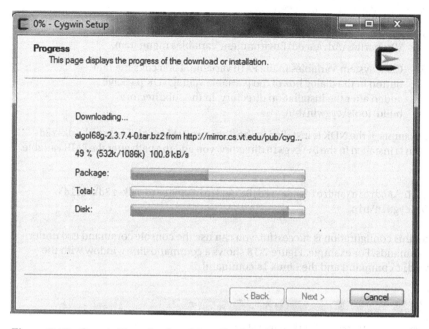

Figure 7-16. *Cygwin Download and Install Selected Components*

12. Installation is complete. Message boxes appear, as shown in Figure 7-17.

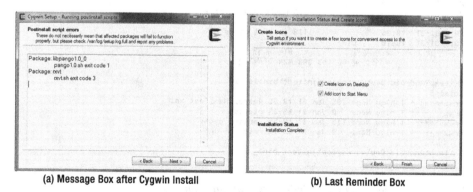

    (a) Message Box after Cygwin Install   **(b) Last Reminder Box**

Figure 7-17. *Cygwin Reminder Boxes after Installation Is Complete*

13. Configure the Cygwin Windows path environment variable.

Follow these steps to add the NDK package installation directory and Cygwin bin directory to the path environment variable:

1. On the desktop, right-click My Computer and select the \Properties\Advanced\Environment Variables menu item.

2. Click System Variables in the PATH variable. Then click the Edit button in the dialog box of the [variable value] NDK package added after the installation directory, in the subdirectory build\tools\cygwin\bin.

For example, if the NDK is installed in the directory D:\Android\android-ndk-r8d and Cygwin is installed in the D:\cygwin directory, you add the path after the PATH variable, as follows:

PATH=...;D:\Android\android-ndk-r8d;D:\Android\android-ndk-r8d\build\tools;D:\cygwin\bin

After this configuration is successful, you can use the console command cmd under Linux commands. For example, Figure 7-18 shows a command-line window with the Windows dir command and the Linux ls command.

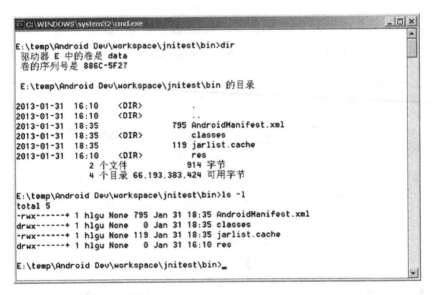

Figure 7-18. Command-Line Window after Installing the NDK

You configure Cygwin's internal environment variables for NDK as follows:

1. Before configuring the NDK Cygwin internal environment variables, you must run Cygwin at least once, otherwise the \cygwin\home directory will be empty. Click the Browse button in Windows Explorer and select the mintty.exe file under the bin subdirectory of the Cygwin installation directory (in this example, it is located at D:\cygwin\bin). The window is shown in Figure 7-19.

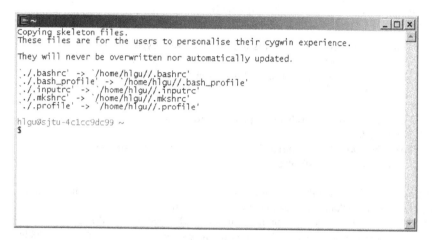

Figure 7-19. *Initial Window when Starting Cygwin for the First Time*

2. Then select the Windows menu \programs\Cygwin\Cygwin terminal. You can directly enter the Cygwin window, as shown in Figure 7-20.

Figure 7-20. *Cygwin Window if it Is Not Being Run for the First Time*

This will create a username (in this case, the Windows logon username hlgu) subdirectory under empty\cygwin\home and generate several files in the directory.

```
D:\cygwin\home\hlgu>dir
2013-01-30   00:42              6,054 .bashrc
2013-01-30   00:52                  5 .bash_history
2013-01-30   01:09              1,559 .bash_profile
2013-01-30   00:42              1,919 .inputrc
2012-12-01   08:58              8,956 .mkshrc
2013-01-30   00:42              1,236 .profile
```

3. Find .bash_profile in the installation directory cygwin\home\<username>\ file. In this case, it is D:\cygwin\home\hlgu\.Bash_profile. To the end of the file, add the following code:

```
NDK=<android-ndk-r4b unzipped_NDK_folder>
export NDK
ANDROID_NDK_ROOT=<android-ndk-r4b unzipped_NDK_folder >
export ANDROID_NDK_ROOT
```

The line <android-ndk-r4b unzipped_NDK_folder > corresponds to the installation directory of the NDK package. (In this example, it's D:\Android\android-ndk-r8d.) Cygwin provides a directory-conversion mechanism. Add /cygdrive/DRIVELETTER/ in front of the directory to refer to the designated directory in the drive. Here, DRIVELETTER is the driver letter of the directory. Consider this example:

```
NDK= /cygdrive/d/Android/android-ndk-r8d
export NDK
ANDROID_NDK_ROOT=/cygdrive/d/Android/android-ndk-r8d
export ANDROID_NDK_ROOT
```

4. Determine whether the command can be run by testing the make command.

```
C:\Documents and Settings\hlgu>make -v
GNU Make 3.82.90
Built for i686-pc-cygwin
Copyright (C) 2010  Free Software Foundation, Inc.
License GPLv3+: GNU GPL version 3 or later <http://gnu.org/
licenses/gpl.html>
This is free software: you are free to change and redistribute it.
There is NO WARRANTY, to the extent permitted by law.
```

If you see this output, it means the make command is running normally. Make sure the version of make is 3.8.1 or above, because all examples in this session need v3.8.1 or above to be able to be compiled successfully.

Now you can test the gcc, g+, gcj, and gnat commands:

```
C:\Documents and Settings\hlgu>gcc -v
Access denied.
C:\Documents and Settings\hlgu>g++ -v
Access denied.
C:\Documents and Settings\hlgu>gcj
Access denied
C:\Documents and Settings\hlgu>gnat
Access denied.
```

If you get the Access denied message, you need to continue the following steps. Otherwise, the installation is completed successfully.

5. Under the bin directory of Cygwin, delete the gcc.exe, g++.exe, gcj.exe, and gnat.exe files.

6. Under the same directory, select the needed gcc, g++, gcj, and gnat files that match the version. For example, version 4 corresponds to gcc-4.exe, g++-4.exe, gcj-4.exe, and gnat-4.exe. Make copies of those files and rename the copied files gcc.exe, g++.exe, gcj.exe, and gnat.exe.

7. Now test again to see if gcc and the other commands can run:

    ```
    C:\Documents and Settings\hlgu> gcc -v
    ```

Using built-in specifications, you can see which commands are available:

```
COLLECT_GCC=gcc
COLLECT_LTO_WRAPPER=/usr/lib/gcc/i686-pc-cygwin/4.5.3/lto-wrapper.exe
Target: i686-pc-cygwin
Configured with: /gnu/gcc/releases/respins/4.5.3-3/gcc4-4.5.3-3/src/gcc-
4.5.3/co
nfigure --srcdir=/gnu/gcc/releases/respins/4.5.3-3/gcc4-4.5.3-3/src/gcc-
4.5.3 --
prefix=/usr --exec-prefix=/usr --bindir=/usr/bin --sbindir=/usr/sbin
--libexecdi
r=/usr/lib --datadir=/usr/share --localstatedir=/var --sysconfdir=/etc
--dataroo
tdir=/usr/share --docdir=/usr/share/doc/gcc4 -C --datadir=/usr/share
--infodir=/
usr/share/info --mandir=/usr/share/man -v --with-gmp=/usr --with-mpfr=/usr
--ena
```

```
ble-bootstrap --enable-version-specific-runtime-libs --libexecdir=/usr/lib
--ena
ble-static --enable-shared --enable-shared-libgcc --disable-__cxa_atexit
--with-
gnu-ld --with-gnu-as --with-dwarf2 --disable-sjlj-exceptions --enable-
languages=
ada,c,c++,fortran,java,lto,objc,obj-c++ --enable-graphite --enable-lto
--enable-
java-awt=gtk --disable-symvers --enable-libjava --program-suffix=-4
--enable-lib
gomp --enable-libssp --enable-libada --enable-threads=posix --with-arch=i686
--w
ith-tune=generic --enable-libgcj-sublibs CC=gcc-4 CXX=g++-4 CC_FOR_
TARGET=gcc-4
CXX_FOR_TARGET=g++-4 GNATMAKE_FOR_TARGET=gnatmake GNATBIND_FOR_
TARGET=gnatbind -
-with-ecj-jar=/usr/share/java/ecj.jar
Thread model: posix
gcc version 4.5.3 (GCC)

C:\Documents and Settings\hlgu>g++ -v
```

Using built-in specifications, like gcc, you can see which commands are available:

```
COLLECT_GCC=g++
COLLECT_LTO_WRAPPER=/usr/lib/gcc/i686-pc-cygwin/4.5.3/lto-wrapper.exe
Target: i686-pc-cygwin
Configured with: /gnu/gcc/releases/respins/4.5.3-3/gcc4-4.5.3-3/src/gcc-
4.5.3/co
nfigure --srcdir=/gnu/gcc/releases/respins/4.5.3-3/gcc4-4.5.3-3/src/gcc-
4.5.3 --
prefix=/usr --exec-prefix=/usr --bindir=/usr/bin --sbindir=/usr/sbin
--libexecdi
r=/usr/lib --datadir=/usr/share --localstatedir=/var --sysconfdir=/etc
--dataroo
tdir=/usr/share --docdir=/usr/share/doc/gcc4 -C --datadir=/usr/share
--infodir=/
usr/share/info --mandir=/usr/share/man -v --with-gmp=/usr --with-mpfr=/usr
--ena
ble-bootstrap --enable-version-specific-runtime-libs --libexecdir=/usr/lib
--ena
ble-static --enable-shared --enable-shared-libgcc --disable-__cxa_atexit
--with-
gnu-ld --with-gnu-as --with-dwarf2 --disable-sjlj-exceptions --enable-
languages=
ada,c,c++,fortran,java,lto,objc,obj-c++ --enable-graphite --enable-lto
--enable-
```

```
java-awt=gtk --disable-symvers --enable-libjava --program-suffix=-4
--enable-lib
gomp --enable-libssp --enable-libada --enable-threads=posix --with-arch=i686
--w
ith-tune=generic --enable-libgcj-sublibs CC=gcc-4 CXX=g++-4 CC_FOR_
TARGET=gcc-4
CXX_FOR_TARGET=g++-4 GNATMAKE_FOR_TARGET=gnatmake GNATBIND_FOR_
TARGET=gnatbind -
-with-ecj-jar=/usr/share/java/ecj.jar
Thread model: posix
gcc version 4.5.3 (GCC)


C:\Documents and Settings\hlgu>gcj
gcj: no input files


C:\Documents and Settings\hlgu>gnat
GNAT 4.5.3
Copyright 1996-2010, Free Software Foundation, Inc.

List of available commands


gnat bind               gnatbind
gnat chop               gnatchop
gnat clean              gnatclean
gnat compile            gnatmake -f -u -c
gnat check              gnatcheck
gnat sync               gnatsync
gnat elim               gnatelim
gnat find               gnatfind
gnat krunch             gnatkr
gnat link               gnatlink
gnat list               gnatls
gnat make               gnatmake
gnat metric             gnatmetric
gnat name               gnatname
gnat preprocess         gnatprep
gnat pretty             gnatpp
gnat stack              gnatstack
gnat stub               gnatstub
gnat xref               gnatxref
Commands find, list, metric, pretty, stack, stub and xref accept project
file sw
itches -vPx, -Pprj and -Xnam=val
```

8. Finally, check out the NDK core command ndk-build script to
    see if it can run.

```
C:\Documents and Settings\hlgu>ndk-build
Android NDK: Your Android application project path contains spaces:
'C:/./ Settings/'
Android NDK: The Android NDK build cannot work here. Please move your
project to a different location.
D:\Android\android-ndk-r8d\build/core/build-local.mk:137: *** Android NDK:
Aborting. Stop.
```

If your output looks like this, it indicates that the Cygwin and NDK have been installed and configured successfully.

Install CDT

CDT is an Eclipse plug-in that compiles C code into .SO shared libraries. In fact, after installing the Cygwin and NDK module, you can compile C code into .SO shared libraries at the command line, which means the core component of Windows NDK is already installed. If you still like using the Eclipse IDE rather than a command-line compiler to compile the local library, you need to install the CDT module; otherwise, skip this step and move ahead to the NDK examples.

If you need to install CDT, use the following steps:

1. Visit Eclipse's official web site at http://www.eclipse.org/ cdt/downloads.php to download the CDT package. As shown on the download page in Figure 7-21, you can click to download a version of the software. In this case, click cdt-master-8.1.1.zip to start the download.

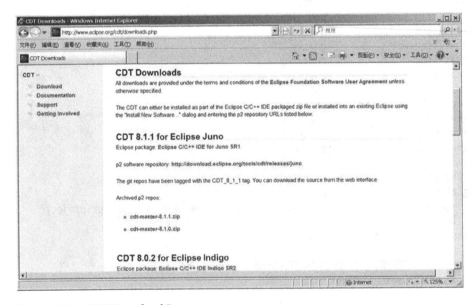

Figure 7-21. *CDT Download Page*

2. Start Eclipse. Select menu \HELP\Install new software and start to install CDT.

3. In the pop-up Install dialog box, click Add, as shown in Figure 7-22.

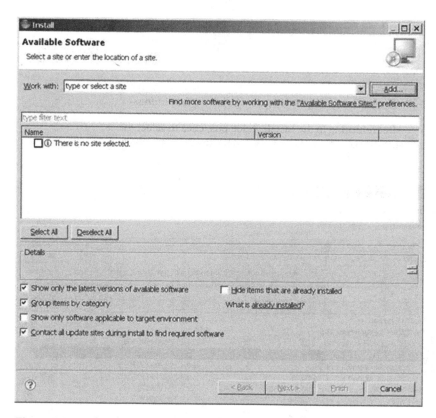

Figure 7-22. *Eclipse Install Software Dialog Box*

4. In the pop-up Add Repository dialog box, enter a name for Name and a software download web site address in Location. You can enter the local address or the Internet address. If you're using an Internet address, Eclipse will go to the Internet to download and install the package, while the local address will direct Eclipse to install the software from the local package. Enter the local address; then you can click the Archive button in the pop-up dialog box and enter the directory and filename for the downloaded cdt-master-8.1.1.zip file, as shown in Figure 7-23. If the file is downloaded from the Internet, the address is http://download.eclipse.org/tools/cdt/releases/galileo/.

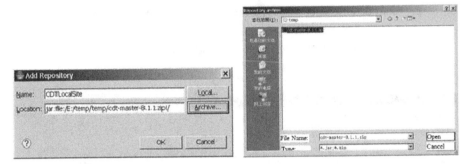

Figure 7-23. *Dialog Box of Eclipse Software Update Install Address*

5. After returning to the Install dialog box, click to select the software components that need to be installed, as shown in Figure 7-24.

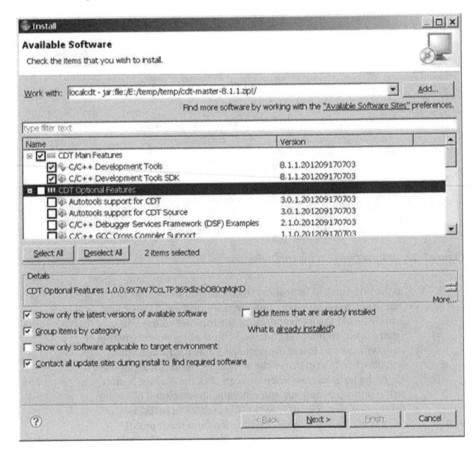

Figure 7-24. *Selection Box for CDT for Components to Install*

Of the components list, the CDT Main Feature is the required component. In this example, we only select this component.

6. A list of detailed information about CDT components to install is displayed, as shown in Figure 7-25.

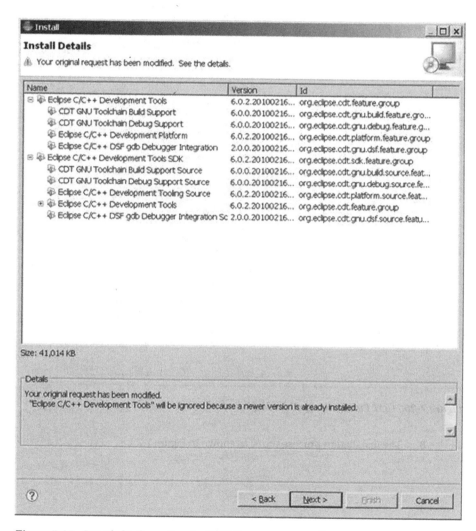

Figure 7-25. *Detailed Information for CDT Component Installation*

7. Review the licenses dialog box. Click "I accept the terms of the license agreement" to continue, as shown in Figure 7-26.

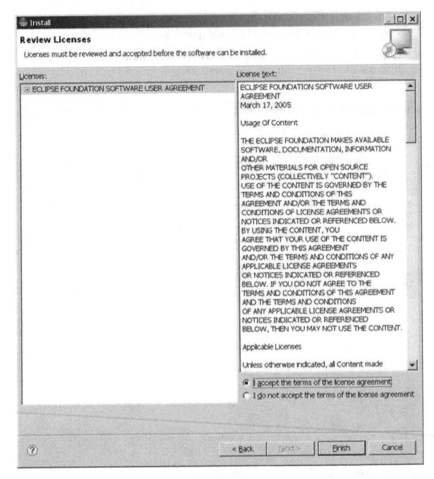

Figure 7-26. *CDT License Review Window*

8. The installation process starts, as shown in Figure 7-27.

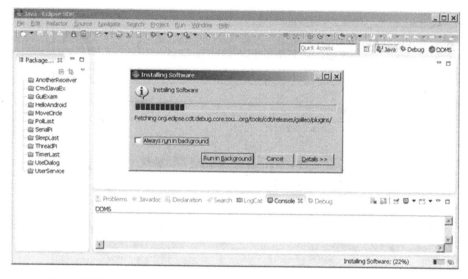

Figure 7-27. *CDT Installation Progress*

9. When the installation process is complete, restart Eclipse to complete the installation.

NDK Examples

This section includes an example to illustrate the use of JNI and NDK. As described previously, NDK can run from the command line and in the Eclipse IDE. We will use both methods to generate the same NDK application.

Using the Command-Line Method to Generate a Library File

The name of this example is jnitest, and it's a simple example to demonstrate the JNI code framework. The steps are outlined in the following sections.

Create an Android App Project

First, you need to create an Android app project, compile the code, and generate the .apk package. Create a project in Eclipse, and name the project jnitest. Choose Build SDK to support the x86 version of the API (in this case the Android 4.0.3), as shown in Figure 7-28. Finally, you generate the project.

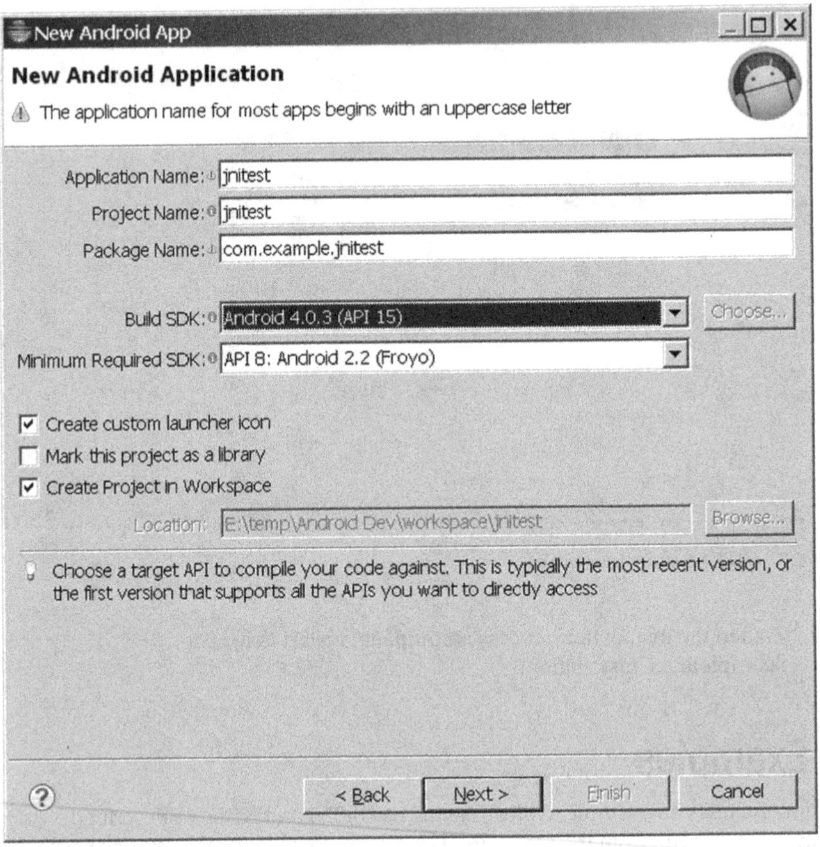

Figure 7-28. jnitest Project Parameters Setup

After the project is generated, the file structure is created as shown in Figure 7-29. Note the directory where the library file (in this case, android.jar) is located, because the following steps will use this parameter.

Figure 7-29. *File Structure of jnitest Project*

Modify the Java Files

Next you modify the Java files, creating code using a C function. In this case, the only Java file is MainActivity.java. You need to modify its code as follows:

```
1.    package com.example.jnitest;
2.    import android.app.Activity;
3.    import android.widget.TextView;
4.    import android.os.Bundle;
5.    public class MainActivity extends Activity
6.    {
7.        @Override
8.        public void onCreate(Bundle savedInstanceState)
9.        {
10.           super.onCreate(savedInstanceState);
11.           TextView tv = new TextView(this);
12.           tv.setText(stringFromJNI() );   // stringFromJNIas a  C
function
13.           setContentView(tv);
14.       }
```

```
15.      public native String stringFromJNI();
16.
17.         static {
18.                         System.loadLibrary("jnitestmysharelib");
19.         }
20.      }
```

The code is very simple. In lines 11 through 13, you use a TextView to display a string returned from the stringFromJNI() function. But unlike the Android application discussed before, there is nowhere in the entire project that you can find the implementation code of this function. So where has the implementation of the function occurred? In line 15 you declare that the function is not a function written in Java, but is instead written by the local (native) libraries, which means the function is outside of Java. Since it's implemented in the local library, the question is what libraries? The answers are described in lines 17–20. The parameter of the static function LoadLibrary of System class describes the name of the library. The library is a Linux shared library named libjnitestmysharelib.so. The application code declared in the static area will be executed before Activity.onCreate. The library will be loaded into memory when it's first used.

Interestingly, when the loadLibrary function loads the library name, it will automatically add the lib prefix before the parameters and the .SO suffix to the end. Of course, if the name of the library file specified by the parameter starts with lib, the function will not add the lib prefix to the filename.

Generate the Project in Eclipse

Only build (build), rather than run. This will compile the project, but the .apk file won't be deployed to the target machine.

When this step is completed, the corresponding .class files will be generated in the project directory called bin\classes\com\example\jnitest. This step must be completed before the next step, because the next step needs the appropriate .class files.

Create a Subdirectory in the Project Root Directory

Name this subdirectory jni. For example, if the project root directory is E:\temp\AndroidDev\workspace\jnitest, you can use the md command to create the jni subdirectory.

```
E:\temp\Android Dev\workspace\jnitest>mkdir jni
```

Then test whether the directory has been built:

```
E:\temp\Android Dev\workspace\jnitest>dir
...
2013-02-01  00:45     <DIR>              jni
```

Create a C Interface File

The so-called C interface file is the C function prototype that works with the local (external) function. Specific to this case are the C function prototypes of the stringFromJNI function. You declare that you need to use the prototype of the external function, but it is in Java format: you need to change it to C formatbuilding C-JNI interface file. This step can be done with the javah command. The command format is:

```
$ javah -classpath <directory of jar and .class documents>
-d <directory of .h documents>  <the package + class name of class>
```

Command parameters are described here:

- -classpath: Represents the classpath

- -d ...: Represents the storage directory for the generated header file

- <class name>: The complete .class classname of a native function being used, which consists of "the package + class name of class" component.

For this example, follow these steps:

1. Enter the root directory from the command line (in this example, it's E:\temp\Android Dev\workspace\jnitest).

2. Then run the following command:

```
E:> javah -classpath "D:\Android\android-sdk\platforms\android-15\android.
jar";bin/classes  com.example.jnitest.MainActivity
```

In this example, the stringFromJNI's class of the native function used is MainActivity, and the resulting file after compiling this class is MainActivity.class, which is located in the root directory of the project bin \classes\com\example directory. The first line of the source code file of its class MainActivity.java shows where the package of the class is:

```
package com.example.jnitest;
```

In the previous command, class name = package name.Class name (be careful not to use the .class suffix), -classpath first needs to explain the Java library path of the entire package (in this case the library file is android.jar; its location is shown in Figure 7-30, namely D:\Android\android-sdk\ platforms\android-15\android.jar). -classpath also needs to explain the target class (MainActivity.class) directory. In this case, it is in the bin\classes directory, under bin\classes\com\example\ MainActivity. class (both are separated by semicolons).

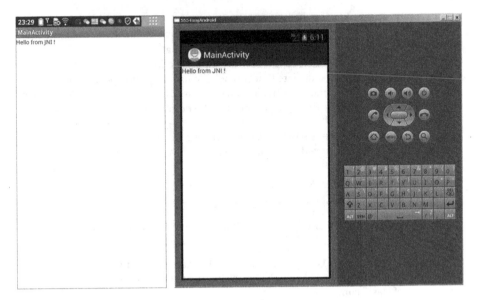

Figure 7-30. jnitest Application Running Interface

After the previous steps, the .h file is generated in the current directory (the project root directory). The file defines the C language function interface.

You can test the output of the previous steps:

```
E:\temp\Android Dev\workspace\jnitest>dir
...
2013-01-31  22:00        3,556 com_example_jnitest_MainActivity.h
```

It is apparent that a new .h file has been generated. The document reads as follows:

```
1.      /* DO NOT EDIT THIS FILE - it is machine generated */
2.      #include <jni.h>
3.      /* Header for class com_example_jnitest_MainActivity */
4.
5.      #ifndef _Included_com_example_jnitest_MainActivity
6.      #define _Included_com_example_jnitest_MainActivity
7.      #ifdef __cplusplus
8.      extern "C" {
9.      #endif
10.     #undef com_example_jnitest_MainActivity_MODE_PRIVATE
11.     #define com_example_jnitest_MainActivity_MODE_PRIVATE OL
12.     #undef com_example_jnitest_MainActivity_MODE_WORLD_READABLE
13.     #define com_example_jnitest_MainActivity_MODE_WORLD_READABLE 1L
14.     #undef com_example_jnitest_MainActivity_MODE_WORLD_WRITEABLE
15.     #define com_example_jnitest_MainActivity_MODE_WORLD_WRITEABLE 2L
16.     #undef com_example_jnitest_MainActivity_MODE_APPEND
```

```
17.    #define com_example_jnitest_MainActivity_MODE_APPEND 32768L
18.    #undef com_example_jnitest_MainActivity_MODE_MULTI_PROCESS
19.    #define com_example_jnitest_MainActivity_MODE_MULTI_PROCESS 4L
20.    #undef com_example_jnitest_MainActivity_BIND_AUTO_CREATE
21.    #define com_example_jnitest_MainActivity_BIND_AUTO_CREATE 1L
22.    #undef com_example_jnitest_MainActivity_BIND_DEBUG_UNBIND
23.    #define com_example_jnitest_MainActivity_BIND_DEBUG_UNBIND 2L
24.    #undef com_example_jnitest_MainActivity_BIND_NOT_FOREGROUND
25.    #define com_example_jnitest_MainActivity_BIND_NOT_FOREGROUND 4L
26.    #undef com_example_jnitest_MainActivity_BIND_ABOVE_CLIENT
27.    #define com_example_jnitest_MainActivity_BIND_ABOVE_CLIENT 8L
28.    #undef com_example_jnitest_MainActivity_BIND_ALLOW_OOM_MANAGEMENT
29.    #define com_example_jnitest_MainActivity_BIND_ALLOW_OOM_MANAGEMENT
16L
30.    #undef com_example_jnitest_MainActivity_BIND_WAIVE_PRIORITY
31.    #define com_example_jnitest_MainActivity_BIND_WAIVE_PRIORITY 32L
32.    #undef com_example_jnitest_MainActivity_BIND_IMPORTANT
33.    #define com_example_jnitest_MainActivity_BIND_IMPORTANT 64L
34.    #undef com_example_jnitest_MainActivity_BIND_ADJUST_WITH_ACTIVITY
35.    #define com_example_jnitest_MainActivity_BIND_ADJUST_WITH_ACTIVITY
128L
36.    #undef com_example_jnitest_MainActivity_CONTEXT_INCLUDE_CODE
37.    #define com_example_jnitest_MainActivity_CONTEXT_INCLUDE_CODE 1L
38.    #undef com_example_jnitest_MainActivity_CONTEXT_IGNORE_SECURITY
39.    #define com_example_jnitest_MainActivity_CONTEXT_IGNORE_SECURITY 2L
40.    #undef com_example_jnitest_MainActivity_CONTEXT_RESTRICTED
41.    #define com_example_jnitest_MainActivity_CONTEXT_RESTRICTED 4L
42.    #undef com_example_jnitest_MainActivity_RESULT_CANCELED
43.    #define com_example_jnitest_MainActivity_RESULT_CANCELED 0L
44.    #undef com_example_jnitest_MainActivity_RESULT_OK
45.    #define com_example_jnitest_MainActivity_RESULT_OK -1L
46.    #undef com_example_jnitest_MainActivity_RESULT_FIRST_USER
47.    #define com_example_jnitest_MainActivity_RESULT_FIRST_USER 1L
48.    #undef com_example_jnitest_MainActivity_DEFAULT_KEYS_DISABLE
49.    #define com_example_jnitest_MainActivity_DEFAULT_KEYS_DISABLE 0L
50.    #undef com_example_jnitest_MainActivity_DEFAULT_KEYS_DIALER
51.    #define com_example_jnitest_MainActivity_DEFAULT_KEYS_DIALER 1L
52.    #undef com_example_jnitest_MainActivity_DEFAULT_KEYS_SHORTCUT
53.    #define com_example_jnitest_MainActivity_DEFAULT_KEYS_SHORTCUT 2L
54.    #undef com_example_jnitest_MainActivity_DEFAULT_KEYS_SEARCH_LOCAL
55.    #define com_example_jnitest_MainActivity_DEFAULT_KEYS_SEARCH_LOCAL
3L
56.    #undef com_example_jnitest_MainActivity_DEFAULT_KEYS_SEARCH_GLOBAL
57.    #define com_example_jnitest_MainActivity_DEFAULT_KEYS_SEARCH_GLOBAL
4L
```

```
58.      /*
59.       * Class:      com_example_jnitest_MainActivity
60.       * Method:     stringFromJNI
61.       * Signature:  ()Ljava/lang/String;
62.       */
63.      JNIEXPORT jstring JNICALL Java_com_example_jnitest_MainActivity_
stringFromJNI
64.         (JNIEnv *, jobject);
65.
66.      #ifdef __cplusplus
67.      }
68.      #endif
69.      #endif
```

In the previous code, pay special attention to lines 63-64, which are C function prototypes of a local function stringFromJNI.

Compile the Corresponding. C File

This is the true realization of a local function (stringFromJNI). The source code file is obtained by modifying the .h file, according to the previous steps.

Create a new .C file under the jni subdirectory in the project. The filename can be created randomly. In this case, it is named jni testccode.c. The contents are as follows:

```
1.      #include <string.h>
2.      #include <jni.h>
3.      jstring Java_com_example_hellojni_HelloJni_stringFromJNI( JNIEnv*
env,  jobject thiz )
4.      {
5.          return (*env)->NewStringUTF(env, "Hello from JNI !");
// Newly added code
6.      }
```

The previous code defines the function implementation and is very simple. Line 3 is the Java code used in the prototype definition of the function stringFromJNI. It is basically a copy of the corresponding content of the .h file obtained from the previous steps (lines 63-64 of com_example_jnitest_MainActivity.h), and slightly modified to make the point. The prototype formats of this function are fixed—JNIEnv* env and jobject thiz are inherent parameters of JNI. Because the parameter of the stringFromJNI function is empty, there are only two parameters in the generated C function. The role of the code in line 5 is to return the string "Hello fromJNI!" as the return value.

The code in line 2 is the header file that contains the JNI function, which is required for any functions that use JNI. As it relates to the string function, line 1 contains the corresponding header file in this case. After you complete the previous steps, the .h file has no further use and can be deleted.

Create the NDK Makefile File in the jni Directory

These documents mainly include the Android.mk and Application.mk files, where Android.mk is required. However, if you use the default configuration of the application, you do not need Application.mk. The four specific steps are as follows:

1. Create a new Android.mk text file in the jni directory in the project. This file tells the compiler about some requirements, such as which C files to compile, the filename for compiled code, and so on. Enter the following:

   ```
   LOCAL_PATH := $(call my-dir)
   include $(CLEAR_VARS)
   LOCAL_MODULE    := jnitestmysharelib
   LOCAL_SRC_FILES := jnitestccode.c
   include $(BUILD_SHARED_LIBRARY)
   ```

The file contents are explained next.

Line 3 represents the generated .SO filename (identifying each module described in your Android.mk file). It must be consistent with parameter values of the System.loadLibrary function in the Java code. This name must be unique and may not contain any spaces.

■ **Note**   The build system automatically generates the appropriate prefix and suffix. In other words, if one is the shared library module named jnitestmysharelib, then a libjnitestmysharelib.so file will be generated. If you name the library libhello-jni, the compiler will not add the lib prefix and will generate libhello-jni.so too.

The LOCAL_SRC_FILES variable in line 4 must contain the C or C++ source code files to be compiled and packaged into modules. The previous steps create a C filename.

■ **Note**   Users do not have to list the header files and include files here, because the compiler will automatically identify the dependent files for you. Just list source code files that are directly passed to the compiler. In addition, the default extension name of C++ source files is .CPP. It is possible to specify a different extension name, as long as you define the LOCAL_DEFAULT_CPP_EXTENSION variable. Don't forget the small dot at the start (.cxx, rather than cxx).

The code in Lines 3 through 4 is very important and must be modified for each NDK application based on their actual configuration. The contents of the other lines can be copied from the previous example.

2. Create an Application.mk text file in the jni directory in the project. This file tells the compiler the specific settings for this application. Enter the following:

```
APP_ABI := x86
```

This file is very simple. You use the object code generated by the application instructions for the x86 architecture, so you can run the application on Intel Atom machines. For APP_ABI parameters, use x86, armeabi, or armeabi-v7a.

3. Next, compile the .c file to the .SO shared library file.

Go to project root directory (where AndroidManifest.xml is located) and run the ndk-build command:

```
E:\temp\Android Dev\workspace\jnitest>ndk-build
D:/Android/android-ndk-r8d/build/core/add-application.mk:128: Android NDK:
WARNI
NG: APP_PLATFORM android-14 is larger than android:minSdkVersion 8 in
./AndroidM
anifest.xml
"Compile x86  : jnitestmysharelib <= jnitestccode.c
SharedLibrary : libjnitestmysharelib.so
Install       : libjnitestmysharelib.so => libs/x86/libjnitestmysharelib.so
```

The previous command will add two subdirectories (libs and obj) in the project. Include an execution version of the .SO file (the command execution information prompt file named libjnitestmysharelib.so) under the obj directory, and it will eventually put the final version under the libs directory.

If the previous steps do not define the Application.mk file of the specified ABI, using the ndk-build command will generate object code of the ARM architecture (armeabi). If you must generate the x86 architecture instructions, you can also use the ndk-build APP_ABI = x86 command to remedy the situation. The architecture of the object code generated by this command is still x86.

4. Deployment: run the project.

After you complete this step, you are almost ready to deploy and run the project. The application running on the interface on the target device is shown in Figure 7-30.

Generating a Library File in the IDE

Recall from the steps described in the previous section the process of compiling the C files into the dynamic library .SO files that can be run on the Android target device. You run the ndk-build command in the command line to complete the process. In fact, you can also complete this step within the Eclipse IDE.

When generating the library files in the IDE, the code in the first four steps are exactly the same as in the previous section. You just have to compile the .C files into .SO shared library files instead. This is explained in detail as follows:

1. Compile the .C file into the .SO shared library file. Right-click on the project name, and select Build Path, Configure Build Path. In the pop-up dialog box, select the Builders branch. Then click the New button in the dialog box. Double-click Program in the prompt dialog box. This process is shown in Figure 7-31.

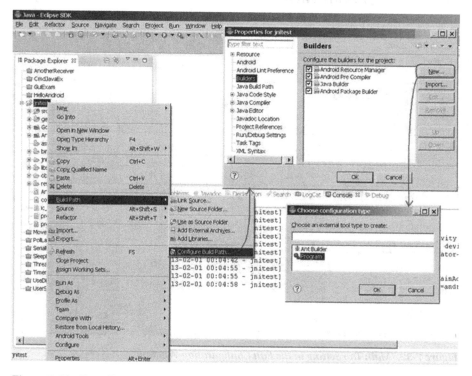

Figure 7-31. *Enter Parameters Settings for the Interface of Compiling C Code in Eclipse*

2. In the Edit Configuration dialog box, enter the following for the Main tab settings:

   - *Location*: The path to the Cygwin bash.exe.

   - *Working Directory*: The bin directory of Cygwin.

- *Arguments:*

  ```
  --login -c "cd '/cygdrive/E/temp/Android Dev/workspace/
  jnitest' && $ANDROID_NDK_ROOT/ndk-build"
  ```

where E/temp/Android Dev/workspace/jnitest is the letter and path for the project. The entire setting is shown in Figure 7-32.

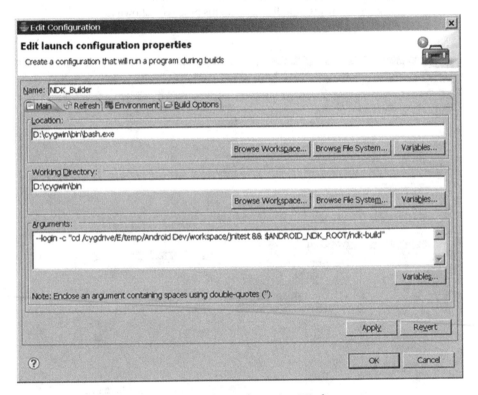

***Figure 7-32.** Main Tab Setting in the Edit Configuration Window*

3. Then configure the Refresh tab, ensuring that these items are selected—The Entire Workspace and Recursively Include Sub-Folders—as shown in Figure 7-33.

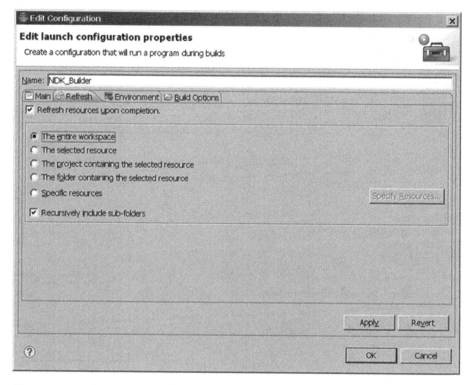

Figure 7-33. *Edit Configuration Window Refresh Tab Settings*

4. Reconfigure the Build Options tab. Check the During Auto
    Builds and Specify Working Set of Relevant Resources items,
    as shown in Figure 7-34.

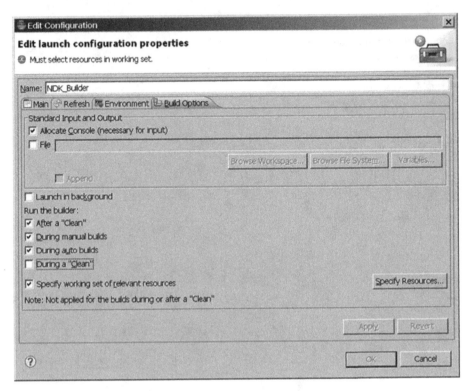

Figure 7-34. *Edit Configuration Window Build Options Tab Settings*

5. Click on the Specify Resources button. In the Edit Working Set dialog box, select the jni directory, as shown in Figure 7-35.

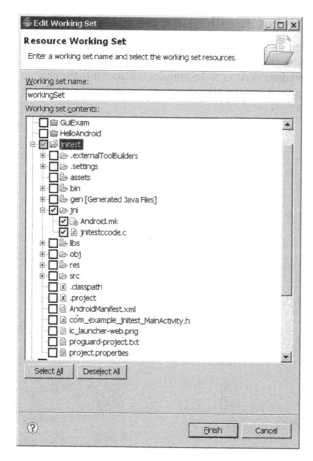

Figure 7-35. *Select Source Code Directories Where Related Files Are Located*

6. When the previous steps are correctly configured, the configuration is saved. It will automatically compile C-related code under the jni directory and output the corresponding .SO library files to the project's libs directory. The libs directory is created automatically. In the Console window you can see the output information for the build, as follows:

```
/cygdrive/d/Android/android-ndk-r8d/build/core/add-application.
mk:128: Android NDK: WARNING: APP_PLATFORM android-14 is larger than
android:minSdkVersion 8 in ./AndroidManifest.xml
Cygwin         : Generating dependency file converter script
Compile x86    : jnitestmysharelib <= jnitestccode.c
SharedLibrary  : libjnitestmysharelib.so
Install        : libjnitestmysharelib.so => libs/x86/libjnitestmysharelib.so
```

Workflow Analysis for NDK Application Development

The process of generating an NDK project described previously works naturally to achieve the C library integration with Java. In the final step, you compile .C files into the .SO shared library files. The intermediate version of the libraries is placed into the obj directory, and the final version is placed into the libs directory. The project file structure is then created, as shown in Figure 7-36.

Figure 7-36. *The jnitest Project Structure after NDK Library Files Generation*

The shared library .SO files are in the directory of the project in the host machine and will be packed in the generated .apk file. The .apk file is essentially a compressed file. You can use compression software like WinRAR to view its contents. For this example, you can find the .apk file in the bin subdirectory of the project directory. Open it with WinRAR, and show the file structure.

The content of the lib subdirectory of .apk is a clone of the lib subdirectory of the project. In Figure 7-36 the generated .SO file is shown in the lib\x86 subdirectory.

When .apk is deployed to the target machine, it will be unpacked, in which case the .SO files will be placed in the /data/dat/XXX/lib directory, where XXX is the application package name. For example, for the previous example, the directory is /data/data/com.example.jnitest/lib. You can view the file structure of the target machine under the Eclipse DDMS; the file structure of the example is shown in Figure 7-37.

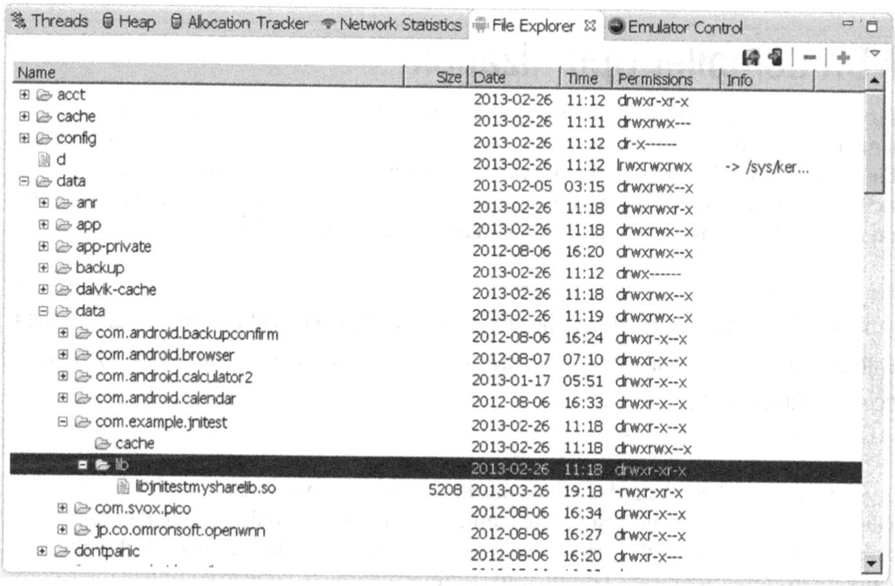

Figure 7-37. *The jnitest Project Structure after NDK Library Files Generation*

In Figure 7-37, you can find the .SO library file under the /data/data/XXX/lib directory, such that when the application is running, the System.loadLibrary function can be loaded into memory to run. Here you see the .SO file in a graphical display of DDMS. Interested readers can try it on the command line, using the adb shell command to view the corresponding contents in the target file directory.

In addition, if you run the jnitest application in an emulator (in this case the target machine is a virtual machine), you'll see the following output in the Eclipse Logcat window:

```
1.  07-10 05:43:08.579: E/Trace(6263): error opening trace file: No such
file or directory (2)
2.  07-10 05:43:08.729: D/dalvikvm(6263): Trying to load lib /data/data/com.
example.jnitest/lib/libjnitestmysharelib.so 0x411e8b30
3.  07-10 05:43:08.838: D/dalvikvm(6263): Added shared lib /data/data/com.
example.jnitest/lib/libjnitestmysharelib.so 0x411e8b30
4.  07-10 05:43:08.838: D/dalvikvm(6263): No JNI_OnLoad found in /data/data/
com.example.jnitest/lib/libjnitestmysharelib.so 0x411e8b30, skipping init
```

5. 07-10 05:43:11.773: I/Choreographer(6263): Skipped 143 frames!
The application may be doing too much work on its main thread.
6. 07-10 05:43:12.097: D/gralloc_goldfish(6263): Emulator without GPU
emulation detected.

Lines 2–3 are reminders about the .SO shared library loaded into the application.

NDK Compiler Optimization

From the previous example, you can see that the NDK tool's core role is to compile the source code into the .SO library file that can run on an Android machine. The .SO library file is placed into the lib subdirectory of the project directory, so that when you use Eclipse to deploy applications, you can deploy the library files to the appropriate location on a target device, and the application can run using the library function.

■ **Note**   The nature of the NDK application is to establish a code framework that complies with the JNI standard. This will enable Java applications to use a local function beyond the scope of the virtual machine.

The key NDK command used to compile the source code into a .SO library file is ndk-build. It's not actually a separate command, but an executable script. It calls the make command in the GNU cross-development tools to compile a project, and make calls, for example, to the gcc compiler to compile the source code to complete the whole process, as shown in Figure 7-38. Of course, you can also directly use .SO shared libraries developed by third parties already in Android applications, thus avoiding the need to write your own library (function code).

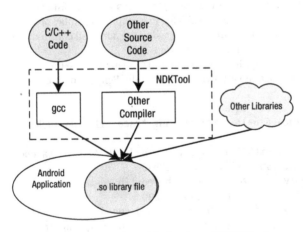

Figure 7-38. *The Working Mechanism of NDK Tools*

As Figure 7-38 shows, core GNU compiler gcc is the core tool in the NDK to complete C/C++ source code compilation. gcc is the standard compiler of Linux, and it can compile and link C, C++, Object-C, FORTRAN, and other source code on the local machine. In fact, the gcc compiler can not only do local compiling, but can also cross-compiling. This feature has been used by the Android NDK and other embedded development tools. In compiler usage, gcc cross-compiling is compatible with native compiling; that is, command parameters and switches of locally compiled code can essentially be ported without modification to cross-compiling code. Therefore, the gcc compiling method described next is generic for both local and cross-compiling.

In **Chapter 9: Performance Optimizations for Android Applications on x86**, we will discuss compiler optimizations in greater detail (that is, how some optimizations can be done automatically by the compiler). For systems based on Intel x86 architecture processors, in addition to the GNU gcc compiler, Intel C/C++ compiler is also a good tool. Relatively speaking, because the Intel C/C ++ compiler fully utilizes the features of the Intel processors, the code optimization results will be better. For Android NDK, both Intel C/C++ compiler and gcc can complete the C/C++ code compilation. Currently, the Intel C/C ++ compiler provides the appropriate usage mechanisms. Ordinary users need a professional license, while gcc is open sourced, free software and is more readily available. The following section uses gcc as an experimental tool to explain how to perform C/C++ module compiler optimization for Android applications.

The gcc optimization is controlled by the optimization options of the compiler switches. Some of these options are machine-independent, and some are associated with the machine. Here we will discuss some important options. For machine-related options, we will describe only the ones that are relevant to Intel processors.

Machine-Independent Compiler Switch Options

The machine-independent options for the gcc compiler switches are the -Ox options, which correspond to different optimization levels. The details are as follows.

-0 or -01

Level 1 optimization, which is the default level of optimization, uses the -0 option. The compiler tries to reduce code size and execution time. For large functions, it needs to spend more compiling time and use a large amount of memory resources for optimizing compiling.

When the -0 option is not used, the compiler's goal is to reduce the overhead of compiling, so that results can be debugged quickly. In this compilation mode, statements are independent. By inserting a breakpoint interrupt program run between the two statements, a user can reassign variables or modify the program counter to jump to other currently executing statements, so you can precisely control the running process. The user can also get results when they want to debug. In addition, if the -0 option is not used, only declared variables of a register can have register allocation.

When you specify the -0 option, the -fthread-jumps and -fdefer-pop options are turned on. On a machine with a delay slot, the -fdelayed-branch option is turned on. Even for machines that support debugging without a frame pointer, the -fomit-frame-pointer option is turned on. Some machines may also activate other options.

-O2

Optimizes even more. GCC performs nearly all supported optimizations that do not involve a space-speed tradeoff. When compared to -O, this option increases compilation time and the performance of the generated code.

-O3

Optimizes yet more. The option -O3 turns on all optimizations specified by -O2 and also turns on the -finline-functions, -funswitch-loops, -fpredictive-commoning, -fgcse-after-reload, -ftree-vectorize, -fvect-cost-model, -ftree-partial-pre, and -fipa-cp-clone options.

-O0

Reduces compilation time and makes debugging produce the expected results. This is the default.

An automatic inline function is often used as a function optimization measure. C99 (C language ISO standard developed in 1999) and C++ both support the inline keyword. The inline function is a reflection of thinking of using inline space in exchange for time. The compiler does not compile an inline-described function into a function, but directly expands the code for the function body, thereby eliminating the function call, returning the call ret instruction and the parameter's push instruction execution. For example, in the following function:

```
inline long factorial (int i)
{
    return factorial_table[i];
}
```

all occurrences of the factorial () call are replaced with the factorial_table [] array references.

When in the optimizing state, some compilers will treat that function as an inline function even if the function does not use inline instructions. It does this only if appropriate in the circumstances (such as the body of the function code is relatively short and the definition is in the header file), in exchange for execution time.

Loop unrolling is a classic speed optimization method and is considered by many compilers as the automatic optimization strategy. For example, the following loop code needs to loop 100 cycles:

```
for (i = 0; i < 100; i++)
{
    do_stuff(i);
}
```

In all 100 cycles, at the end of each cycle, the cycle conditions have to be checked to do a comparative judgment. By using a loop-unrolling strategy, the code can be transformed as follows:

```
for (i = 0; i < 100; )
{
    do_stuff(i); i++;
    do_stuff(i); i++;
    do_stuff(i); i++;
    do_stuff(i); i++;
    do_stuff(i); i++;
    do_stuff(i); i++;
    do_stuff(i); i++;
    do_stuff(i); i++;
    do_stuff(i); i++;
    do_stuff(i); i++;
}
```

As you can see, the new code reduces the comparison instruction from 100 to 10 times, and the time used on conditions comparison can be reduced by 90 percent.

Both methods described previously will increase the optimization of the object code. This is a typical space for time-optimization ideas.

Intel Processor-Related Compiler Switch Options

The m option of gcc is defined for the Intel i386 and x86 - 64 processors family. The main command options are explained in Table 7-3.

Table 7-3. *Intel Processor-Related gcc Switch Options*

Switch Options	Note	Description
-march=cpu-type -mtune=cpu-type		Generated code for the specified type of CPU. CPU type can be i386, i486, i586, Pentium, i686, Pentium 4, and so on
-msse		
-msse2		
-msse3		
-mssse3	gxx-4.3 new addition	
-msse4.1	gcc-4.3 new addition	The compiler automatic vectorization. Use or not use MMX, SSE, SSE2 instructions. For example, -msse represents programming into instruction, and –mno-sse means not programmed into the SSE instruction
-msse4.2	gcc-4.3 new addition	
-msse4	Include 4.1, 4.2 ,gcc-4.3 new addition	
-mmmx		
-mno-sse		
-mno-sse2		
-mno-mmx		
-m32 -m64		Generated 32/64 machine code

In Table 7-3, -march is the CPU type of the machine, and -mtune is the CPU type that the compiler wants to optimize (by default it is the same as with -march). The -march option is "tight constraint," and -mtune is "loose constraint." The -mtune option can provide backward compatibility.

Compiler optimization options with -march = i686, -mtune = pentium4 is optimized for the Pentium 4 processor, but can be run on any i686 as well.

For -mtune = pentium-mmx compiled procedures, the Pentium 4 processor can be run.

-march=cpu-type

This option will generate cpu-type instructions that specify the type of machine. The -mtune = cpu-type option is available only for optimizing code generated for cpu-type. By contrast, -march = cpu-type generates code not run on non-gcc for the specified type of processor, which means that -march = cpu-type implies the -mtune = cpu-type option.

The cpu-type option values that are related to Intel processors are listed in Table 7-4.

Table 7-4. *The Main Optional Value of* -march *Parameters of* gcc *for* cpu-type

cpu-type Value	Description
native	This selects the CPU to generate code at compilation time by determining the processor type of the compiling machine. Using -march=native enables all instruction subsets supported by the local machine (hence the result might not run on different machines). Using -mtune=native produces code optimized for the local machine under the constraints of the selected instruction set.
i386	Original Intel i386 CPU.
i486	Intel i486 CPU. (No scheduling is implemented for this chip.)
i586	Intel Pentium CPU with no MMX support.
pentium	
pentium-mmx	Intel Pentium MMX CPU, based on Pentium core with MMX instruction set support.
pentiumpro	Intel Pentium Pro CPU.
i686	When used with -march, the Pentium Pro instruction set is used, so the code runs on all i686 family chips. When used with -mtune, it has the same meaning as "generic."
pentium2	Intel Pentium II CPU, based on Pentium Pro core with MMX instruction set support.
pentium3 pentium3m	Intel Pentium III CPU, based on Pentium Pro core with MMX and SSE instruction set support.
pentium-m	Intel Pentium M; low-power version of Intel Pentium III CPU with MMX, SSE, and SSE2 instruction set support. Used by Centrino notebooks.
pentium4 pentium4m	Intel Pentium 4 CPU with MMX, SSE and SSE2 instruction set support.
prescott	Improved version of Intel Pentium 4 CPU with MMX, SSE, SSE2, and SSE3 instruction set support.
nocona	Improved version of Intel Pentium 4 CPU with 64-bit extensions, MMX, SSE, SSE2, and SSE3 instruction set support.
core2	Intel Core 2 CPU with 64-bit extensions, MMX, SSE, SSE2, SSE3, and SSSE3 instruction set support.

(continued)

Table 7-4. (*continued*)

cpu-type Value	Description
corei7	Intel Core i7 CPU with 64-bit extensions, MMX, SSE, SSE2, SSE3, SSSE3, SSE4.1, and SSE4.2 instruction set support.
corei7-avx	Intel Core i7 CPU with 64-bit extensions, MMX, SSE, SSE2, SSE3, SSSE3, SSE4.1, SSE4.2, AVX, AES, and PCLMUL instruction set support.
core-avx-i	Intel Core CPU with 64-bit extensions, MMX, SSE, SSE2, SSE3, SSSE3, SSE4.1, SSE4.2, AVX, AES, PCLMUL, FSGSBASE, RDRND, and F16C instruction set support.
atom	Intel Atom CPU with 64-bit extensions, MMX, SSE, SSE2, SSE3, and SSSE3 instruction set support.

Traditional gcc is a local compiler. These command options can be added to gcc to control gcc compiler options. For example, say you have an int_sin.c file.

```
$ gcc int_sin.c
```

The previous command uses the -O1 optimization level (default level) and will compile int_sin.c into an executable file, called a.out by default.

```
$ gcc int_sin.c -o sinnorm
```

The previous command uses the -O1 optimization level (default level) to compile int_sin.c into an executable file; the executable filename is specified as sinnorm.

```
$ gcc int_cos.c -fPIC -shared -o coslib.so
```

The previous command uses the -O1 optimization level (default level) to compile int_cos.c into a shared library file called coslib.so. Unlike the previous source code files compiled into an executable program, this command requires that the source code file int_cos.c not contain the main function.

```
$ gcc -O0 int_sin.c
```

The previous command compiles int_sin.c into the executable file with the default filename. The compiler does not perform any optimization.

```
$ gcc -O3 int_sin.c
```

The previous command uses the highest optimization level -O3 to compile the int_sin.c file to the executable file with the default filename.

```
$ gcc -msse int_sin.c
```

The previous command compiles int_sin.c into an executable file using SSE instructions.

```
$ gcc -mno-sse int_sin.c
```

The previous command compiles int_sin.c into an executable file without any SSE instructions.

```
$ gcc -mtune=atom int_sin.c
```

The previous command compiles int_sin.c into an executable file that can use the Intel Atom processor instructions.

From the previous example compiled by gcc locally, you have some experience using the compiler switch options for the gcc compiler optimizations. For the gcc native compiler, the gcc command can be used directly in the switch options to achieve compiler optimization. However, from the previous example, you know that the NDK does not directly use the gcc command. Then how do you set the gcc compiler switch option to achieve the NDK optimization?

Recall that using the NDK example, you used the ndk-build command to compile C/C++ source code; the command first needed to read the makefile Android.mk. This file actually contains the gcc command options. Android.mk uses LOCAL_CFLAGS to control and complete the gcc command options. The ndk-build command will pass LOCAL_CFLAGS runtime values to gcc, as its command option to run the gcc command. LOCAL_CFLAGS passes the values to gcc and uses them as the command option to run gcc command.

For example, you amended Android.mk as follows:

```
1.  LOCAL_PATH := $(call my-dir)
2.  include $(CLEAR_VARS)
3.  LOCAL_MODULE        := jnitestmysharelib
4.  LOCAL_SRC_FILES     := jnitestccode.c
5.  LOCAL_CFLAGS        := -O3
6.  include $(BUILD_SHARED_LIBRARY)
```

Line 5 is newly added. It sets the LOCAL_CFLAGS variable script.

When you execute the ndk-build command, which is equivalent to adding a gcc -O3 command option. It instructs gcc to compile the C source code at the highest optimization level O3. Similarly, if you edit the line 5 to:

```
LOCAL_CFLAGS        := -msse3
```

You instruct gcc to compile C source code into object code using SSE3 instructions.

Interested readers can set LOCAL_CFLAGS to a different value, comparing the target library file size and content differences. Note that the previous example jnitest C code is very simple and does not involve complex tasks. As a result, the size or content of the library files are not very different when compiled from different LOCAL_CFLAGS values.

So, can there ever be a significant difference in the size or content of the library file? In fact, the answer is yes. In this regard, we will give practical examples in the following chapters.

Overview

With this chapter behind you, you should have a comprehensive knowledge of the Android native development kit and understand how it can be used to create Android applications for the Intel platform. We also covered the Intel C++ compiler and its options. It is important to remember that the Intel C++ compiler is just one of the possible compilers that can be used for Intel Android applications. We talked at length about the Java native interface that exists to interact with your NDK applications, and how it operates. We also covered various code samples to best explain the various basic optimizations that exist for the Intel C++ compiler.

CHAPTER 8

■ ■ ■

Debugging Android

Not all problems have a technological answer, but when they do, that is the more lasting solution.

—Andy Grove, semiconductor manufacturing pioneer

The processes for identifying runtime issues and possible problematic code in an Android OS-targeted application or in the Android system software stack are remarkably similar. The challenges and approaches are the same, regardless of whether the underlying platform architecture is based on Intel architecture and the latest-generation Atom processor or on ARM architecture. This chapter provides an overview of the available debug methodologies for Android-targeted software on Intel architectures. We will also touch on the setup and configuration of application and system software debug environments targeting Android and Intel architectures in the early part of the chapter. In the process of doing so, we will also point out where the experience differs when developing for ARM architecture.

Prerequisites

This chapter covers the Intel USB driver that is necessary to enable remote application debugging on an Intel Atom processor-based device running Android OS. Additionally we will also look at the Intel Atom x86 System Image for the Android Emulator. If no physical debug target is available, having a virtual Intel Atom processor-based device emulated inside the Android SDK's device emulation layer is the next best option. These two prerequisites in conjunction with the Android SDK build the foundation for cross-development targeting an Intel Atom processor-based tablet or smartphone.

Intel USB Driver for Android Devices

This section looks at the Intel Android USB driver package, which enables you to connect your host development machine to an Android device that contains an Intel Atom processor inside. In this first example, we assume a Windows development host. Similar principles apply to Linux or OS X host systems.

1. Download the installer package from
   http://www.intel.com/software/android.

2. Run the installer and accept the Windows User Account
   Control (UAC) prompt, if applicable.

3. You will see the screen in Figure 8-1. Click Next to continue.
   (If the installer detects an older version of the driver, accept to
   uninstall it.)

Figure 8-1. *USB Device Driver Installation Start Screen*

4. Read and agree to the Intel Android USB Driver End-User
   License Agreement (EULA).

5. You will be prompted to select components. Click the Next
   button to proceed.

6. Choose the path for the installation and click Install.

7. The installer will proceed to install the Android USB drivers.
   This may take a few minutes (see Figure 8-2).

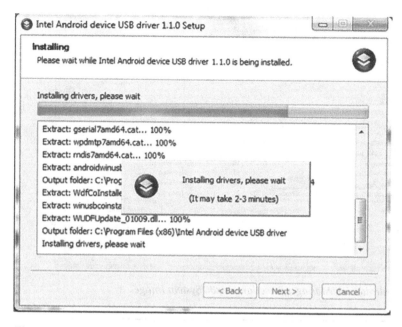

Figure 8-2. USB Device Driver Installation Progress Screen

8. After the driver installation is completed, click OK on the pop-up note and then click on Finish to close the installation program.

Installing the Intel Atom x86 System Image for Android Emulator

For the alternative of debugging on the development host using the Android Virtual Device Manager, the first prerequisite is the availability of the appropriate system image.

Using the Android Emulator requires both an Intel Atom x86 System Image and the Android SDK to be installed. Please refer to the Android developer web site (http://developer.android.com/sdk/installing.html) for Android SDK installation instructions, or refer to **Chapter 6: Installing the Android SDK for Intel Application Development**. The Android SDK Manager allows you to download and install the Intel Atom Android x86 Emulator Image add-on, and then the necessary Intel Atom x86 System Image.

Follow these steps:

1. Start the Android SDK Manager program.

2. Under Packages ➤ Android 4.x.x (API 1x), check the box to select Intel Atom x86 System Image by Intel Corporation.

3. Once selected, click the Install Package button, as shown in Figure 8-3.

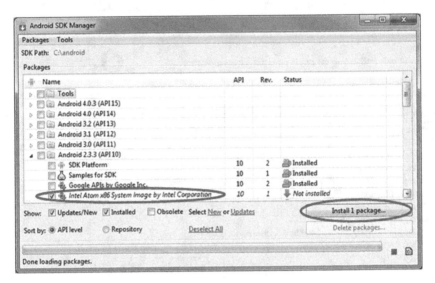

Figure 8-3. Android SDK Manager Selection for x86 System Image

---

■ **Note**   You may have more than one package to install, based on other packages that you
or the Android SDK Manager program selected.

---

4. Review the Intel Corporation license agreement. If you accept
    the terms, select the Accept option and click the Install
    button, as shown in Figure 8-4.

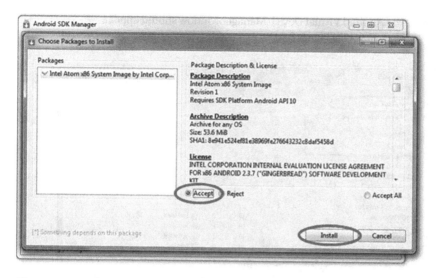

Figure 8-4. *Android SDK Manager—Accepting Licensing Terms*

5. At this point, the Android SDK Manager will download and install the add-on to your Android SDK add-ons folder (<sdk>/add-ons/). The download and install will take several minutes, depending on your connection speed.

6. Select Manage AVDs from the Tools menu (see Figure 8-5).

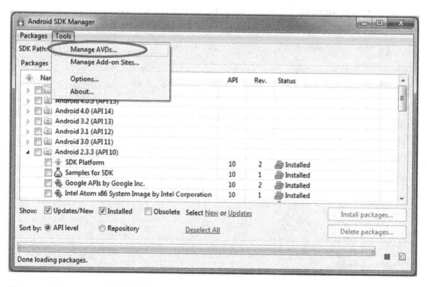

Figure 8-5. *Android SDK Manager—Manage Android Virtual Devices*

7. The Android Virtual Device Manager window should appear. Click New (see Figure 8-6).

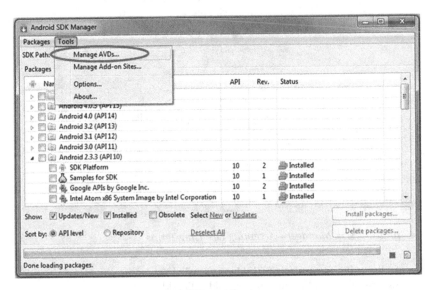

Figure 8-6. *Adding a New Android Virtual Device*

8. Enter a name for your virtual device in the Name field. Spaces are not allowed in the name.

9. Select Intel Atom x86 System Image (Intel Corporation) – API Level 10 from the Target field drop-down list (see Figure 8-7).

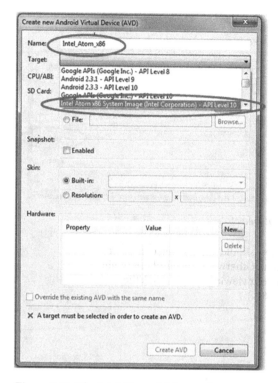

Figure 8-7. *The Intel Atom x86 System Image as a Virtual Device Target*

10. Once you select your configuration settings, click the Create AVD button.

11. The new virtual device should appear on the Android Virtual Device Manager. Select the new device and click the Start button, as shown in Figure 8-8.

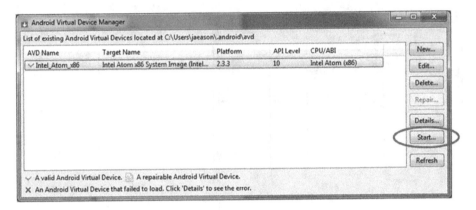

Figure 8-8. *Starting an Android Virtual Device*

12. The Launch Options window should appear. Select the screen size and DPI for your system. Otherwise, the emulator might exceed the dimensions of your viewing screen. Click the Launch button (see Figure 8-9).

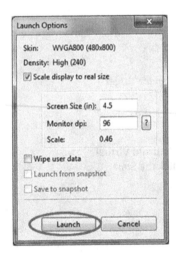

Figure 8-9. *Virtual Device Launch Options*

13. After a few moments, the emulator will launch and show you the screen in Figure 8-10.

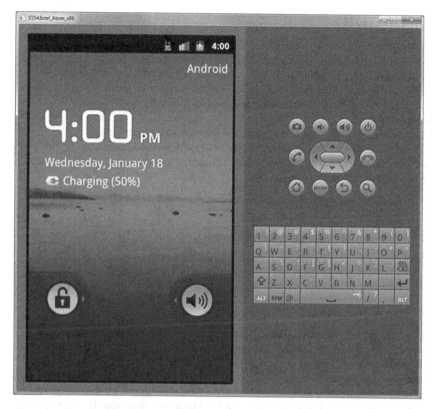

Figure 8-10. *AVD Emulation of Intel Architecture-Based Android Device*

Application Debugging Using the Android Debug Bridge

The Android Debug Bridge (ADB) is a command-line tool that handles debug communication between a debugger on the host—usually GDB, DDMS (Dalvik Debug Monitor Server), or ADT—and an Android image running on the target. The target image could be running on device emulation or running on a physical development device, which you communicate with via a USB-OTG (on-the-go) or USB-to-Ethernet dongle. In short, ADB is the glue that makes application debugging on Android possible.

The device you are connecting to or emulating could cover a wide range of form factors. Typically it would be a smartphone or tablet. It could also be a medical tablet or an embedded device in an industry setting, home energy management, warehousing, or any number of intelligent systems applications.

Setting up the Android Debug Bridge to allow remote debugging of a platform based on the Intel Atom processor does not differ very much from debugging on other architectures.

Setting Up ADB

First you need the Android SDK, including ADB installed on the development host. Instructions for this can be found at http://developer.android.com/sdk/installing.html.

If your target image is running on a physical device, you need to include USB-OTG or USB-to-Ethernet support. For USB-to-Ethernet support, a kernel configuration change and rebuild is required. Your OEM will provide you with the necessary information if desired.

The standard method for remote application debug is to use the existing USB-OTG interface of most Android devices. The setup is described in detail at the Android developer web site at http://developer.android.com/guide/developing/device.html.

The key steps are:

1. Declare your application as "debuggable" in your Android manifest.

2. Turn on USB Debugging on your device.

3. On the device, go to Settings ➤ Applications ➤ Development and enable USB debugging (on an Android 4.x.x device, the setting is located in Settings ➤ Developer Options).

4. Set up your system to detect your device.

If you're developing on Windows, you need to install a USB driver for ADB—visit http://developer.android.com/tools/extras/oem-usb.html for driver downloads and prerequisites.

If you're developing on Ubuntu Linux, you need to add a udev rules file that contains a USB configuration for each type of device you want to use for development. In the rules file, each device manufacturer is identified by a unique vendor ID, as specified by the ATTR{idVendor} property. For a list of vendor IDs, see http://developer. android.com/tools/device.html#VendorIds.

To set up device detection on Ubuntu Linux, log in as root and create this file:

/etc/udev/rules.d/51-android.rules

Use this format to add each vendor to the file:

SUBSYSTEM=="usb", ATTR{idVendor}=="????", MODE="0666", GROUP="plugdev"

The MODE assignment specifies read/write permissions, and GROUP defines which UNIX group owns the device node.

Execute:

chmod a+r /etc/udev/rules.d/51-android.rules

When plugged in over USB, you can verify that your device is connected by executing ADB devices from your SDK platform-tools/directory. If connected, you'll see the device name listed as a device.

With the Android OS booted on the SDK, connect a USB-OTG cable to the (USB mini b) port on the SDK and connect the other end of the cable (USB A) to your development host.

If everything is working, you should be able to run the following command to see the attached device:

```
$ adb devices
* daemon not running. starting it now *
* daemon started successfully *
List of devices attached
0123456789ABCDEF  device
```

■ **Note**   To see which device name is assigned to this connection on the Linux dev. host, you can look at dmesg to find the address of the usb-storage: device found at <num> and then run an ls -l /dev/bus/usb/* listing to find that number.

ADB on Windows

Download and install Eclipse Classic from http://www.eclipse.org/downloads/.

Download the Android SDK package for Windows from http://developer. android.com/sdk/index.html (android-sdk_r18-windows.zip or installer_r18-windows.exe).

After installing the Android SDK, adb.exe will be located at <install-dir>\ android-sdk\platform-tools.

ADB Host-Client Communication

Thus far we focused on installing ADB on the development host. In reality, it is a client-server program that includes three components:

- A client that runs on your development machine. You can invoke a client from a shell by issuing an ADB command. Other Android tools, such as the ADT plug-in and DDMS, also create ADB clients.

- A server that runs as a background process on your development machine. The server manages communication between the client and the ADB daemon running on an emulator or device.

- A daemon that runs as a background process on each emulator or device instance.

When you start an ADB client, the client first checks whether there is an ADB server process already running. If there isn't, it starts the server process. When the server starts, it binds to a local TCP port 5037 and listens for commands sent from ADB clients—all ADB clients use port 5037 to communicate with the ADB server.

The server then sets up connections to all running emulator/device instances. It locates emulator/device instances by scanning odd-numbered ports in the range 5555 to 5585, which is the range used by emulators/devices. When the server finds an ADB daemon, it sets up a connection to that port. Note that each emulator/device instance acquires a pair of sequential ports—an even-numbered port for console connections and an odd-numbered port for ADB connections. For example:

```
Emulator 1, console: 5554
Emulator 1, adb: 5555
Emulator 2, console: 5556
Emulator 2, adb: 5557 …
```

As shown, the emulator instance connected to ADB on port 5555 is the same as the instance whose console listens on port 5554.

Once the server has set up connections to all emulator instances, you can use ADB commands to control and access those instances. Because the server manages connections to emulator/device instances and handles commands from multiple ADB clients, you can control any emulator/device instance from any client (or from a script).

Starting ADB

Type adb shell. You will get a # sign to indicate that the connection was successful.

```
$ adb shell
#
```

Key ADB Device Commands

The commands listed in Table 8-1 help to transfer the debuggee application onto the target device or emulation from the command line. This can be very helpful, especially if no ssh terminal connection is available.

Table 8-1. *Key ADB Device Commands*

Command	Description
adb push <local> <remote>	Copies file/dir to device
adb pull <remote> [<local>]	Copies file/dir from device
adb sync [<directory>]	Copies host->device only if changed (-l means list but don't copy) (See adb help all)
adb shell	Runs the remote shell interactively

(continued)

Table 1-5. (*continued*)

Command	Description
adb shell <command>	Run the remote shell command
adb emu <command>	Runs the emulator console command
adb logcat [<filter-spec>]	Views the device log
adb forward <local> <remote>	Forwards socket connections Forward specs are one of: tcp:<port> localabstract:<unix domain socket name> localreserved:<unix domain socket name> localfilesystem:<unix domain socket name> dev:<character device name> jdwp:<process pid> (remote only)
adb jdwp	Lists PIDs of processes hosting a JDWP transport
adb install [-l] [-r] [-s] <file>	Pushes this package file to the device and installs it (-l means forward-lock the app) (-r means reinstall the app, keeping its data) (-s means install on SD card instead of internal storage)

More details on ADB setup and usage can be found at http://developer.android. com/guide/developing/tools/adb.html.

Using the Android Debug Tools Plug-in for Eclipse

For devices based on Intel architecture, the setup process does not vary significantly from what is described at http://developer.android.com/sdk/eclipse-adt.html#installing. The Android Debug Tools (ADT) plug-in provides full Eclipse IDE integrated application debug for emulators based on Intel architecture as well as target devices. It provides two different debug perspectives with different feature sets. You can switch between either one as needed and they both provide different strengths when debugging applications.

The Debug Perspective in Eclipse

The Debug Perspective in Eclipse, shown in Figure 8-11, gives you access to the following tabs:

- *Debug*. Displays previously and currently debugged Android applications and its currently running threads.

- *Variables*. When breakpoints are set, displays variable values during code execution.

- *Breakpoints.* Displays a list of the set breakpoints in your application code.

- *LogCat.* Allows you to view system log messages in real time. The LogCat tab is also available in the DDMS perspective.

Figure 8-11. *Debug Perspective in Eclipse*

You can access the Debug Perspective by clicking Window ➤ Open Perspective ➤ Debug. Refer to the appropriate documentation for the Eclipse debugger for more information.

The DDMS Perspective

The DDMS Perspective in Eclipse, shown in Figure 8-12, lets you access all of the features of DDMS from within the Eclipse IDE. The following sections of DDMS are available to you:

- *Devices.* Shows the list of devices and AVDs that are connected to ADB.

- *Emulator Control.* Lets you carry out device functions.

- *LogCat.* Lets you view system log messages in real time.

- *Threads.* Shows currently running threads within a VM.

- *Heap.* Shows heap usage for a VM.

- *Allocation Tracker.* Shows the memory allocation of objects.

- *File Explorer.* Lets you explore the device's file system.

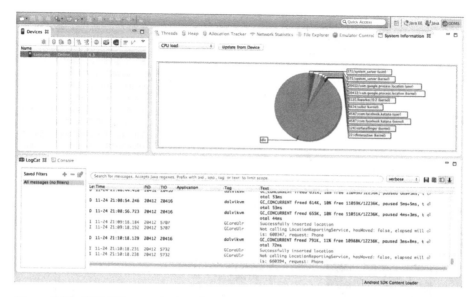

Figure 8-12. *DDMS Perspective in Eclipse*

Application Runtime Environment for Debugging

The difference when debugging an Android application targeted for a device based on Intel architecture comes in when setting up the debug target device.

Selecting the target device using the Android Virtual Device Manager that is part of the Android SDK, you go to Window ➤ AVD Manager in the Eclipse IDE's pull-down menu. There you need to make sure to select Intel Atom (x86) as the EABI target for the OS image and the device emulation (see Figure 8-13).

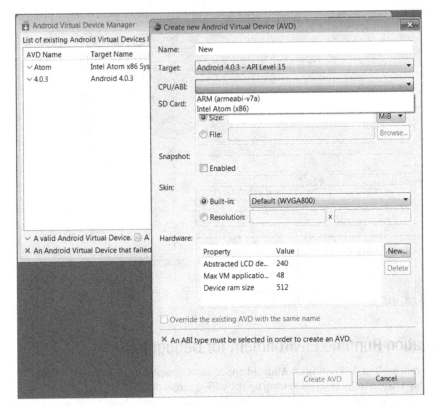

Figure 8-13. *Selection of a Device Based on the Intel Atom Processor in Android Virtual Device Manager*

If you followed the steps outlined at the beginning of the chapter for setting up ADB and establishing a debug bridge to a physical device, you will see a device chooser entry in the Eclipse IDE from which you can pick the target for application deployment and debug.

Otherwise, debugging an Android application targeted for Intel architecture is not different from debugging an Android application that targets ARM architecture.

Intel Hardware Accelerated Execution Manager

The Intel Hardware Accelerated Execution Manager (HAXM) is a hardware-assisted virtualization engine (hypervisor) that uses Intel Virtualization Technology (VT) to speed up Android app emulation on a host machine. In combination with Android x86 emulator images provided by Intel and the official Android SDK Manager, Intel HAXM allows for faster Android emulation on Intel VT–enabled systems. For more information on installing and using Intel HAXM, refer to **Chapter 11: Using Intel Hardware Accelerated Execution Manager to Speed-up Android on x86 Emulation**.

The x86 Android 4.0.4 (Ice Cream Sandwich) emulator system image enables you to run an emulation of Android on your development machine. In combination with the Android SDK, you can test your Android applications on a virtual Android device based on Intel architecture, thereby taking full advantage of the underlying Intel architecture and Intel Virtualization Technology.

In order to install the emulator system image, you use the Android SDK Manager. Intel HAXM can be installed through the Android SDK Manager (see Figure 8-14). Intel HAXM requires the Android SDK to be installed (version 17 or higher). For more information, refer to the Android developer web site (http://developer.android.com/sdk/).

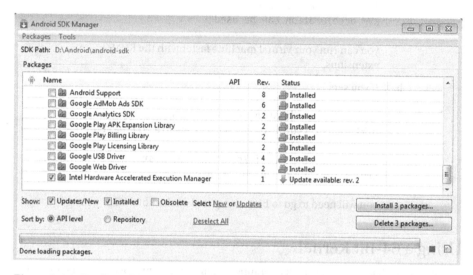

Figure 8-14. *Intel Hardware Accelerated Execution Manager Download*

Intel HAXM is available for Linux, Windows, and OS X host operating systems. As an example we outline the installation on Ubuntu 64-bit OS, as this is Google's main validated and supported platform for Android builds.

The next section contains the quick steps for how to install KVM, enable it on the Ubuntu host platform, and start the Intel Android x86 emulator with Intel hardware-assisted virtualization (hypervisor). When the AVD takes advantage of Intel HAXM, the operating system will run significantly faster and smoother than without hypervisor.

KVM Installation

1. To see if your processor supports hardware virtualization, you can review the output from this command:

   ```
   $ egrep -c '(vmx|svm)' /proc/cpuinfo
   ```

   If this command returns 0, your CPU doesn't support hardware virtualization.

2. Next, install CPU checker:

```
$ sudo apt-get install cpu-checker
```

3. Now you can check if your CPU supports KVM:

```
$kvm-ok
```

    a. If you see:

```
"INFO: Your CPU supports KVM extensions
INFO: /dev/kvm exists
KVM acceleration can be used"
```

you can run your virtual machine faster with the KVM extensions.

    b. If you see:

```
"INFO: KVM is disabled by your BIOS
HINT: Enter your BIOS setup and enable Virtualization
Technology (VT),
and then hard poweroff/poweron your system
KVM acceleration can NOT be used"
```

you will need to go to BIOS setup and enable Intel VT.

Using a 64-Bit Kernel

Running a 64-bit kernel on the host operating system is recommended but not required. To serve more than 2GB of RAM for your VMs, you must use a 64-bit kernel. On a 32-bit kernel install, you'll be limited to 2GB RAM at maximum for a given VM. Also, a 64-bit system can host both 32-bit and 64-bit guests. A 32-bit system can only host 32-bit guests.

1. To see if your processor is 64-bit, you can run this command:

```
$ egrep -c ' lm ' /proc/cpuinfo
```

If 0 is printed, it means that your CPU is not 64-bit. If 1 or higher is printed, it is. Note: lm stands for long mode, which equates to a 64-bit CPU.

2. To see whether your running kernel is 64-bit, just issue the following command:

```
$ uname -m
```

The return value x86_64 indicates a running 64-bit kernel. If you see i386, i486, i586, or i686, you're running a 32-bit kernel.

Install KVM

To install KVM, follow these steps:

1. For Ubuntu 12.04 or later:

    ```
    $ sudo apt-get install qemu-kvm libvirt-bin ubuntu-vm-builder
    bridge-utils
    ```

    You can ignore the Postfix Configuration request shown in Figure 8-15 by selecting
No Configuration.

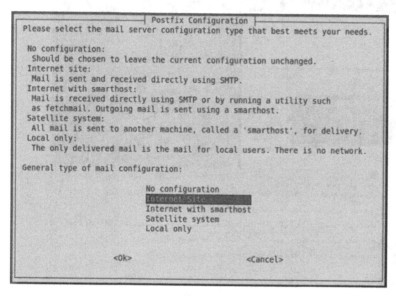

Figure 8-15. KVM Install Postfix Configuration Settings

2. Next, add your <username> account to the group kvm and
    libvirtd:

    ```
    $ sudo adduser your_user_name kvm
    $ sudo adduser your_user_name libvirtd
    ```

After the installation, you need to log in again so that your user account becomes an
active member of the kvm and libvirtd user groups. The members of this group can run
virtual machines.

To verify installation, you can test whether your install has been successful with the
following command:

```
$ sudo virsh -c qemu:///system list
```

Starting the Android Virtual Device

The Android for x86 Intel Emulator (see Figure 8-16) can be started using the following command:

```
$ <SDK directory>/tools/emulator-x86 -avd Your_AVD_Name -qemu -m
2047 -enable-kvm
```

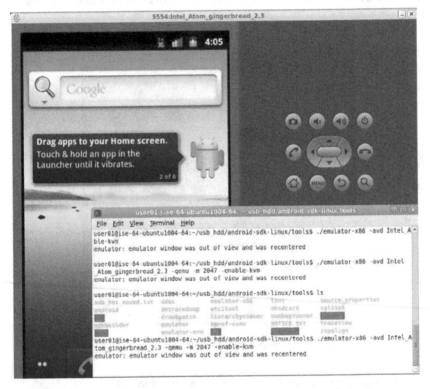

Figure 8-16. *AVD Running Android in the Intel Architecture Emulation Layer*

with Your_AVD_Name being a name of your choice; -qemu provides the options to qemu, and -m specifies the amount of memory for the emulated Android (that is, guest). If you use too small a value for your memory, it is possible that performance will suffer because of frequent swapping activities.

Using AVD Manager in Eclipse to Launch a Virtual Device

The following steps are recommended by Google to start debugging an application using AVD from within the Eclipse IDE:

1. In Eclipse, click your Android project folder and then select Run ➤ Run Configurations.

2. In the left panel of the Run Configurations dialog, select your Android project run configuration or create a new configuration.

3. Click the Target tab.

4. Select the Intel architecture-based AVD you created previously.

5. In the Additional Emulator Command Line Options field, enter:

   ```
   -qemu -m 2047 -enable-kvm
   ```

6. Run your Android project using this run configuration.

Running Android Within Oracle VirtualBox

Running a full Android OS image on a desktop PC inside an Oracle VirtualBox virtual machine can be a valuable alternative to KVM and QEMU on Windows host systems, especially for those developers looking to develop and debug native code on Android.
   In this section, we share some details about:

- Building the Android 4.0.x VirtualBox installer for x86 from the official Google x86 VirtualBox target vbox-x86-eng (included in Android 4.0.1 source tree).

- Using a Linux 2.6 kernel provided by Intel to add specific features for VirtualBox.

- How to use installer.vdi to install Android ICS 4.0 into VirtualBox.

In addition to Google's AVD emulator supported by Intel Hardware Accelerated Execution Manager (Intel HAXM) technology, Android for x86 VirtualBox is running a true virtualized Intel architecture-based environment. It thus provides another fast, high-performance tool for developers and partners for quick application development and testing. Booting Android 4.0.x in VirtualBox on a typical Intel Core i5 host system takes about 10 seconds. Speed, performance, and user experience account for the popularity of VirtualBox among Android developers, especially when targeting platforms based on Intel architecture. Availability of Android tablets and smartphones on the market based on Intel architecture is still somewhat limited, and it can be more convenient to start development using a virtual environment on the development host system instead of relying on USB debug communication. Especially with both the development host and the Android target device based on Intel architecture, this becomes a valid and interesting alternative.

Google x86 VirtualBox Build Targets for Android 4.x

If you have been using Google's Android 4.0.x source repository before, you probably noticed that Google provides an x86 version of the VirtualBox target vbox_x86-eng. Using the lunch command before starting the build, the first three targets that Google provides for Android 4.0.x are:

```
$ lunch
1. full-eng
2. full_x86-eng
3. vbox_x86-eng
```

With the vbox_x86-eng (#3) target, application developers and system developers alike can create android_disk.vdi and android installer.vdi packages. These can then be used to run Android 4.x inside VirtualBox for application development and system integration on Windows, Linux, and OS X.

Downloading the Source Tree and Installing the Repository

To install, initialize, and configure the repository, follow these steps (you can find more information at http://source.android.com/source/downloading.html):

```
$ mkdir ~/bin
$ PATH=~/bin:$PATH
$ curl https://dl-ssl.google.com/dl/googlesource/git-repo/repo > ~/bin/repo
$ chmod a+x ~/bin/repo
$ mkdir ANDROID_TOP_PATH
$ cd ANDROID_TOP_PATH
```

To get a list of available branches (from your Android repository checkout root), use this command:

```
$ git --git-dir .repo/manifests/.git/ branch -a
```

Run repo init to obtain a current list of the available repository sub-branches with all the most recent updates:

```
$ repo init -u https://android.googlesource.com/platform/manifest
-b android-4.0.1_r1
```

To use the Gerrit code-review tool, you will need an e-mail address that is connected to a registered Google account. Make sure this is a live address at which you can receive messages. The kernel version and build number will be assigned to your build, and information will be displayed on the Android/Settings/About Phone/ page.

A successful initialization will end with a message stating that Repo is initialized in your working directory. Your client directory should now contain a .repo directory where files such as the manifest are stored.

To pull down files to your working directory from the repositories, as specified in the default manifest, run

```
$ repo sync
```

By default, access to the Android source code is anonymous. To protect the servers against excessive usage, each IP address is associated with a quota.

Building a Custom Kernel with Mouse Support

Since Android is meant for touch screen devices, it doesn't include support for a mouse pointer by default. Additionally it may not include a driver for hardwired Ethernet support, as most Android devices are exclusively using wireless radios for network communication. To add these capabilities, you need to rebuild the kernel with mouse support as well as any additional features that you require. To do so, follow these steps:

1. Download the Android x86 Emulator Image add-on through the Android SDK Manager.

2. Create a new folder and untar kernel_sdk_x86.tar.gz into it to create a folder with the kernel source tree.

3. Switch to the directory that holds your kernel files.

4. Now that you have the kernel source, the configuration needs to be modified to match the hardware being used as the VirtualBox host system and rebuilt. The menuconfig graphical user interface provided by the kernel sources will allow to do this conveniently:

```
$ cp ANDROID_TOP_PATH/your_kernel_path/arch/x86/configs/vbox_defconfig
.config
$ make CC=gcc-4.4 CXX=g++-4.4 ARCH=x86 menuconfig
```

This will take a few seconds to compile and load. Once it does load, you can use

- Up/Down arrows to navigate

- Enter to select (to expand)

- Y (or space) to include

To enable mouse support, navigate to Device Driver ➤ Input Device Support ➤ Mice.

▪ **Note**   menuconfig can be used to ensure that all features required to support your application or system integration are available. For application developers, it is equally important to test and validate the application on default Android builds. Only then can maximum compatibility with Android devices from multiple different device manufacturers be guaranteed.

Having made the necessary change to the kernel configuration, you can now compile it. It doesn't take too long, so I picked a low −j value. It is important to note that if you omit the CC and CCX parameters, the compile will terminate prematurely (on this setup), without an explicit error, as it will use version 4.6.

```
$ make CC=gcc-4.4 CXX=g++-4.4 ARCH=x86 −j8
```

The −j parameter provides the number of available cores for compilation. This example assumes a quad-core system with Intel Hyper-Threading Technology enabled.

After the build is completed successfully, the last line of the build log will say

```
Kernel: arch/x86/boot/bzImage is ready
```

Add Patched Kernel

The kernel image bzImage needs to be renamed to kernel-vbox and copied to /ANDROID_TOP_PATH/prebuilt/android-x86/kernel/kernel-vbox:

```
$ cp /ANDROID_TOP_PATH/kernel/arch/x86/boot/bzImage
/ANDROID_TOP_PATH/prebuilt/android-x86/kernel/kernel-vbox
```

Reduce Compile Time Using CCACHE

You can greatly reduce the compile time for subsequent compilations by using the compiler cache. To set up a 50GB cache, do the following:

1. Install the CCcache program and create a directory for your ccache:

    ```
    $ sudo apt-get install ccache
    $ sudo mkdir /ANDROID_TOP_PATH/ccache
    $ sudo chown $LOGNAME  /ANDROID_TOP_PATH/ccache
    ```

2. Set up your environment variables for ccache support by modifying ~/.bashrc:

    ```
    $ sudo gedit ~/.bashrc
    ```

3. Add the following:

    ```
    export CCACHE_DIR=/ANDROID_TOP_PATH/ccache
    export USE_CCACHE=1
    ```

4. Set the ccache sizes.

    ```
    $ ccache -F 100000
    $ ccache -M 50G
    ```

Build Android 4.0.x with New Kernel

To set up the environment:

```
$ /ANDROID_TOP_PATH/> source build/envsetup.sh
```

For ICS 4.0.1, you will see:

```
including device/samsung/maguro/vendorsetup.sh
including device/samsung/tuna/vendorsetup.sh
including device/ti/panda/vendorsetup.sh
including sdk/bash_completion/adb.bash
```

To ensure you pick a valid target when using the lunch command, it is convenient to simply do the following:

```
$ lunch
```

and pick the desired target from the list:

```
1. full-eng
2. full_x86-eng
3. vbox_x86-eng
4. full_maguro-userdebug
5. full_tuna-userdebug
6. full_panda-eng
Which would you like? [full-eng]
```

■ **Note** Make sure you select 3. vbox_x86-eng.

```
PLATFORM_VERSION_CODENAME=REL
PLATFORM_VERSION=4.0.1
TARGET_PRODUCT=vbox_x86
TARGET_BUILD_VARIANT=eng
TARGET_BUILD_TYPE=release
TARGET_BUILD_APPS=
TARGET_ARCH=x86
TARGET_ARCH_VARIANT=x86
HOST_ARCH=x86 HOST_OS=linux
HOST_BUILD_TYPE=release
BUILD_ID=ITL41D
```

Run make:

```
$ make -j8
```

Build the VirtualBox Disk and Android Installer

Finally, build the Android_disk.vdi and installer_vdi together:

```
$ make android_disk_vdi  installer_vdi  -j8
```

If the build is successful, you will see this output in the build log:

```
Done with VirtualBox bootable disk image -
[ out/target/product/vbox_x86/android_disk.vdi ]-
Done with VirtualBox bootable installer image -
[ out/target/product/vbox_x86/installer.vdi ]-
```

With android_disk.vdi, you can select New ➤ Create New Virtual Machine in VirtualBox. You can use android_disk.vdi as an existing disk image to base the virtual machine on, which will now automatically boot Android 4.0.x.

Setting up the start parameters for VirtualBox is straightforward. Go to Settings ➤ About This Phone to see the build information shown in Figure 8-17.

Figure 8-17. *Android 4.0.x Build Information Inside Oracle VirtualBox*

Using an Android Installer Disk to Create a Large Virtual Partition

Even if the file size in VirtualBox is expanded to 550MB, it is still too small to load applications for testing. An Android installer disk is needed to install Android into a much larger partition (preferably larger than 4GB).

First select Machine ➤ New from the VirtualBox menu bar and use the Create New Virtual Machine Wizard to create a larger disk under the IDE controller configuration entry.

Then in Settings ➤ Storage of your virtual machine, add the installer.vdi as the primary IDE slave, as shown in Figure 8-18. Now you can install Android on the 4GB hard disk you just created.

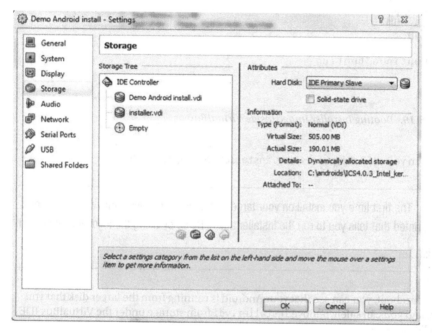

Figure 8-18. *Configuring Storage Settings for Virtual Machine*

1. Start the emulator.

2. Use F12 to get to the BIOS boot menu. Boot to the secondary drive.

3. Use grub to select the Install option: 2. Boot from the primary slave (see Figure 8-19).

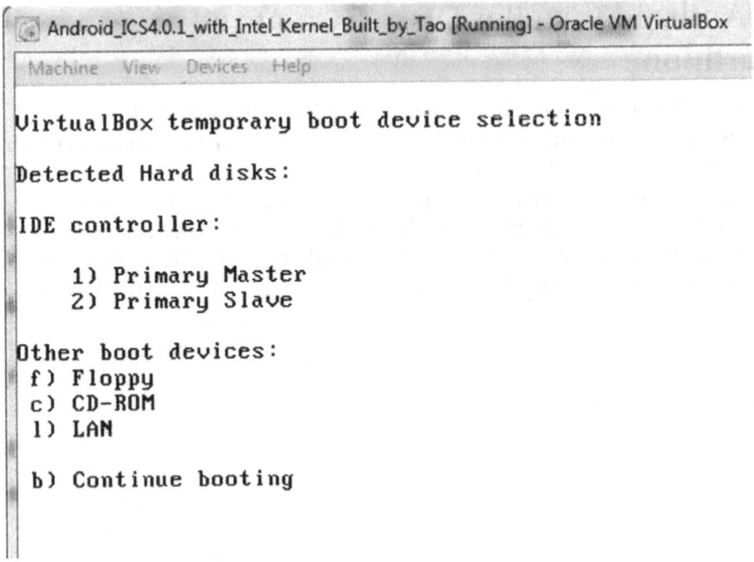

```
Android_ICS4.0.1_with_Intel_Kernel_Built_by_Tao [Running] - Oracle VM VirtualBox

 Machine    View    Devices    Help

VirtualBox temporary boot device selection

Detected Hard disks:

IDE controller:

     1) Primary Master
     2) Primary Slave

Other boot devices:
 f) Floppy
 c) CD-ROM
 l) LAN

 b) Continue booting
```

Figure 8-19. *Booting Installer Image Inside VirtualBox*

When you see Done processing installer config, type reboot.

■ **Note**   The first time you install on your target virtual disk, the install may fail. A message will be printed that tells you to run the installer again. Do so by using the following command:

```
$ installer
```

After reboot, you can see that your Android is running from the larger disk that you create, and you can safely remove installer.vdi from storage under the VirtualBox IDE controller settings.

Serial Port

Serial port support in the virtual machine is enabled by default. However, the COM1 serial port needs to be initialized and configured before it can be used. The following instructions cause VirtualBox to create a named pipe called .vbox_pipe in your home directory. On the command line, enter:

```
$ VBoxManage modifyvm Android --uart1 0x03f8 4
$ VBoxManage modifyvm Android --uartmode1 server /home/user/.vbox_pipe
```

Alternatively from in the VirtualBox GUI, use the Serial Ports tab in the Virtual Machine Settings menu to enable COM1 as a host pipe. Select Create Pipe for it to be created as /home/user/.vbox_pipe.

To connect to this named pipe, use:

```
$ socat unix-client:$HOME/.vbox_pipe stdout
```

■ **Note** VirtualBox might not understand environment variables (such as $HOME), so you will have to specify a full explicit path, such as /home/user/.vbox_pipe.

Ethernet

The Ethernet port (eth0) is enabled for DHCP in the image. To connect to it via ADB, you will need to look up the DHCP address that has been assigned.

If you are using a bridged ethernet, you may obtain this address from a shell prompt, either from the serial port or from Developer Tools ➤ Terminal Emulator using this command:

```
$ netcfg
```

If you are using a host-only adapter, vboxnet0, you should use the address 192.168.56.101.

Final Notes

Now you have a VirtualBox image running Android 4.0.x completely built from Google's official vbox-x86 target (see Figure 8-20).

Figure 8-20. *Android OS Fully Booted Inside the VirtualBox Virtual Machine*

Debugging with GDB, the GNU Project Debugger

The Android NDK includes the GDB, the GNU debugger, which allows you to start, pause, examine, and alter a program. On Android devices and more generally on embedded devices, GDB is configured in client/server mode. The program runs on a device as a server and a remote client. The developer's workstation connects to it and sends debugging commands similar to a local application. GDB itself is a command-line utility. You'll first look at its basic usage model before looking at the Eclipse CDT integration.

When debugging with GDB, gdbserver running on the device handles debug communication. However, you still might be using an underlying USB-to-Ethernet dongle driver with ADB to communicate to the transport layer on which gdbserver communicates via TCP/IP with GDB running on the development host.

There is a gdbclient application that sets up the debug communication environment and launches gdbserver on the debuggee device.

```
usage: gdbclient EXECUTABLE :PORT [PROG_PATH]
EXECUTABLE   executable name (default app_process)
PORT         commection port (default :1234)
PROG_PATH    executable full path on target (ex /system/bin/mediaserver)
```

If PROG_PATH is set, gdclient tries to launch gdbserver and attach it to the running PROG_PATH.

To launch gdbserver explicitly, you use the following command:

```
# gdbserver :1234 --attach 269
Attached; pid = 269
Listening on port 1234
```

The step-by-step debug session launch instructions that follow illustrate how ADB is still underlying the debug communication even if GDB (not ADT or DDMS) is used for debugging. Assume that port 1234 is being used.

The lunch process is as follows:

```
gdbserver :1234 /system/bin/executable
```

To attach to an existing process:

```
gdbserver :1234 --attach pid
```

On your workstation, forward port 1234 to the device with adb:

```
adb forward tcp:1234 tcp:1234
```

Start a special version of gdb that lives in the "prebuilt" area of the source tree:
prebuilt/Linux/toolchain-eabi-4.x.x/bin/i686-android-linux-gdb (for Linux)
or
prebuilt/darwin-x86/toolchain-eabi-4.x.x/bin/i686-android-linux-gdb (for Darwin).

If you can't find either special version of GDB, run this

```
$find prebuilt -name i686-android-linux-gdb
```

in your source tree to find and run the latest version. Make sure to use the copy of the executable in the symbols directory, not the primary Android directory, because the one in the primary directory has been stripped of its symbol information.

In GDB, tell GDB where to find the shared libraries that will be loaded:

```
set solib-absolute-prefix /absolute-source-path/out/target/product/product-name/
symbols
set solib-search-path /absolute-source-path/out/target/product/product-name/
symbols/system/lib
```

The path to your source tree is *absolute-source-path*. Make sure you specify the correct directories—GDB might not tell you if you make a mistake. Connect to the device by issuing the gdb command:

```
(gdb) target remote :1234
```

The :1234 tells GDB to connect to the localhost port 1234, which is bridged to the device by ADB.

Now you can start debugging native C/C++ code running on Android with GDB the same way you are used to. If you also have Eclipse installed, which you probably do if you are using the Android SDK for Dalvik/Java-based application development, Eclipse and the GDB integration of Eclipse can be used directly to add breakpoints and inspect a program.

Indeed, using Eclipse, you can insert breakpoints easily in Java as well as in C/C++ source files. You simply clicking in the left margin of the text editor. Java breakpoints work out of the box thanks to the ADT plug-in, which manages debugging through the Android Debug Bridge. This is not true for CDT, which is, of course, not Android-aware. Thus, inserting a breakpoint will do nothing unless you configure CDT to use the NDK's GDB, which itself needs to be bound to the native Android application in order to debug it. First, enable debugging mode in the application by following these steps:

1. An important thing to do, but something that is really easy to forget, is to activate the debugging flag in your Android project. This is done in the application manifest AndroidManifest.xml. Do not forget to use the appropriate SDK version for native code:

```
<?xml version="1.0" encoding="utf-8"?> <manifest ...>
<uses-sdk android:minSdkVersion="10"/> <application ...
android:debuggable="true"> ...
```

2. Enable the debug flag in the manifest. This automatically activates debug mode in native code. However, the APP_OPTIM flag also controls debug mode. If it has been manually set in Android.mk, then check that its value is set to debug (and not release) or simply remove it:

```
APP_OPTIM := debug
```

3. Now configure the GDB client that will connect to the device. Recompile the project and plug your device in or launch the emulator. Run and leave your application. Ensure the application is loaded and its PID is available. You can check it by listing processes using the following command (use Cygwin in Windows):

```
$ adb shell ps |grep gl2jni
```

One line should be returned:

```
app_75 13178 1378 201108 68672 ffffffff 80118883 S com.android.
gl2jni
```

4. Open a terminal window and go to your project directory. Run the ndk-gdb command (located in the Android NDK folder, for example android-ndk-r8\):

    ```
    $ ndk-gdb
    ```

    This command should not return a message, but will create three files in the obj\local\x86 directory:

    •   gdb.setup. This is a configuration file generated for GDB client.

    •   app_process. This file is retrieved directly from your device. It is a system executable file, launched when the system starts up and forked to start a new application. GBD needs this reference file to find its marks. In some ways, it is the binary entry point of your app.

    •   libc.so. This is also retrieved from your device. It is the Android standard C library (commonly referred as bionic) used by GDB to keep track of all the native threads created during runtime.

5. In your project directory, copy obj\local\x86\gdb.setup and name it gdb2.setup. Open it and remove the following line, which requests the GDB client to connect to the GDB server running on the device (to be performed by Eclipse):

    ```
    (gdb) target remote :1234
    ```

6. In the Eclipse main menu, go to Run | Debug Configurations and create a new debug configuration in the C/C++ application item called GL2JNIActivityDefault. This configuration will start the GDB client on your computer and connect to the GDB server running on the device.

7. In the Main tab (see Figure 8-21), set the project to your own project directory. Set the C/C++ application to point to obj\ local\ x86\app_process using the Browse button (you can use an absolute or relative path).

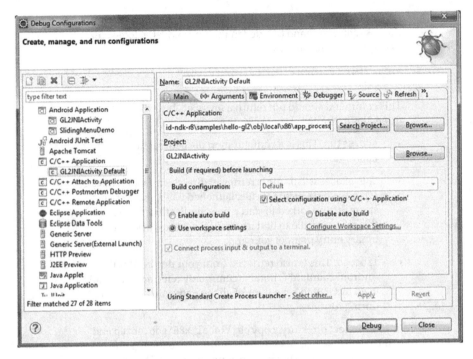

Figure 8-21. *Debug Configurations for C/C++ Application*

8.   Switch the launcher type to Standard Create Process Launcher (see Figure 8-22) using the link Select Other link at the bottom of the window.

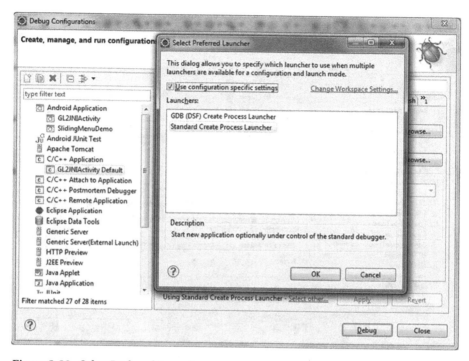

Figure 8-22. *Select Preferred Launcher*

9. Go to the debugger file and set the debugger type to
gdbserver. Set the GDB debugger to android-ndk-r8\
toolchains\x86-4.4.3\prebuilt\windows\bin\i686-
android-linux-gdb.exe. The GDB command file
(see Figure 8-23) needs to point to the gdb2.setup file located
in \obj\local\x86 (you can use an absolute or relative path).

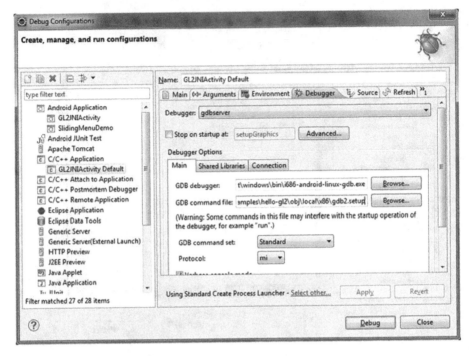

Figure 8-23. *Debugger Setting Panel*

10. Go to the Connection tab (see Figure 8-24) and set Type to TCP. Keep the default values for hostname or IP address and port number (localhost, 5039).

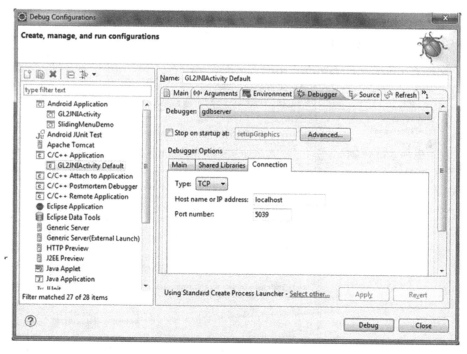

Figure 8-24. *Connection Settings on the Debugger Setting Panel*

11. Now, let's configure Eclipse to run a GDB server on the device. Make a copy of `android-ndk-r8\ndk-gdb` and open it with a text editor. Find the following line:

    ```
    $GDBCLIENT -x 'native_path $GDBSETUP'
    ```

    Comment it out because GDB client is going to be run by Eclipse itself:

    ```
    #$GDBCLIENT -x 'native_path $GDBSETUP'
    ```

12. In the Eclipse main menu, go to Run | External Tools | External Tools | Configurations (see Figure 8-25), and create a new configuration `GL2JNIActivity_GDB`. This configuration will launch GDB server on the device.

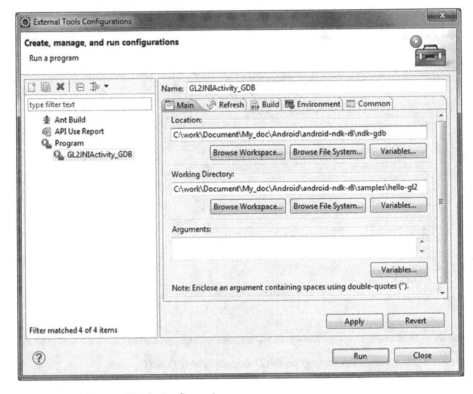

Figure 8-25. *External Tools Configurations*

13. On the Main tab, set the Location pointing to the modified
    ndk-gdb in android-ndk-r8. Set the working directory to your
    application directory location. Optionally, set the Arguments
    text box:

    - Verbose: To see in detail what happens in the Eclipse
      console.

    - Force: To automatically kill any previous session.

    - Start: To let the GDB server start the application instead of
      getting attached to the application after it has been started.
      This option is interesting if you debug native code only and
      not Java.

14. Now, launch your application as usual.

15. Once the application starts, you could launch ndk-gdb by console directly or launch the external tool configuration GL2JNIActivity_GDB, which is going to start the GDB server on the device. The GDB server receives debug commands sent by the remote GDB client and debugs your application locally.

16. Open jni\gl_code.cpp and set a breakpoint (see Figure 8-26) in setupgraphics by double-clicking the left margin of the text editor (or right-clicking and selecting Toggle Breakpoint).

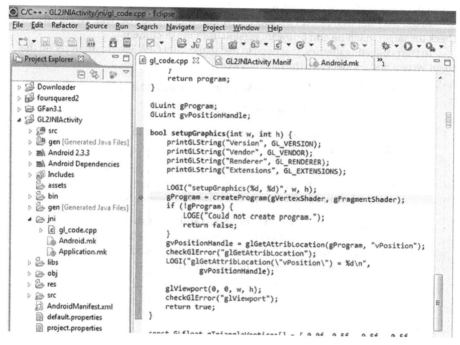

Figure 8-26. *Setting Breakpoints*

17. Finally, launch the GL2JNIActivity default C/C++ application configuration to start the GDB client. It relays debug commands from Eclipse CDT to the GDB server over a socket connection. From the developer's point of view, this is almost like debugging a local application.

The Intel Graphics Performance Analyzer (Intel GPA)

There are also some specific tools for debugging graphics performance. The Intel GPA System Analyzer is one of the Intel Graphics Performance Analyzers (GPA) with new support for Intel-based Android devices, and is intended for application and driver engineers to optimize their OpenGL ES workloads.

This section provides instructions for how to configure and use Intel GPA with your Android device over a USB connection. When connected to an Android device, the Intel GPA System Analyzer provides OpenGL ES API, CPU, and GPU performance metrics, and also provides multiple graphics pipeline state overrides to aid with your analysis of OpenGL ES application performance.

To use the Intel GPA System Analyzer on Android x86-based devices, you need to check the target machine and firmware version from the document.

To start collecting metrics, you need to install the Intel GPA System Analyzer on the client system and connect it to the target device:

1. Install Intel GPA 2013 on the Windows/Linux client machine.

2. Launch the Intel GPA System Analyzer.

3. Make sure that the Android device(s) is connected to the client system using a USB cable.

4. Wait up to 10 seconds while your client system is detecting the target device(s). Found devices appear in the window. The list of the target devices refreshes every five to six seconds.

5. Find the device you want to connect to and click Connect (see Figure 8-27). The Intel GPA System Analyzer will copy the required components to the target device and generate the list of installed applications. You can interrupt the connection process by clicking Stop.

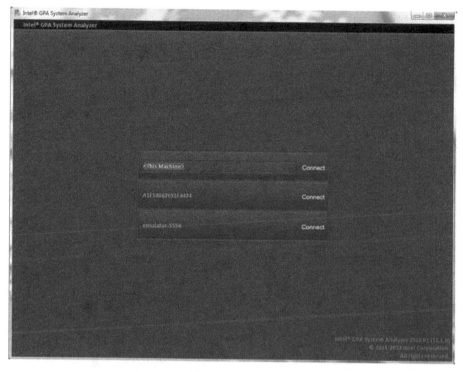

Figure 8-27. *Select the Connected Device*

6. Select the desired application from the list of available ones. The Application List screen (see Figure 8-28) displays all user and system applications installed on the Android device.

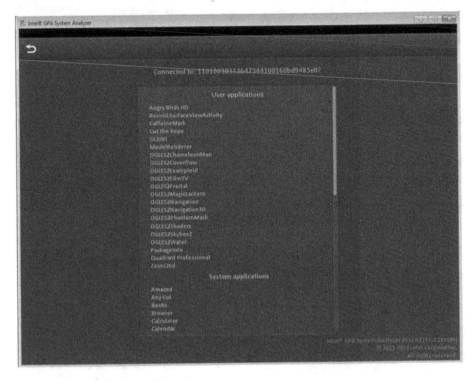

Figure 8-28. *Applications List*

7. The application will be launched and you will see its data in the Intel GPA System Analyzer window.

8. To switch to a different application, click Back. Note that the running application will be forced to close.

9. To switch to a different target device, click Back. The PowerVR graphics architecture consists of the following core modules that convert the submitted 3D application data into a rendered image—Tile Accelerator (TA), Image Synthesis Processor (ISP), and the Texture & Shading Processor (TSP). Intel GPA metrics in the "GPU" group correspond to one of these core modules, and the order of metrics in the Metrics List depends on the order of the core modules in the graphics pipeline (see Figure 8-29).

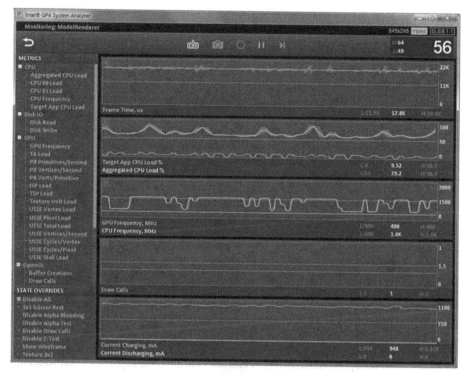

Figure 8-29. Intel GPA System Analyzer Window

System Debug of Android OS Running on an Intel Atom Processor

Until now this chapter has focused on developing and debugging applications, whether they use Android's Java runtime alone or run natively as x86 Intel Architecture binaries and shared objects.

For the system integrator and device manufacturer it might be necessary to work on the device driver and system software stack layer as well. This is especially true if additional platform-specific peripheral device support needs to be implemented or if the first operating system port to a new Intel Atom processor-based device is undertaken.

In the following chapters, you'll look at the Joint Test Action Group IEEE 1149.1 (JTAG) standard-based debug solutions for this purpose as well as architectural differences between the ARM and Intel architectures that can impact system-level debugging.

JTAG Debugging

For true firmware, operating system-level, and device driver debugging, the most commonly used method in the world is using a JTAG debug interface. Historically speaking, the Joint Test Action Group was formed by industry leaders in the 1980s to define a standard for testing access ports and printed circuit boards. The IEEE adopted their standard in the 1990s as the IEEE 1149.1 Standard Test Access Port and Boundary-Scan Architecture. For the sake of brevity, the testing standard is usually referred to as JTAG. From its original use for circuit board testing, it has developed into the de facto interface standard for OS-independent and OS-level platform debugging.

More background information on JTAG and its usage in modern system software stack debugging is available in the article, "JTAG 101; IEEE 1149.x and Software Debug" by Randy Johnson and Stewart Christie (see http://www.intel.com/content/www/us/en/intelligent-systems/jtag-101-ieee-1149x-paper.html).

From the OEM's perspective and that of their partner application and driver developers, understanding the interaction between the driver and software stack components running on the different parts of the system-on-chip (SoC) integrated intelligent system or smartphone form factor device is critical for determining platform stability. From a silicon validator's perspective, the low-level software stack provides the test environment that emulates the kind of stress factors the platform will be exposed to in real-world use cases. In short, modern SoCs require understanding the complete package and its complex real-world interactions, not just positive unit test results for individual hardware components. This is the level of insight a JTAG-based system software debug approach can provide. This can be achieved by merging the in-depth hardware awareness JTAG inherently provides with the ability to export state information of the Android OS running on the target.

Especially for device driver debug, it is important to understand both the exact state of the peripheral device on the chipset and the interaction of the device driver with the OS layer and the rest of the software stack.

If you are looking at Android from the perspective of system debugging—looking at device drivers and the OS kernel—it is really just a specialized branch of Linux. Thus it can be treated like any 2.6.3x or higher Linux.

The Intel Atom processor Z2460 supports IEEE-1149.1 and IEEE-1149.7 (JTAG) Boundary Scan and MPI Parallel Trace Interface (PTI), as well as Branch Trace Storage (BTS)-based instruction tracing through Intel's JTAG-compliant eXtended Debug Port (XDP).

Various JTAG vendors offer system debug solutions with Android support, including the following:

- Wind River (http://www.windriver.com/products/JTAG-debugging/)

- Lauterbach (http://www.lauterbach.com)

- Intel (http://software.intel.com/en-us/articles/embedded-using-intel-tools)

Android OS Debugging,

What complicates debugging an Android-based platform is that Android aggressively takes advantage of low power idle states and sleep states to optimize for power consumption. Thus the real challenge becomes debugging through low power states and either maintaining JTAG functionality through some of the low power states or, when this is not possible, reattaching JTAG as soon as the chipset power domain for JTAG is re-enabled.

Many OS-level issues on these types of platforms tend to center around power mode changes and sleep/wake-up sequences.

A system debugger, whether debug agent-based or using a JTAG device interface, is a very useful tool to help satisfy several of the key objectives of OS development.

The debugger can be used to validate the boot process and to analyze and correct stability issues like runtime errors, segmentation faults, or services not being started correctly during boot.

It can also be used to identify and correct OS configuration issues by providing detailed access and representations of page tables, descriptor tables, and instruction trace. The combination of instruction trace and memory table access can be a very powerful tool to identify the root causes for stack overflow, memory leak, or even data abort scenarios.

Figure 8-30 shows the detailed access to page translation attributes and descriptor tables as provided by the Intel JTAG debugger. With the high level of flexibility that is available on x86 in defining the depth of translation tables and granularity of the addressed memory blocks, this level of easy access and visibility of the memory layout becomes even more important for system development on the OS level.

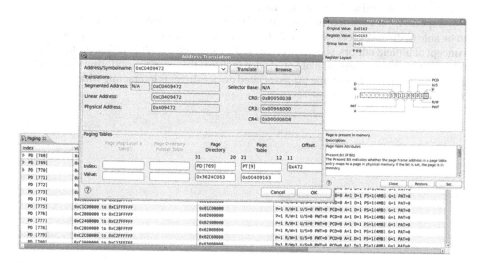

Figure 8-30. *Example of Debugger Views for Memory Configuration*

This highlights two key differences between developing and configuring the Android OS software stack on Intel architecture and many other architectures. The selector base and offset addressing model—combined with the local descriptor table (LDT) and global descriptor table (GDT)—allow for deep, multilayered address translation from physical to virtual memory with variable address chunk granularity as well. This is a powerful capability for custom memory configuration in a compartmentalized environment with protected isolated memory spaces. If used incorrectly it can, however, also increase memory access times.

One other difference between Intel architecture and others is handling system interrupts. On ARM, for instance, you have a predefined set of hardware interrupts in the reserved address space from 0x0 through 0x20. These locations then contain jump instructions to the interrupt handler. On Intel architecture, a dedicated hardware interrupt controller is employed. The hardware interrupts are not accessed directly through memory space, but by accessing the Intel 8529 interrupt controller. The advantage of this approach is that the interrupt handler already allows for direct handling of I/O interrupts for attached devices. In architectures that don't use a dedicated interrupt controller, the IRQ interrupt usually has to be overloaded with a more complex interrupt handler routine to accomplish this.

Device Driver Debugging

A good JTAG debugger solution for OS-level debugging should furthermore provide visibility of kernel threads and active kernel modules along with other information exported by the kernel. To allow for debugging dynamically loaded services and device drivers, a kernel patch or a kernel module that exports the memory location of a driver's initialization method and destruction method may be used.

Especially for system configuration and device driver debugging, it is also important to be able to directly access and check the contents of device configuration registers. The concept of bitfield editors, shown in Figure 8-31, can be very useful for this. A *bitfield editor* is a bitwise visualization of SoC device registers that allows monitoring changes to a device state in real time while the associated device driver is interacting with it.

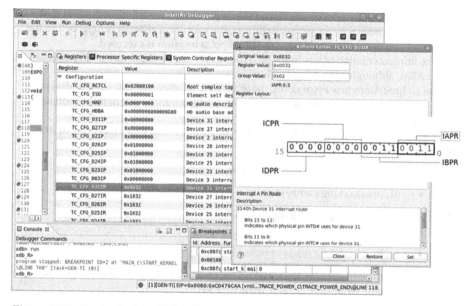

Figure 8-31. *Device Register Bitfield Editor View*

Analyzing the code after the Android-compressed zImage kernel image has been unpacked into memory is possible by simply releasing run control in the debugger until start_kernel is reached. This implies that the vmlinux file that contains the kernel symbol information has been loaded. At this point the use of software breakpoints is possible. Prior to this point in the boot process, only breakpoint-register–based hardware breakpoints should be used, to avoid the debugger attempting to write breakpoint instructions into uninitialized memory. The operating system is then successfully booted once the idle loop mwait_idle has been reached.

Additionally, if your debug solution provides access to Branch Trace Store (BTS) based instruction trace, this capability can, in conjunction with all the regular run control features of a JTAG Debugger, be used to force execution stop at an exception. You can then analyze the execution flow in reverse to identify the root cause of the runtime issues.

Hardware Breakpoints

Just as on ARM architecture, processors based on Intel architecture support breakpoint instructions for software breakpoints as well as hardware breakpoints for data and code. On ARM architecture, you usually have a set of dedicated registers for breakpoints and data breakpoints (called *watchpoints*). The common implementation tends to provide two of each. When these registers contain a value, the processor checks against accesses to the set memory address by the program counter register or a memory read/write. As soon as the access happens, execution is halted. This is different from software breakpoints in that their execution is halted as soon as a breakpoint instruction is encountered. Since the breakpoint instruction replaces the assembly instruction that would normally be at a given memory address, the execution effectively halts before the instruction that normally would be at the breakpoint location is executed.

The implementation of hardware breakpoints on Intel architecture is very similar to that on ARM, although it is a bit more flexible.

On all Intel Atom processor cores, there are four DR registers that store addresses, which are compared against the fetched address on the memory bus before (sometimes after) a memory fetch.

You can use all four of these registers to provide addresses that trigger any of the following debug run control events:

- 00. Break on instruction execution

- 01. Break on data write only

- 10. Undefined OR (if architecture allows it) break on I/O reads or writes

- 11. Break on data reads or writes but not instruction fetch

Thus, all four hardware breakpoints can be used as breakpoints or watchpoints. Watchpoints can be write-only or read-write (or I/O).

Cross-Debug: Intel Atom Processor and ARM Architecture

Many developers targeting the Intel Atom processor have experience developing primarily for RISC architectures with fixed instruction length. MIPS and ARM are prime examples of ISAs with fixed lengths. In general, the cross-debug usage model between an Intel Atom processor and ARM architecture processor is very similar. Many of the conceptual debug methods and issues are the same.

Developing on an Intel architecture-based development host for an Intel Atom processor target does, however, offer two big advantages, especially when the embedded operating system of choice is a derivative of one of the common standard operating systems like Linux or Windows. The first advantage is the rich ecosystem of performance, power analysis, and debug tools available for the broader software development market on Intel architecture. The second advantage is that debugging functional correctness and multithreading behavior of the application may be accomplished locally. This advantage will be discussed later in the chapter.

There are a few differences between Intel Atom processors and ARM processors that developers should know. These differences are summarized in the next two subsections.

Variable Length Instructions

The IA-32 and Intel 64 instruction sets have variable instruction lengths. The debugger cannot just inspect the code in fixed 32-bit intervals, but must interpret and disassemble the machine instructions of the application based on the context of these instructions. The location of the next instruction depends on the location, size, and correct decoding of the previous one. In contrast, on ARM architecture all the debugger needs to monitor is the code sequence that switches from ARM mode to Thumb mode or enhanced Thumb mode and back. Once in a specific mode, all instructions and memory addresses are 32-bit or 16-bit in size. Firmware developers and device driver developers who need to precisely align calls to specific device registers and may want to rely on understanding the debugger's memory window printout should understand the potential impact of variable length instructions.

Hardware Interrupts

One other architectural difference that may be relevant when debugging system code is how hardware interrupts are handled. On ARM architecture the following exception vectors are mapped from address 0x0 to address 0x20:

- 0. Reset

- 1. Abort

- 2. Data Abort

- 3. Prefetch Abort

- 4. Undefined Instruction

- 5. Interrupt (IRQ)

- 6. Fast Interrupt (FIRQ)

This memory area is protected and cannot normally be remapped. Commonly, all of the vector locations at 0x0 through 0x20 contain jumps to the memory address where the real exception handler code resides. For the reset vector that implies that at 0x0 will be a jump to the location of the firmware or platform boot code. This approach makes the implementation of hardware interrupts and OS signal handlers less flexible on ARM architecture, but also more standardized. It is easy to trap an interrupt in the debugger by simply setting a hardware breakpoint at the location of the vector in the 0x0 through 0x20 address range.

On Intel architecture, a dedicated hardware interrupt controller is employed. The following interrupts cannot be accessed directly through the processor memory address space, but are handled by accessing the Intel 8259 Interrupt Controller:

- 0. System timer

- 1. Keyboard

- 2. Cascaded second interrupt controller

- 3. COM2—serial interface

- 4. COM1—serial interface

- 5. LPT—parallel interface

- 6. Floppy disk controller

- 7. Available
- 8. CMOS real-time clock
- 9. Sound card
- 10. Network adapter
- 11. Available
- 12. Available
- 13. Numeric processor
- 14. IDE—Hard disk interface
- 15. IDE—Hard disk interface

As you can see the list of interrupts, the controller already allows for direct handling of hardware I/O interrupts of attached devices, which are handled through the IRQ interrupt or fast interrupt on an ARM platform. This feature makes the implementation of proper interrupt handling at the operating system level easier on Intel architecture especially for device I/O. The mapping of software exceptions like data aborts or segmentation faults is more flexible on Intel architecture as well and corresponds to an interrupt controller port that is addressed via the Interrupt Descriptor Table (IDT). The mapping of the IDT to the hardware interrupts is definable by the software stack. In addition, trapping these exceptions cannot as easily be done from a software stack agnostic debug implementation. In order to trap software events that trigger hardware interrupts on Intel architecture, some knowledge of the OS layer is required. It is necessary to know how the OS signals for these exceptions map to the underlying interrupt controller. Most commonly, even in a system-level debugger, a memory mapped signal table from the operating system will trap exceptions instead of attempting to trap exceptions directly on the hardware level.

Single Step

ARM architecture does not have an explicit single-step instruction. On Intel architecture, an assembly-level single step is commonly implemented in the debugger directly through such an instruction. On ARM, a single instruction step is implemented as a "run until break" command. The debugger is required to do some code inspection to ensure that all possible code paths are covered (especially if it's stepping away from a branch instruction or such). From a debugger implementation standpoint, this does generate slight overhead but is not excessive, since this "run until break" implementation will be frequently needed for high-level language stepping anyway. Software developers in general should be aware of this difference since this can lead to slightly different stepping behavior.

Virtual Memory Mapping

The descriptor table and page translation implementation for virtual memory mapping is surprisingly similar, at least conceptually. On Intel architecture, the Global Descriptor Table (GDT) and Local Descriptor Table (LDT) enable nested coarseness adjustments to memory pages to be mapped into the virtual address space. Figure 8-32 uses the page translation feature of the debugger to graphically represent the linear-to-physical address translation on Intel architecture.

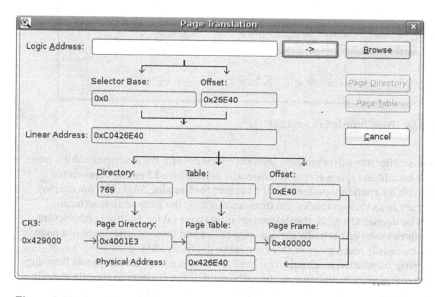

Figure 8-32. *Page Translation on Intel Architecture*

On ARM, the first level and second level page tables define a more direct and at maximum, a one- or two-level–deep page search for virtual memory. Figure 8-33 shows a sample linear address to physical address translation.

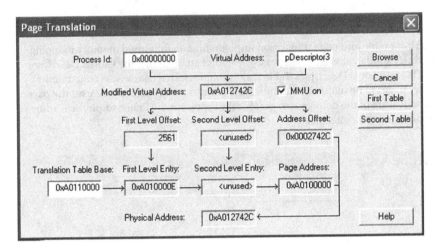

Figure 8-33. *Page Translation on ARM*

Intel architecture offers multiple levels of coarseness for the descriptor tables, page tables, 32-bit address space access in real mode, and 64-bit addressing in protected mode, which is dependent on the selector `base:offset` model. ARM does not employ `base:offset` in its various modes. On Intel architecture, the page table search can implicitly be deeper. On ARM, the defined set is two page tables. On Intel architecture, the descriptor tables can actually mask nested tables and thus the true depth of a page table run can easily reach twice or three times the depth on ARM.

The page translation mechanism on Intel architecture provides for greater flexibility in the system memory layout and mechanisms used by the OS layer to allocate specific memory chunks as protected blocks for application execution. However, it does add challenges for the developer to have a full overview of the memory virtualization and thus avoid memory leaks and memory access violations (segmentation faults). On a full featured OS with plenty of memory, this issue is less of a concern. Real-time operating systems with more visibility into memory handling may be more exposed to this issue.

Considerations for Intel Hyper-Threading Technology

From a debugging perspective, there is really no practical difference between a physical processor core and a logical core that has been enabled via Intel hyper-threading technology. Enabling hyper-threading occurs as part of the platform-initialization process in your BIOS. Therefore, there is no noticeable difference from the application standpoint between a true physical processor core and an additional logical processor core. Since this technology enables concurrent execution of multiple threads, the debugging challenges are similar to a true multi-core debug.

SoC and Interaction of Heterogeneous Multi-Core

Dozens of software components and hardware components interacting on SoCs increase the amount of time it takes to root-cause issues during debug. Interactions between the different software components are often time-sensitive. When trying to debug a code base with many interactions between components, single-stepping through one specific component is usually not a viable option. Traditional `printf` debugging is also not effective in this context because the debugging changes can adversely affect timing behavior and cause even worse problems (also known as "Heisenbugs").

SVEN (System Visible Event Nexus)

SVEN is a software technology (and API) that collects real-time, full-system visible software "event traces." SVEN is currently built into all media/display drivers and is the primary debug tool for the Intel media processor CE3100 and Intel Atom processor CE4100 platforms. SVEN provides debug, performance measurement, and regression testing capabilities.

Ultimately, SVEN is simply a list of software events with high-resolution timestamps. The SVEN API provides developers a method for transmitting events from any operating system context and firmware. The SVEN Debug infrastructure consists of a small and fast "event transmit" (SVEN-TX) library and a verbose capture and analysis (SVEN-RX) capability.

This so-called System Visible Event Nexus in the form of the SVEN-TX library provides an instrumentation API with low and deterministic overhead. It does not cause any additional timing-dependent effects. There are no changes in the behavior of the system because of the instrumentation observation. In other words, there is no software Heisenberg effect. The events to monitor can be issued by any software component on the entire platform. These can be interrupt service routines (ISRs), drivers, applications, and even firmware.

A real-time monitor interface named SVEN-RX provides real-time and offline analysis of the data exported by the SVEN-TX API. SVEN-RX can monitor an executing system and analyze failures on the executing application. In addition, it provides detailed information for fine-grained performance tuning.

Lastly, the SVEN Debug console is a command-line utility that attaches to the Nexus and observes all events being generated by the SVEN-TX instrumented code (drivers, user apps, and libraries). A scriptable filter dynamically accepts or rejects any describable event category (for example, only record events from MPEG decoder). Scriptable "triggers" stop recording events to halt local capture of events leading up to a failure. A Reverse Engineer feature transfers all register reads/writes from a physical address to the unit and External Architecture Specification (EAS) registers.

The SVEN debug console can save the recorded events collected from the SoC to a disk file for offline debugging.

Signal Encode/Decode Debug

The SVEN Debug console has a built-in Streaming Media Decoder (SMD) buffer flow monitor that checks on SMD ports/queues for data flow between drivers. It also samples the SMD circular buffer utilization over time. Its health monitor is capable of triggering an execution stop and data capture if, for example, it fails to detect video flip or an audio decode within a specified period of time.

SVEN Benefits

SVEN enables an accelerated platform debug process providing the developers with all of the required evidence for problem triage. The included automation tools can diagnose most of the common system failures automatically. In short, it speeds up the development cycle on complex Intel Atom processor–based SoC designs by reducing the time it takes the developer to understand issues that occur in the data exchanges and handshake between all of the system components.

Overview

This chapter covered the configuration and installation details of the necessary drivers and debug tools. In addition, we highlighted some of the underlying architectural differences that may impact debug, but usually only for those developers who are interested in development very close to the system layer.

As you have seen in the overview of available debug solutions and debug configurations, there is a full set of debug environments available covering the needs of the Java application developer, the native C/C++ code developer, as well as the system software stack developer.

Debugging on Intel architecture is supported with the standard Android SDK and Android NDK toolsets provided by Google. In addition Intel as well as other ecosystem players provide debug solutions that expand on these available debug tools and provide solutions for system software stack debug as well as graphics performance debug.

If you are familiar with debugging and developing for Android running on ARM architecture, the same debug methods apply to Intel architecture. The available debug tools and development tools infrastructure is based on the Android SDK and extended by solutions from Intel, as well as ecosystem partners that are often also familiar from ARM. Thus there should be few surprises when debugging software on an Intel Atom processor–based Android device versus ARM-based devices.

CHAPTER 9

Performance Optimizations for Android Applications on x86

Like so many other things in life, you rarely get only what you optimize for.

— Erik Naggum

Performance optimization is one of the important goals that every application developer always wants to pursue, no matter if the application is for a general desktop Windows computer or an Android device. Android is a resource-limited system and thus requires very strict resource utilization in space and processing time. Compared with a desktop system, the performance optimization for Android applications is therefore far more critical.

Different applications require a different focus for optimization. Performance optimization for an Android system generally falls into three categories:

- Optimization of the application's running speed

- Code size

- Optimization for lower power consumption

Generally speaking, storage space and cost for Android on Intel Atom is not a bottleneck, so in this chapter, we will focus on performance optimization that makes an application run faster.

We will first introduce the basic principles of SOC performance optimization. We'll follow that with an introduction of principles and methodologies of performance optimization for Android applications running on Intel architectures. We will discuss application development for Android using the Native Development Kit, and share specific case studies using the certain tools such as the Intel Graphics Performance Analyzers.

Basic Concepts of Performance Optimization

Optimization aims at reducing the time needed to complete a specific task accurately and according to specification. This is achieved by structural adjustments, or refactoring, of the application based on the optimization of either hardware or software.

There are several basic principles related to the results of the performance optimization of an application that need to be followed:

- *Equal-value principle*: There is no change in the result of application execution after performance optimization.

- *Efficacy principle*: After performance optimization, the targeted code runs faster.

- *Combined-value principle*: Sometimes, performance optimization gains performance improvement in certain aspects, but degrades performance in others. Combined overall performance needs to be considered when deciding whether or not a performance optimization is needed.

One of important considerations for performance optimization is trading time with space. For example, in order to do a function calculation, the values of the function can be pre-calculated and put into a program storage zone (memory) as a table. When a program is running, instead of spending time on doing repetitive calculations of the function to get the value, the program can directly get the value from the table in order to reduce the execution time. For search operations, this could be done on a large space using hash methods.

The approach picked most frequently for performance optimization is the reduction of the instructions and executions frequency. For example, from the point of view of data structures and algorithms, the instructions for comparison and exchange in bubbling sequencing need to execute $O(n^2)$ times. However, by using a quick sort, the instruction time reduces to $O(n \log n)$ times. In loop optimizations, code compilation can extract irrelevant public code out of the loop and reduce the execution time of public code from n to 1, thus dramatically reducing the execution frequency. In addition, in-line functions supported by C and C++ can be used to change function calls, the instruction of function calls, and the implementation of the return instructions.

Selection of a Faster Instruction

The same function can be realized by utilizing different instructions. Different instructions take different machine clock cycles, and thus the execution times are quite different. This gives us the opportunity to choose to use a faster instruction.

Reducing computational strength is a typical example of performance optimization achieved by selecting a faster instruction set. For example, to multiply an integer by 4, the operation can be done by shifting the operator two digits to the left to complete. The shift instruction takes much fewer clock cycles and runs much faster than multiplication and division instructions.

Another example of this category of optimization is to use special instructions provided by the hardware to replace the generic instructions for faster instruction execution. For example, the Intel Atom processor provides Streaming SIMD Extensions (SSE) instruction set support. For vector operations, SSE instructions should always be used to accomplish the operation, as they run much faster due to the benefit of instruction-level parallel processing. The ordinary addition instruction width for Intel Atom is 32 bits, while SSE instructions are capable of four times 32-bit data processing. As a result, the optimized codes using SSE instructions shorten the time consumed dramatically.

Improve the Degree of Parallelism

The degree of parallelism can be improved at multiple levels, including instruction, expression, function, and threads.

Many modern embedded processors including the Intel Atom processor support instruction pipeline execution. This enables an optimization method called instruction-level parallelism. A code chain can be decomposed of several units of code that are not dependent on the chain and can be executed in parallel in the pipeline.

In addition, many embedded system processors, such as the Intel Atom processor, physically support the concurrent execution of threads. The use of an appropriate number of concurrent threads rather than a single thread can increase running speed. In order to take advantage of thread concurrency optimization, programmers need to consciously adopt multithreading technology; sometimes optimization needs to be done with compiler support.

Effective Use of the Register Cache

Writes and reads that go to and from the cache registers are much faster than those that go to and from memory. The goal of cache optimization is to try to put data and instructions that are being used and will be used often into the cache in order to improve the cache hit rate and reduce cache conflicts. Cache optimization often appears in the optimization process for a nested loop. Register optimization involves effectively using the register and keeping frequently used data in the register as much as possible.

Cache is based on locality. That is, cache assumes the data to be used is located in the most recent data that is already in use or is in the vicinity of their own register. This is called the *locality principle* or *principle of locality*, and it deeply affects hardware, software, and system design and performance. Instructions and data required by the processor are always first read by cache access. If high-speed cache has the needed data, the processor always accesses high-speed cache directly. In this situation, such an access is called a high-speed *cache hit*. If high-speed cache does not contain the needed data, this is referred to as a failed hit or *cache miss*.

If this happens, the processor needs to copy data from memory to high-speed cache. If the corresponding location of high-speed cache already is already occupied by other data, the data that are no longer needed in cache will need to be expelled and written back to memory. Failed hits will result in a sharp rise in access time; therefore the goal in increasing cache efficiency is used to improve the hit rate and lower failure rates. The data exchange between cache and memory is performed via a block unit, which is used to copy needed data or write-back blocks into memory.

Locality describes the way that accessed or referenced data locations are collected into predictable clusters for easy future reference by the processor. There are two important cases of locality, explained briefly as follows:

- *Spatial locality*: When a particular data object is referenced, it is statistically likely that *nearby* data will be referenced in the near future. A section of adjacent data is marked off as a single block for the processor to gain faster access to that location.

- *Temporal locality*: When a particular data object is referenced, it is also statistically likely that the *same* data will be referenced again in the near future. The referenced data is moved into cache memory so that it can be referenced more quickly in its new location.

Methodology of Performance Optimizations

There are many methods and techniques for performance optimization. One or more comprehensive optimization principles can be utilized simultaneously, such as modifying the source code to run faster. According to the type of criteria for the classification, optimization methods can be divided into different categories.

Machine-dependent optimization can be done only on specific hardware or architecture. For example, the optimizations of switching ordinary vector instruction computing to SSE instructions, which are dependent on many low-level details of the Intel Atom processor, can only be used on the Intel processors that support SSE instructions. It is difficult to use this optimization on other machines with different architecture, such as ARM, or unspecified architectures. In general, the complexity of a machine-independent optimization is higher than that of the machine-dependent optimization and difficult to achieve.

Performance Optimization Approaches

In the ideal scenario, the compiler should be able to compile any code that we write and optimize it into the most efficient machine code. But the reality is that the compiler can actually automate only some of all possible optimizations because some optimizations may be blocked by default by the compiler's optimization blocker. In general, depending on how much of a role the human or automated tools will play, the performance optimization approaches can be divided into three main categories:

- Performance optimizations done automatically by a compiler

- Performance optimizations done with the assistance of development tools

- Performance optimizations done manually by a programmer

The following sections present several approaches and methods for developers to achieve performance optimization.

Performance Optimizations Automatically Done by a Compiler

Modern compilers automatically complete the most common code optimizations. These automatic optimizations done by a compiler are also known as compiler optimizations or compiling optimizations. A compiler optimization needs to be triggered by the appropriate extensions option or switch variable.

C/C++ code optimization for Android applications can be achieved by the GNU Compiler Collection tools located in the Native Development Kit. We will cover this topic in detail in the next chapter.

Performance Optimizations Assisted by Development Tools

It is very difficult to achieve an overall comprehensive optimization of a large program. Fortunately, for applications based on Intel architecture, many useful tools are available to help the user complete the optimization. For example, Intel Profiler, Graphics Performance Analyzer (GPA), Power Monitoring Tool, and other tools can help users to analyze a program and guide them through complete optimization.

VTune and GPA are part of Intel's product development tools and can only be used for Intel processors such as the Intel Atom processor. Intel Profiler is a GNU chain tool and can be used for all types of processors. It can be used to create a profiling process that shows which areas of the program execute frequently and use more computing resources and which areas are less frequently implemented. The profiling data provides valuable information for developers to complete the optimization.

A typical example of profile-guided optimization (PGO) is the optimization of the switch statement (such as the switch-case statement of C#). In this example, according to the profile of the collected sample run, after getting the actual frequency of occurrence of each case statement, the case statement is sorted in the switch statement by frequency sequence. The most frequently occurring statements are moved to the front (the performance of these statements require a minimum number of comparisons), so as to achieve optimal results with the least number of comparisons. In GNU terminology, the process is known as profile-guided optimization (PGO).

Like the GNU Profiler, Intel VTune is capable of locating hotspots in the program. The hotspot zone refers to the segment of programming code that takes a long execution time (which means more computing power). With VTune, programmers can find the time-consuming code segment and then take measures to optimize that code. VTune has a much higher resolution (fine granularity) and more functions for positioning the hotspot than the GNU profiler, including displaying the assembly code of the program, failed cache hits, and branch misprediction events for Intel processors.

Intel GPA was originally a development tool used for graphics processing unit (GPU) analysis. It has now been developed into a comprehensive tool for CPU speed analysis, customization, and device power consumption analysis. Intel GPA can be used to get CPU load, operating frequency, and power consumption information. It can guide the user to optimize the application, especially multithreaded optimization. Intel GPA is not only a speed optimization tool but also a very handy power optimization tool.

With optimization tools, developers no longer need to get disoriented and confused when trying to find a starting point for optimization of a large program. These tools allow you to easily locate the areas that are most in need of optimization, which are the codes segments that are potentially the most problematic. Quickly finding the hotspot allows you to achieve your optimization with less time and effort. Of course, typical performance optimization is complicated. The tool only plays a guiding and supporting role—the real optimization still needs to be completed by the compiler or developer manually.

Use of High-Performance Libraries

High-performance libraries are sets of software libraries that are usually developed by a hardware original equipment manufacturer (OEM) and which provide some commonly used operations and services. These library codes are carefully optimized based on a combination of processor features and have higher computing speeds than ordinary codes. In short, high-performance databases are libraries optimized through various methods that utilize the full potential of the processor. For example, Intel Integrated Performance Primitives (Intel IPP) libraries have been optimized based on SSE instructions for the processor, hyper-/multithreaded parallel pipelined execution, and a waterfall process. Compared with nonoptimized code, Intel IPP libraries can increase the processing power of Intel processors and save power consumption. For some important code and algorithms, using high-performance libraries is actually a simple, practical optimization method and offers the benefit of "standing on the shoulders of giants." Intel IPP is one of Intel's high-performance libraries. It is a library of functions for Intel processors including the Intel Atom processor and Intel Chipsets. Intel IPP is powerful; it can be used for mathematical calculations, signal processing, multimedia, image and graphics processing, vector calculations, and other fields. Intel IPP uses a C/C++ programming interface.

Performance Optimizations Done Manually

In various stages of optimization, the human factor should not be ignored. Some high-level global optimizations, such as the optimization of algorithms and data structures, cannot be done by a compiler automatically. The optimization must be completed manually by people. As a programmer, in order to write efficient code, it is necessary to learn the various algorithms and optimization techniques to develop good programming habits and style. Even if the compiler can automatically complete the optimization, additional assistance from the programmers is still needed to write efficient code at the following levels:

- *Source code (that is, high-level language) level optimization*: This optimization is done by the programmers at the source code level. The programmer uses the expression of a high-level language source code to modify and transform the program.

- *Assembly language level optimization*: Sometimes using high-level language is not enough to reach the optimal results, and programmers may need to modify the codes to bring them down to the assembly-language level. In some key computing areas, although the process of assembly-level optimization is cumbersome, the performance benefit of the outcome is worth it.

- *Compiling instruction-level optimization*: This is an optimization accomplished by performers through additions and modifications of compiler directives, such as the typical compiler directive modification "pragma" and/or increasing the degree of parallelism in OpenMP.

Program-interactive optimization is truly a reflection of the art of the programming, and the level of accomplishment fulfills the ideal of the "unity of human and machine." This unity is the focus of this chapter. Relatively speaking, optimizations performed at the compiling phase of the assembly-language level or the instruction level require a programmer to have comprehensive expertise in processor architecture, hardware, system, and so on. As a result, for Android systems on Intel architecture, we recommend the performance optimization at the source-code level. In the following example, we focus on the introduction of performance optimization on Android multithreaded design.

There is no doubt that optimization can be done in several ways that are related to each other and structurally undividable, while each has its own unique function. The overall process is shown in Figure 9-1.

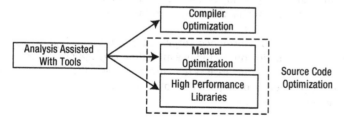

Figure 9-1. *Recommended User Optimization*

As Figure 9-1 shows, compiler optimization, manual optimization, and high-performance library functions are tied together. They are final steps in optimization. The use of both manual optimization and high-performance libraries is needed in order to modify the source code. Before starting those optimizations, analyzing the programs using optimization tools has proved to be very beneficial to developers and is a must-have step.

Performance Tuning with Intel VTune

For the Linux platform, profile analysis is the most important type of software performance analysis. Profile analysis generally involves the user analyzing and identifying the source code that needs to be optimized with the assistance of various tools. The best tool for the analysis of the performance profile of software running on Intel processors is the Intel VTune family of products.

Intel VTune Performance Amplifier (commonly referred to as VTune analyzer or VTune) is performance analysis software and a useful optimization tool for Intel processors. With the capability to analyze the program's performance, VTune can assist and guide the programmers and compiler to optimize various applications. VTune provides a user-friendly graphical user interface that does not require you to recompile the application. Performance analysis can be done directly on the executable application. VTune is applicable to a wide range of applications from embedded systems to supercomputers, has cross-platform capability, and can run on Android, Tizen, Windows, Linux, Mac OS, and so on.

VTune is based on a hotspot area analysis to guide and support the performance optimization of the application. Hotspots are code segments that require excessively long execution times. In addition to the hotspot analysis, the user needs to consider what causes the hotspot and how to resolve it. For advanced users, VTune can be used to track key function calls, monitor special CPU events (such as a cache miss), and perform a series of other advanced features.

Intel has continuously added features to VTune Performance Analyzer, and in 2012 it renamed the tool. Formerly known as Intel VTune Performance Analyzer with an Intel Thread Profiler, the company changed its name to Intel VTune Amplifier XE. The updated tool includes all of the features and functionality of the Intel Parallel amplifier and also has some advanced features for programmers who need to explore issues in depth. Its main functions are described in the following sections.

As shown in Figure 9-2, the VTune Performance Amplifier lists the entire elapsed time of the program as well as information on the top five most time-consuming functions (when the functions of the program are less than five, it lists only the actual function number), such as the percentage of elapsed time of the total elapsed time of entire program used by the top five functions.

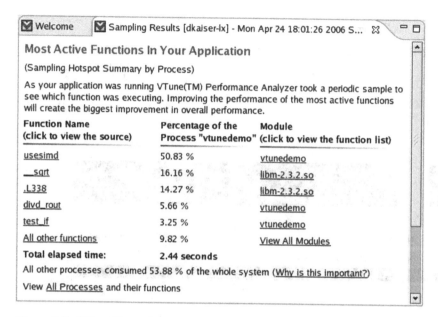

Figure 9-2. *VTune Elapsed Time and Statistics*

VTune provides run-time statistics that as specific as pointers to individual lines of code, which can help users to locate which sections of code are the most time-consuming. As shown in Figure 9-3, VTune displays the running time of the program source code statements (ticks, clock ticks) occupied by the percentage of the total time consumed and instructions completed (instructions retired).

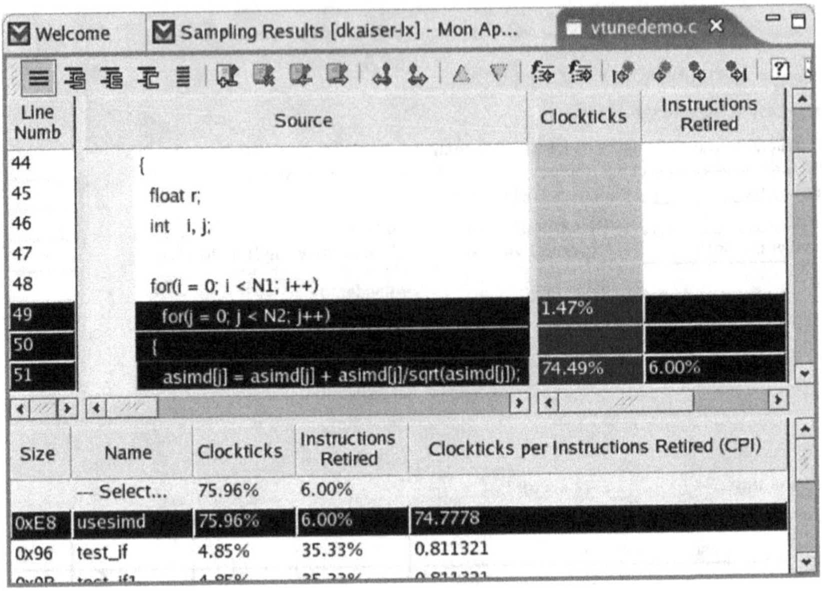

Figure 9-3. *VTune displays the most time-consuming lines of source codes*

VTune shows the program function call relations in an intuitive way in a call graph as shown in Figure 9-4, in which the function calls are displayed in graphical form. Highlighted in the display, the function call relationship from the root to the current function is called the *critical path* (also known as *focus function*).

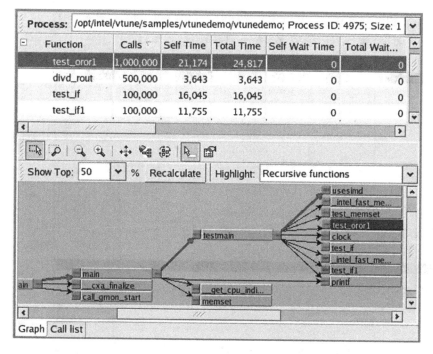

Figure 9-4. *VTune Call Graph for a Function Call Relationship*

VTune can be displayed directly in an assembly code in the source code corresponding to the target file. Figure 9-5 shows the assembly code corresponding to the function of a program. With this feature, users can do a compilation analysis, locate the time-consuming code, and perform assembly-level optimization.

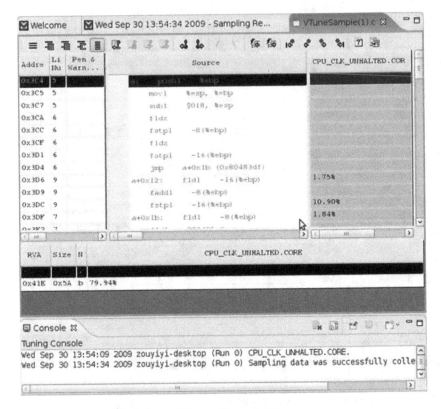

Figure 9-5. *Assembly Codes and Source Codes in VTune*

VTune provides a graphical interface that displays the statistics for time and other processor events, including cache miss, branch misprediction, and other information. Figure 9-6 shows the statistics for processor events corresponding to four threads of the application. Each of the four threads includes three bars: the top bar, which represents the average consumption of the number of clock ticks of executing instructions that occurred (Clockticks per Instruction Retired); the middle bar, which shows the highest number of clock ticks consumed (Clockticks); and the bottom bar, which indicates the instruction that has been completed (Instructions Retired).

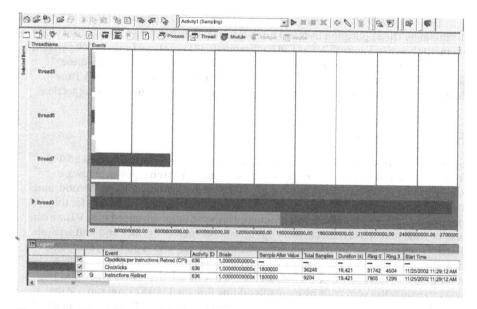

Figure 9-6. *VTune Display of Other Processor Events*

VTune can display the CPU usage of the application and the distribution of the degree of concurrency for an application. Information can be used to analyze the degree of parallelism. Figure 9-7 is a 1000HC screenshot of an application on a device using the Intel Atom N270 processor.

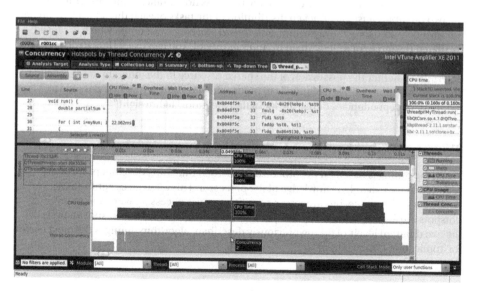

Figure 9-7. *Thread and CPU Usage Distribution*

The Intel Atom N270 is a single-core processor, but it supports Intel Hyper-Threading Technology. The application uses two threads to calculate a degree of parallelism of the moment shown in Figure 9-7. The CPU utilization (CPU time) can be up to 200 percent.

By comparing the VTune features previously described, we can classify these features by how the tuning is used (optimization analysis). In summary, the VTune function tuning can be divided into the three levels described in the following sections.

System Tuning

System tuning is what VTune Amplifier XE is designed for but is not the main goal of application optimization. The purpose of system tuning is to change the hardware configuration, such as network bandwidth, disk read/write operations per second, and hit failure, on the memory page. System tuning and optimization are mainly for the original equipment manufacturer's products. However, as an advanced tool, VTune can also be used to reach certain auxiliary optimizations, such as the lock and wait analysis. Here, VTune can measure the waiting time of the network socket object to complete disk write I/O, which can be configured to reduce the thread-to-block waiting time. Another use to run a hot spot analysis and find a hot spot. If the results are applicable, you can parallelize your code by manually adding threaded tasks or you can use the compiler to automatically parallelize the code using Intel Thread Building Blocks (Intel TBB). Of course, you can also adjust or tune the algorithm by checking the function-call relationship and removing duplicate computing to reduce the number of function calls.

In another scenario, where the program has been parallelized, you need VTune to run *parallel analysis* to determine the degree of parallelism of the program and hotspot analysis to find the hotspot as well as the degree of parallelism at the hotspot. When the degree of parallelism at the hotspot is low (such as in the case of functions consuming most of the CPU time where the thread is not parallel to the other threads), the two possible causes are uneven distribution of the tasks of each thread, which can be optimized by adjusting the algorithm, and *thread blocking* (wait time), which is caused by shared resources or a "lock" held by another thread. You can use VTune to do lock and wait for the analysis to find out the cause of obstruction. In this case, you need to determine whether the possession of the shared resource in the other threads is needed and time is optimized. The solution is to reduce the hot zone as much as possible to reduce data dependencies or use the locks that are more "lightweight."

Tuning Based on the Microarchitecture of the Processor

When the tuning is based on the processor's microarchitecture, developers are often required to have detailed knowledge of the processor. This often gives application developers a hard time, but processor-specific tuning is necessary when too many hotspots are found (or too many hotspot functions are called) in the hotspot analysis. Of the two different levels of tuning previously described, algorithm tuning is the most useful for application optimization.

VTune's two modes

When VTune is in local mode, the analysis of the program being tested and VTune itself work on the same machine. In remote mode, the testing of the application takes place on one machine and VTune is installed on another machine. For desktop machines, VTune is generally used in local mode, which is relatively simple. The Android system is commonly used in remote mode. Here, VTune is installed on an Ubuntu/Win/MAC development system, where most development and the SDK are located, and the Android device is connected to the development system by a USB network cable or a Wi-Fi network.

Intel offers a free trial version of VTune for noncommercial use, which generally lasts for one year. Special discount prices for student and academic institutions are also available. Readers can go to Intel's official web site (http://www.intel.com) to download the Linux version of VTune Amplifier XE. Before downloading, Intel will let you fill in your email information, and the serial number will be sent to you. The following is an excerpt from the Intel VTune Amplifier XE 2011 download.

You have registered Intel VTune Amplifier XE for Linux* (formerly VTune Performance Analyzer for Linux*). You will be receiving an email which includes the serial numbers listed below as well as the download links for your future reference:

... ...

```
Serial Number:XXXX-XXXXXXXX

File to download: Install Package for IA-32 and Intel 64 (143 MB)
```

... ...

```
Intel VTune Amplifier XE for Linux*

Download:

Install Package for IA-32 and Intel 64
```

... ...

When readers go to the download link, the serial number will be shown as XXXX-XXXXXXXX. Download the software package entitled vtune_amplifier_xe_2011_update4.tar.gz (file size about 150 MB) to your local drive and install.

Note that to install and use VTune on an Android device, you will need the corresponding driver support. The driver needs to be compiled and generated using Android course codes. Typical users rarely have access to or are familiar with the source code of the Android devices. Driver preparation is generally produced by the Android device OEM. Most manufacturers are reluctant to install related drivers to commercial-grade devices (such as mobile phones), and even root privileges are not open. For non-OEM users, using VTune locally on an Android device is still a challenge, as there are some system-level configurations that only Android system engineers can handle. However, Intel is stepping up development and improving the use of VTune on Android, and it is estimated that in the near future, application developers, students, and the academic world can get access to the powerful VTune tool and use it locally on an Android device.

Intel Graphics Performance Analyzers

Intel Graphics Performance Analyzers (Intel GPA) are a suite of optimization and analysis tools used only for Intel processors that support Intel Core and Intel Atom processor-based hardware platforms. Intel GPA provides a graphical user interface for the CPU/GPU speed analysis and customization features. It enables developers to find performance bottlenecks and optimize applications for devices based on the Intel chipset platform. Intel GPA consists of the System Analyzer, Frame Analyzer, and the Software Development Kit (SDK).

Introduction

Intel GPA supports all Android devices running on Intel Atom processors. The suite offers the following features:

- A real-time display of dozens of key indicators including CPU, GPU, and OpenGL ES API

- Several graphics pipeline tests, which are provided instantly to isolate graphics bottlenecks

- Compatibility with Microsoft Windows or Ubuntu OS as host development systems

Intel GPA currently only supports real Android devices using Intel Atom processors – it does not support analysis of the Android Virtual Device (AVD). Intel GPA for Android uses a typical hardware deployment model often used in Android application cross-development, in which the host system (Windows or Ubuntu) and the target device (Android Intel-based devices) are connected via a USB connection to monitor Android applications. Android GPA operates on the Android Debug Bridge utility (adb, here tied to a local server) to achieve the monitoring of the application on the target Android devices. The adb (server) runs on Android devices, and the GPA runs on the host system as the adb client applications to achieve target machine monitoring. The GPA configuration is shown in Figure 9-8.

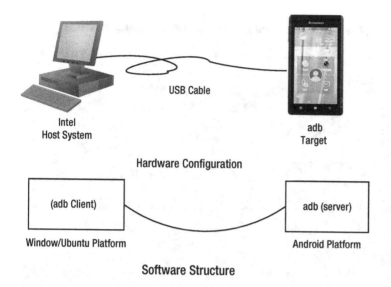

Figure 9-8. *Intel GPA Configuration for Monitoring Applications on an Android Device*

Developers should be cautious given that Intel GPA is based on adb to work. Since both Eclipse and DDMS also use adb, Intel GPA may not work properly if GPA, DDMS, and Eclipse are running at the same time due to a server conflict. It is best to turn off other Android software development tools, such as Eclipse or DDMS, when using Intel GPA. Figure 9-9 shows the Intel GPA graphic interface in the process of monitoring an app running on an Android device.

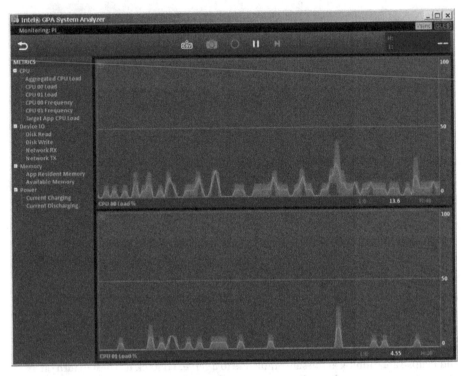

Figure 9-9. *GPA Graphic Interface Monitoring an App Running on an Android Device*

As shown in Figure 9-9, which is screenshot for a Lenovo K800 smartphone, the GPA interface displays two frames and a toolbar pane. The Metrics toolbar displays the indicators being measured, which are organized in a tree structure, as follows:

- Under the CPU metric are the Aggregated CPU Load, the CPU XX Load, the CPU XX Frequency, the Target App CPU Load, etc. The CPU XX numbers are determined by how many CPUs are monitored by Intel GPA. To get CPU information such as the number of cores, model, and frequency, we can use the cat/ proc/cpuinfo command at a terminal window. The Lenovo K800 smartphone in the figure uses a single-core Intel Atom Z2460 processor. The figure shows two logical processors as the processor supports for Intel Hyper Threading Technology (Intel HTT). Thus, the two items shown in CPU Load and CPU Frequency are indexed as 00 and 01. In CPU XX Load, XX is the CPU number: it displays the load status for CPU XX, while CPU XX Frequency displays the frequency status for CPU XX. The Aggregated CPU Load is the total load of the CPU. The Target App CPU Load is the CPU load of the app on the target device.

- Under the Device IO metric are the Disk Read, the Disk Write, the Network RX, and the Network TX items, which list the statuses and information for the disk read, disk write, and packets sent and received over the network, respectively.

- Under the Memory metric are App Resident Memory, Available Memory, etc.

- Under the Power metric are Current Charging and Current Discharging, which provide the status of charging and discharging.

By default, the right pane shows two real-time status display windows. These windows display the oscilloscope-like status of the specified indicators. The horizontal axis features the elapsed time and the vertical axis features the value of the corresponding indicator. The user can drag and drop an index entry from the left pane to one of two windows and the real-time indicator of the entry will be displayed in the window. In Figure 9-9, in which the CPU 00 Load has been dragged and dropped to the top display window and the CPU 01 Load onto the bottom display window, the vertical axis shows the CPU utilization. The maximum utilization is 100 percent.

Above the real-time status display window is the toolbar, offering tools such as taking a screenshots and pausing the display. Users can use these tools to achieve some auxiliary functions.

Installation

Hosting Intel GPA can be done in Windows or Ubuntu. The following section gives examples of the Intel GPA installation process for the Windows platform. Users can refer to Intel GPA release notes or related Intel GPA web site for the installation process and usage on the Ubuntu platform.

Intel GPA requires having version 4.0 or higher of the .NET Framework installed to run on the Windows platform. The installation of Intel GPA on the Windows platform consists of two major steps: the first step is to install the .Net Framework and the second step is the real Intel GPA installation. Detailed step-by-step instructions for installing Intel GPA on Windows host platform follow.

1. **Install .Net Framework.**

   .Net Framework v4.0 is used for these instructions. Make sure the latest Windows service pack and critical updates are installed on your computer. If the platform is a 64-bit version of XP or Windows 2003, you may need to install the Windows Imaging Component. To install it, visit http://www.microsoft.com/en-us/download/details. aspx?id=17851 and download .Net Framework 4.0.

   Next, double click dotNetFx40_Full_setup.exe. The pop-up window interface shown in Figure 9-10(a) appears to start the installation. Follow the step-by-step installation prompts to complete the installation.

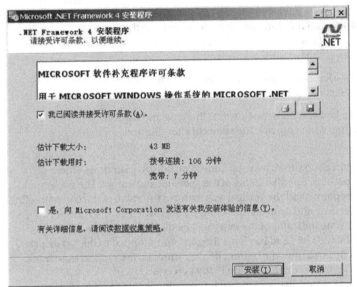

(a). Net Framework Installation Start Windows

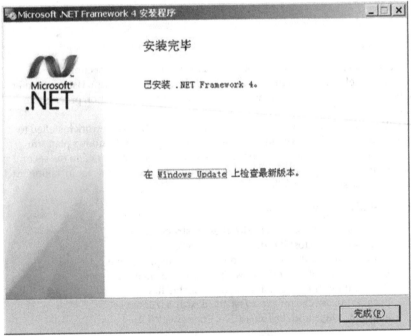

(b). Installation Complete Window

Figure 9-10. *Net Framework 4.0 Installation Interface*

2. **Install Intel GPA**

The installation prerequisites follow: Make sure the latest Windows service pack and critical updates are installed on your computer. Users can go directly to the official Intel web site to download Intel GPA (here, version gpa_12.5_release_187105_windows.exe is used for the test): http://intel.com/software/gpa or http://software.intel.com/en-us/vcsource/tools/intel-gpa, as shown in Figure 9-11. Double click gpa_12.5_release_187105_windows.exe to run the program. This is a self-extracting file. Uncompressed files are saved into the same folder where the original file is located. Double click the setup.exe in the extracted folder to install.

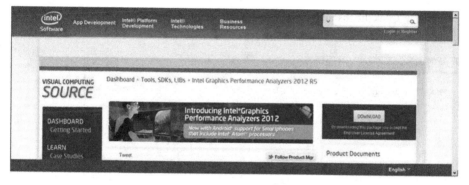

Figure 9-11. Intel GPA Software Download Site

Double click gpa_12.5_release_187105_windows.exe to run the program, which is a self-extracting file; uncompressed files are saved into the same folder where the original file is located.

Next, double click the setup.exe in the extracted folder as shown above to install.

If .Net Framework is not installed, the Intel GPA Prerequisite Setup will appear and prompt users with the necessary information, as shown in Figure 9-12.

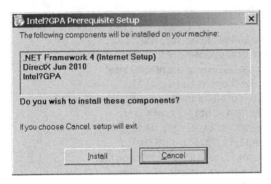

Figure 9-12. *Intel GPA Installation Pop-Up that Appears When .Net Framework Is Not Found*

Click the Install button. The dialog box appears as shown in Figure 9-13.

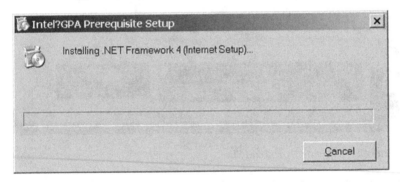

Figure 9-13. *Installation Dialog Box*

One you have installed the prerequisites, you will be returned to the first step to install Intel GPA. The installation progress bar for Intel GPA is shown in Figure 9-14.

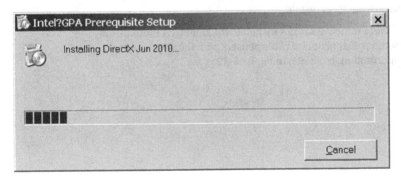

Figure 9-14. *Progress Bar for the Installation of Intel GPA*

Once Intel GPA loads, as shown in Figure 9-15(a), click Next to continue. Intel GPA will test for compatibility and hardware support and remind you of the next step, as shown in Figure 9-15(b). Click Confirm to continue.

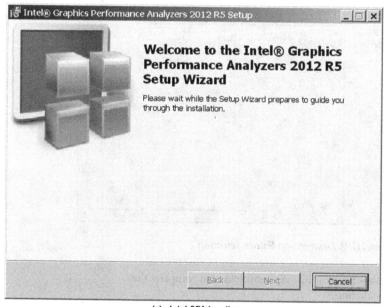

(a). Intel GPA Loading

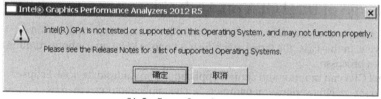

(b). Confirm or Cancel message

Figure 9-15. *Message Boxes for Intel GPA Installation*

Figure 9-16 shows the destination folder selection box (in this example, you would choose D:\GPA\2012 R5).

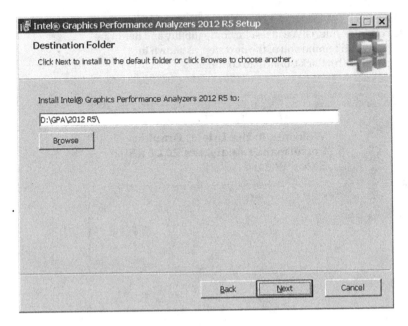

Figure 9-16. Intel GPA Destination Folder Selection

Follow the step-by-step instructions to complete the installation.

Sample Usage of Intel GPA on Android

The following example demonstrates how to use Intel GPA to monitor an application on an Android device. In this case, the target machine is a Lenovo K800 smartphone running on an Intel Atom processor.

Before Intel GPA can monitor and control applications on Android devices, Eclipse must be used to set specific application parameters. The applications can then be generated and deployed by Eclipse, run, and monitored.

The application we will use here as an example for Intel GPA monitoring is MoveCircle. The operation interface is shown in Figure 9-17(a).

The application is a simple drag-around game. The user interface is a simple circle. When the user touches any point inside the circle and drags it around, a black circle will follow the touch point and move around. When the user stops touching the spot in the circle, the circle will become still. At this point, the circle does not move when the user drags it outside the circle (that is, the initial touch point within that circle). If the user presses the phone's Back button, the Exit dialog box will pop up. Selecting Exit will allow you to exit the application, as shown in Figure 9-17(b).

(a). Application in Progress   (b). Exit Interface

Figure 9-17. *The MoveCircle Application*

The major computing tasks of the application take place in the dragging of the circle. You are required to constantly calculate the circle's new location and refresh (redraw) the display.

Following are the steps for Intel GPA monitoring of the sample application:

1. Build and deploy the application in Eclipse that will be monitored by Intel GPA.

2. Use general procedures to create an application project. Name the application MoveCircle.

3. Write the related code for the project. The document framework is shown in Figure 9-18.

Figure 9-18. *Document Framework of the Application MoveCircle*

4. Edit the AndroidManifest.xml file and add the following code:

```
1.   <manifest xmlns:android="http://schemas.android.com/apk/
     res/android"
2.        package="com.example.movecircle"
3.        android:versionCode="1"
4.        android:versionName="1.0" >
5.
6.     <uses-sdk
7.         android:minSdkVersion="8"
8.         android:targetSdkVersion="15" />
9.         <uses-permission android:name="android.
           permission.INTERNET"/>
10.
11.     <application
12.         android:icon="@drawable/ic_launcher"
13.         android:debuggable="true"
14.         android:label="@string/app_name"
15.         android:theme="@style/AppTheme" >
16.         <activity
17.             android:name=".MainActivity"
18.             android:label="@string/title_activity_main" >
19.             <intent-filter>
20.                 <action
21.     android:name="android.intent.action.MAIN" />

22.                 <category android:name="android.intent.
                    category.LAUNCHER" />
23.             </intent-filter>
24.         </activity>
```

```
25.        </application>
26.
27.        </manifest>
```

In line 9, we add a description of uses-permission elements, which is the same level of the application, and we grant the application's Internet write/read access. In line 13, we specify that the application is debuggable.

5. Generate the application package and deploy the application to the real target device. Be sure to close Eclipse before starting the next step.

6. Start Intel GPA on the host machine to monitor the application

    a. Connect the Android phone to the PC. Make sure the screen is not locked or you may get error the error Unsuccessful Phone Connection.

    b. Make sure to turn off all tools that use the adb server, such as Eclipse and DDMS. Otherwise, you may get the error Unsuccessful Phone Connection. (This step can be skipped) Make sure the adb server is started and running (See Figure 9-19).

```
C:\Documents and Settings>adb devices
    List of devices attached
    Medfield04749AFB                device
```

Figure 9-19. ADB Server Displaying Our Medfield Device

7. Select the Windows menu "\start\program\Intel Graphics Performance Analyzers 2012 RS\Intel GPA System Analyzer" to start Intel GPA.

8. The Intel GPA initial window then pops up, suggesting the machine that will be monitored, as shown in Figure 9-20. Since the tuning target is a phone in this case, select the phone (in this case the Medfield04749AFB) by clicking the Connect button to the right of name of the phone.

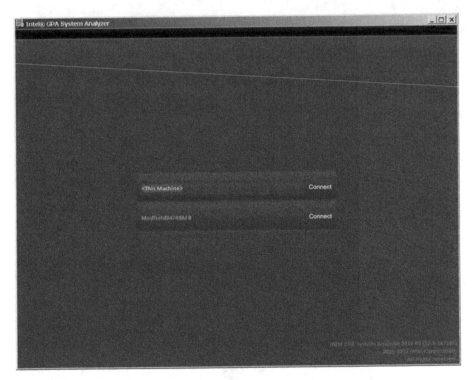

Figure 9-20. Intel GPA Interface for Connecting to the Monitored Device

9. Once you are connected, Intel GPA does an initial analysis of the applications installed on the monitored smartphone, dividing the apps into two groups: analyzable applications and nonanalyzable applications, as shown in Figure 9-21.

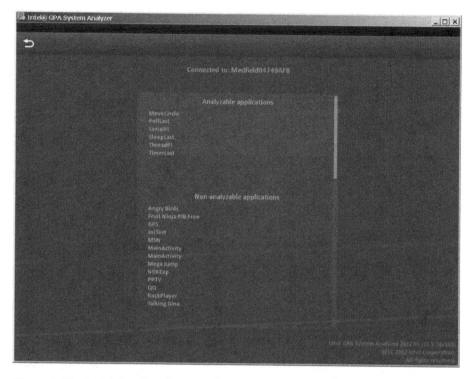

Figure 9-21. *Initial Interface (Apps List) After Intel GPA Is Connected to the Monitored Phone Device*

At the top of the window is an Analyzable applications category that can be tuned or debugged by Intel GPA. Non-analyzable applications are listed in the bottom panel. In the analyzable application list, you can see the MoveCircle application that we are using as the example for the Intel GPA monitoring exercise. The reason that an application is not analyzable by Intel GPA is usually because its parameters are not set in the way we described in earlier in this session.

10. Click the name of the application that you want Intel GPA to monitor in the Analyzable applications window (in this case, MoveCircle). An icon of a rolling circle showing ongoing progress appears on the left side of the app (MoveCircle). See Figure 9-22.

213

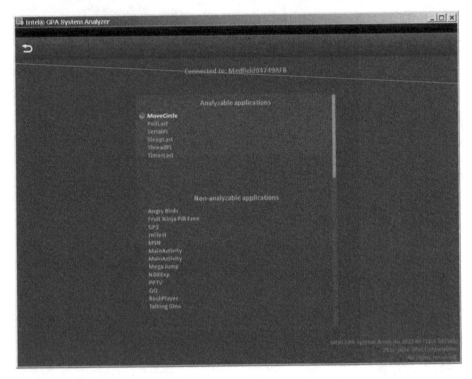

Figure 9-22. *App Initialization Interface in Intel GPA*

While this is happening, the application start-up screen is displayed on the phone. The screen will prompt you with the message Waiting For Debugger, as shown in Figure 9-23. Note that you should not click the Force Close button but instead wait until the message box automatically closes in the interface.

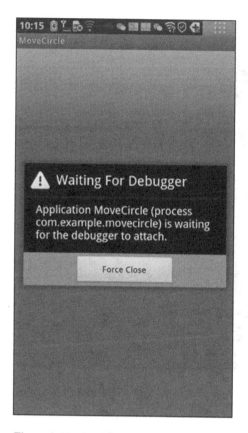

Figure 9-23. *Initial Message Appearing on Target Phone When Intel GPA Starts Monitoring the Application*

11.   Next, Intel GPA monitoring interface appears, as shown in Figure 9-24.

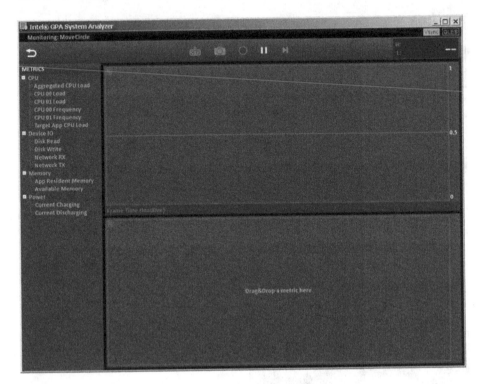

Figure 9-24. *Initial Monitoring Interface Shown on Intel GPA when the Application Is Started*

While this takes place, the MoveCircle app starts to run on the phone, as shown in Figure 9-25.

Figure 9-25. *The MoveCircle App That is Shown on the Target Phone Device*

Drag and drop the CPU 00 Load to the top real-time status display panel in the display window, and drag and drop the CPU 01 Load onto the bottom real-time status display panel in the display window. Click and drag the MoveCircle around for a few seconds and then stop the interaction for a few seconds. The corresponding Intel GPA monitoring screen is shown in Figure 9-26.

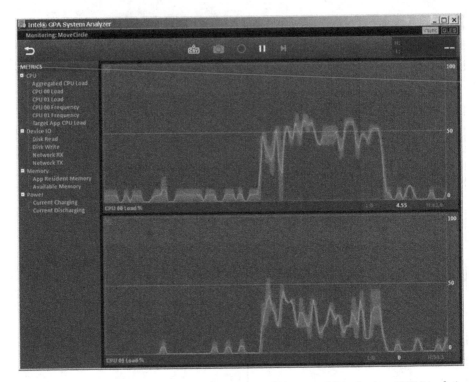

Figure 9-26. *Intel GPA Monitoring the MoveCircle App and Displaying CPU Loads in Real Time*

In Figure 9-26, we can see a rule: when we drag the circle, the two CPU loads will both rise to a certain height; when we do not interact with the app, the two CPU loads will immediately drop to near 0 percent. The application's main computing tasks are concentrated in dragging and moving the circle, and there is no or low CPU load when the circle is not being moved.

To end the Intel GPA analysis, exit the app, as shown in Figure 9-17(b). Intel GPA will return to the starting interface shown in Figure 9-20.

The previous example only demonstrates monitoring of the CPU load. An interested reader can try other app examples and other monitoring metrics. Using the MoveCircle app as an example, we chose the Disk Read metric for the top display window and the Disk Write metric for the bottom display window. We then switched apps and reviewed some photo files. When we returned to the MoveCircle app, the instant action of disk read shows the existence of Disk Read activity, as shown in Figure 9-27.

Figure 9-27. Intel GPA Monitoring Window Showing Disk Read for the MoveCircle App and Other Apps

Android Multithreaded Design

The Intel Atom processor supports hyperthreading and multicore configurations. A multithreaded design is a good way to increase the degree of parallelism and improve performance. The Intel Atom N-series processors support the parallel execution of multiple threads. Although most Intel Atom Z series processors for mobile phones and other mobile devices are single core, they support Intel Hyper-Threading Technology. Thus the Z series processors form two or four logical CPUs and also physically support a certain degree of parallel execution.

Note that the word used here is parallel rather than concurrent. For some tasks, we can follow the classic methodology in parallel computing called "divide and conquer" and divide them into two or more basic units. We assign those units to different threads to be executed at the same time. In this way, the performance potential of the processor is fully utilized, accelerating execution speed such that the software runs faster and more efficiently.

Based on the Java multithreaded programming interface, Android extensions provide a more powerful multithreaded programming interface for Android developers. With the aid of this programming interface, developers can easily implement multithreaded development and design at the Java language level without needing to use the cumbersome underlying operating system called interface.

Android Framework or a Thread

The Android threaded programming framework is based on Java. There are two methods to realize multithreaded programming in Java. The first is to inherit from the Thread class and override the run method. The second is to implement the Runnable interface and run method.

Java Thread Programming Interface

The general code framework for the first approach to realizing multithreaded programming, to inherit from the thread, is as follows: first, define the thread class (in this case, the thread class named MyThread) and its code as shown in Figure 9-28.

```
// Thread inheritance, custom thread
class MyThread extends Thread        {
        public MyThread()     {
        super();
        // Call the parent class builder to create objects
        }


        @Override
        // To write run code in the run method of the thread body
        public void run(){
                // The real Run Code of the thread.
        }
}
```

Figure 9-28. *A Sample Custom Thread Class*

Then, create an instance of our custom Thread class and start it, as shown in Figure 9-29.

```
MyThread myThread = new MyThread(); //create a new thread
myThread.start(); //Start the Thread
```

Figure 9-29. Starting the Thread

Wait for the thread to finish, and handle the cases if something goes wrong, as shown in Figure 9-30.

```
try {
        myThread.join();      // Wait for thread process to end
} catch (InterruptedException e) {
        //Handle the fail cases
}
```

Figure 9-30. Waiting for the Thread to Finish

The second approach to realizing multithreaded programming in Java uses the Runnable interface implementation. The following is the general code framework for Runnable. The first step is to create a custom Runnable interface, as shown in Figure 9-31.

```
// implement runnable interface
class MyRunnableThread implements Runnable {
        public void run() {
                // actual implementation codes of the thread
        }
}
```

Figure 9-31. Custom Runnable

Next, you need to actually start the thread and give it a Runnable. This can be done as shown in Figure 9-32.

```
// create custom runnable interface implementation object
MyRunnableThread target = new MyRunnableThread();


//create a Thread object and give it our runnable
Thread myThread = new Thread(target);


//Start Thread
myThread.start();
```

Figure 9-32. *Starting the Thread*

These two approaches have the same effects, but the occasions on which they are used are different. Developers who are familiar with Java know that it does not have *multiple inheritance*, so it uses Interface Implement instead. To separately implement a thread, you can use the first approach, thread inheritance.

But some classes have themselves been inherited from another class. In such cases, if you want the thread to run, you have to use the second method (the Runnable interface method) to achieve thread implementation. In this method, you can declare that the class implements the Runnable interface and then put the code that will be run as a thread into the run function. In this way, it will not affect its previous inheritance hierarchy and can also to run as a thread.

Note the following points about Java's threading framework:

1. In Java runtime, the system implements a thread scheduler for thread execution, which is used to determine a time by which a thread will run on the CPU.

2. In Java technology, the thread is usually preemptive without the need for a time slice allocation process (which assigns to each thread the process of equal CPU time). In the preemptive scheduling model, all threads are in a ready-to-run state (waiting state), but in fact only one thread is running. The thread continues to run until it terminates or a higher-priority thread becomes runnable. In that case, the low-priority thread terminates and gives the right to run to the high-priority thread.

3. The Java thread scheduler supports this preemptive scheme for threads with different priorities, but the scheduler itself does not support the time slice rotation of threads with the same priority.

4. If the operating system on which Java runtime is running supports the rotation of the time slice, then the Java thread scheduler supports the time slice rotation of the same priority thread.

5. The system's thread scheduler should not be excessively relied upon. For example: the low-priority thread must also get a chance to run.

For more detailed information on Java multithreaded programming methods for Android applications, developers can refer to related Java programming books.

Threaded Programming Extensions and Support

When Android is running, the Dalvik virtual machine supports multiple concurrent CPUs. That being said, if the machine has more than one logical processor, the Dalvik virtual machine will follow certain strategies to automatically be assigned different threads to run on different CPUs. In this way, Android can physically run different threads in parallel. In addition to the thread programming interfaces provided by Java, Android also provides important extensions and support. The first is the Looper-Message mechanism.

Android's interface, including a variety of activity, is running in the main thread of the application (also known as the UI thread, the Interface thread, or the default thread). By default, the application has only one thread, which is the main thread. Thus the application is considered to be single-threaded. Some time-consuming tasks (computing), if they are run on the main thread by default, will cause the interaction of the main interface to fail to respond for a long time. To prevent the main interface interaction from remaining at a standstill for a long time, those time-consuming tasks should be allocated to the independent thread to execute.

The independent thread running behind the scenes (also known as the assistive thread or background thread) often needs to communicate with the interface of the main thread, such as by updating the display interface. If the behind-the-scenes thread calls a function of an interface object to update the interface, Android will give the execution error message CalledFromWrongThreadException.

For example, in an application (in this case GuiExam), if a worker thread directly calls the setText function of the TextView object in the interface to update the display, the system will immediately encounter an error and terminate the running application, as shown in Figure 9-33.

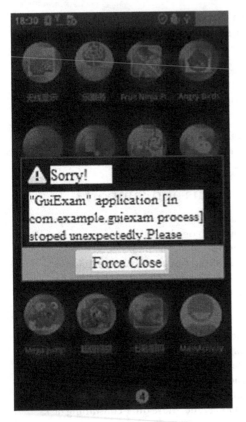

Figure 9-33. *Running Error Message When Worker Thread Directly Calls a Function of the UI object*

In order to enable the worker thread and the main thread interface to communicate well, you need to understand the Looper-Message mechanisms. In order to solve such problems, Android has a mechanism called *message queue*, in which the threads can be combined by the message queue, processing Handler and Looper components to exchange information.

Message

The Java class Message defines the information exchanged between threads. When a thread behind the scenes needs to update the interface, it sends a message containing the data to the UI thread (the main thread).

Handler

The Handler class is the main processor of the Message class, and is responsible for sending messages and the execution and processing of the message content. The behind-the-scenes thread, making use of the processing object passed in, calls the sendMessage function to send a message. To use the Handler class, you need a method with which to implement the class handleMessage, which is responsible for handling the message operation content, such as updating the interface. The handleMessage method usually requires subclassing.

The Handler class itself is not used to open up a new thread. A Handler is more like the secretary of the main thread, a flip-flop, and is responsible for managing the updated data from the subthread and then updating the interface in the main thread. The behind-the-scenes thread processes the sendMessage () method to send a message, and the Handler will call back (which is automatically invoked) processing in the handleMessage method to process the message.

Message Queue

The message queue is used to store the messages sent by a Handler, according to the first-in/first-out rule for execution. For each message queue, there will be a corresponding Handler. The Handler uses two methods to send messages to the message queue: sendMessage or post. These two types of messages will be inserted at the end of message queue according to the first-in/first-out rule. Messages sent by these two methods are executed in slightly different ways: a Message sent by sendMessage is a message queue object and will be processed by the handleMessage function of the Handler, whereas a Message sent through the post method is a runnable object and will be implemented automatically.

Android has no global message queue and automatically builds a message queue for the main thread (one of the UI threads), but the message queue has not been established in the subthread, so Looper.getMainLooper () must be called to get the Looper of the main thread. The main thread loop will not go to NULL, but to call Looper.myLooper () to get Looper of the current thread loop, it is possible for a NULL.

Looper

The Looper class is the housekeeper of each thread's message queue. A Looper is a bridge between the Handler and message queues. Program components first pass the message to the Looper through the Handler, and then the Looper puts the Message in the queue.

For the main thread of default UI of the application, the system has established the message queue and Looper, and there is no need to write the message queue and looper operation code in the source code. Even having said that, both are "transparent" for the default main thread. However, the Handler is not transparent to the default main thread. In order to send messages to the main thread and handle them, users must establish their own Handler object.

AsyncTask

In addition to using the Looper-Message mechanisms to achieve the communication between the worker thread and the main GUI thread, you can use a technique called *the asynchronous tasks* (AsyncTask) *mechanism* to implement the communication. The general procedure for using the AsyncTask framework is described as follows:

1. Implement the AsyncTask according one or several of the following methods:

    -   onPreExecute(): begin preparatory work before Execution.

    -   doInBackground(Params...): start background execution, inside this call the publishProgress method to update real-time task progress.

    -   onProgressUpdate(Progress...): after the publishProgress method is called, the UI thread will call this method to show the progress of the task interface; for example, by displaying a progress bar.

    -   onPostExecute(Result): after the completion of the implementation of the operation, send the results to the UI thread.

    Of these four functions, none may be manually called. In addition to the doInBackground (Params...) method, the other three are UI thread called, causing the following requirements:

    -   The AsyncTask instance must be created in the UI thread.

    -   The AsyncTask.execute function must be called in the UI thread.

Keep in mind that the task can only be executed once. Multiple calls will result in inconsistent and indeterminate results.

Thread Example

The running interface Application GuiExam is shown in Figure 9-34. Here we use an example to illustrate the use of Android-threaded programming.

| (a). App Start | (b). App Running | (c). App Stopped |

Figure 9-34. *Demo UI of Multithreaded Code Framework*

As shown in Figure 9-34, the demo app has three main activities buttons: Start Thread Run, Stop Thread Run, and Exit App; the first two buttons are used to control the operation of the auxiliary thread. When you click the Start Thread Run button, the thread starts running, as shown in Figure 9-34(b). When you click Stop Thread Run, the thread run ends, as shown in Figure 9-34(c). The worker thread refreshes output text displays TextView each period of time (in this case 0.5 s), displaying on screen "Done Step. X increments from 0 to X. Click 'Exit' to close the activities and exit the application demo."

The structure of the demo app and the procedures follow:

1. Edit the main activity file (in this example: activity_main. xml), delete the originalTextView window component, and then add three buttons and two TextView window components. The properties of Button's ID are respectively: @+id/startTaskThread, @+id/stopTaskThread, @+id/ exitApp. The TextView property is respectively startTaskThread, exitApp, taskThreadOutputInfo, and stopTaskThread. There is one ID of TextView for which the property is set as @+id/taskThreadOuputInfo to display the text output of the worker thread. The TextView Outline for the Demo App is shown in Figure 9-35.

227

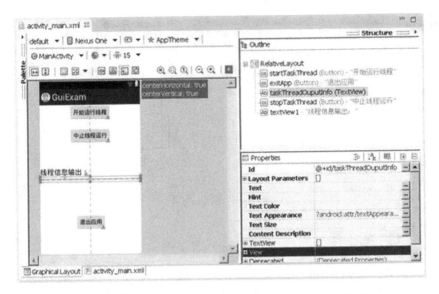

Figure 9-35. Multithreaded Code Framework in activity_main.xml of Demo App

    2.   Edit the source code MainActivity.java of activity_main class.
          The content is listed below:

```
1.     package com.example.guiexam;
2.     import android.os.Bundle;
3.     import android.app.Activity;
4.     import android.view.Menu;
5.     import android.widget.Button;
6.     import android.view.View;
7.     import android.view.View.OnClickListener;
8.     import android.os.Process;
9.     import android.widget.TextView;
10.    import android.os.Handler;
11.    import android.os.Message;

12.    public class MainActivity extends Activity {
13.            private Button btn_StartTaskThread;
14.            private Button btn_StopTaskThread;
15.            private Button btn_ExitApp;
16.            private TextView threadOutputInfo;
17.            private MyTaskThread myThread = null;
18.            private Handler mHandler;;

19.            @Override
20.            public void onCreate(Bundle savedInstanceState) {
```

```
21.              super.onCreate(savedInstanceState);
22.              setContentView(R.layout.activity_main);
23.              threadOutputInfo = (TextView)findViewById(R.
                 id.taskThreadOuputInfo);
24.              threadOutputInfo.setText("Thread Not Run");

25.              mHandler = new Handler() {
26.                  public void handleMessage(Message msg) {
27.                      switch (msg.what)
28.                      {
29.                      case MyTaskThread.MSG_REFRESHINFO:
30.                          threadOutputInfo.setText((String)(msg.obj));
31.                          break;
32.                      default:
33.                          break;
34.                      }
35.                  }
36.              };

37.              btn_ExitApp = (Button) findViewById(R.id.exitApp);
                 // Code for <Exit App>Button
38.              btn_ExitApp.setOnClickListener(new /*View.*/OnClickListener()
     {
39.                  public void onClick(View v) {
40.                                    finish();
41.                      Process.killProcess(Process.myPid());
42.                  }
43.              });

44.              btn_StartTaskThread = (Button) findViewById(R.
                 id.startTaskThread);
45.     // Code for<Start Thread Run>
46.              btn_StartTaskThread.setOnClickListener(new /*View.*/
                 OnClickListener(){
47.                  public void onClick(View v) {
48.                      myThread = new MyTaskThread(mHandler);
                         // Create a thread
49.                      myThread.start();        // Start Thread
50.                      setButtonAvailable();
51.                  }
52.              });

53.              btn_StopTaskThread = (Button) findViewById(R.
                 id.stopTaskThread);
54.     //code for <Stop Thread Run>
55.              btn_StopTaskThread.setOnClickListener(new /*View.*/
                 OnClickListener(){
```

```
56.                    public void onClick(View v) {
57.                        if (myThread!=null && myThread.isAlive())
58.                            myThread.stopRun();
59.                        try {
60.                            if (myThread!=null){
61.                                myThread.join();
62.    // Wait for Thread Run to end
63.                                myThread =null;
64.                            }
65.                        } catch (InterruptedException e) {
66.                            // Empty statement block, ignored forcibly
                                abort exception
67.                        }
68.                        setButtonAvailable();
69.                    }
70.                });
71.                setButtonAvailable();
72.            }

73.            @Override
74.            public boolean onCreateOptionsMenu(Menu menu) {
75.                getMenuInflater().inflate(R.menu.activity_main, menu);
76.                return true;
77.            }

78.            private void setButtonAvailable()        // New function is used to
                                                          set the button optional
79.            {
80.                btn_StartTaskThread.setEnabled(myThread==null);
81.                btn_ExitApp.setEnabled(myThread==null);
82.                btn_StopTaskThread.setEnabled(myThread!=null);
83.            }
84.    }
```

In lines 17 and 18 of the code just given, we define the variable myThread of the defined thread class as MyTaskThread and the default main thread handler object as mHandler, respectively. From line 25 to line 36, we define the Handler class. The What attribute field of the message class indicates the type of message. The custom handler class uses a switch-case statement for different handlers depending on the type of message, of which MSG_REFRESHINFO is the message type of custom thread class MyTaskThread, which means that the worker thread requires an updated interface display message. The purpose of lines 29 to 31 is to process the message. The code is very simple; it updates the widget display of TextView according to the message with the parameter object.

Lines 47 to 49 consist of the response code given when the start running threads button is clicked. It first creates the custom thread object and then calls the Thread.start function to make the self-defined thread class MyTaskThread run, which runs execution code in the run function as a single thread. Line 49 calls the custom setButtonAvailable function to set each button's option (that is, grayed as not selectable, or white, which is selectable).

Lines 55 to 65 are the code responsible for the Stop Thread Run button. Line 55 first determines whether the thread already exists or is running, and then stops a thread run in line 56 by calling the defined stop-the-thread prototype function from the custom thread class MyTaskThread and then calling the Thread.join () function. It then waits for the thread run to end. Finally, it sets the optional status of the interface buttons.

Lines 75 to 80 consist of a customized function, which is used to determine the optional status of each button: white as selectable; gray as not selectable.

3. Create a new class MyTaskThread in the application. This class inherits from Thread and is used to implement the worker thread. The source code file MyTaskThread.java of this class is as follows:

```
1.    package com.example.guiexam;
2.    import android.os.Handler;
3.    import android.os.Message;
4.
5.    public class MyTaskThread extends Thread {
6.            private static final int stepTime = 500;
7.    // Execution timeof each step(unite:ms)
8.            private volatile boolean isEnded;
9.    //mark if the thread is running. Used to stop thread run
10.           private Handler mainHandler;
11.   //Handler used to send message
12.           public static final int MSG_REFRESHINFO = 1;
              // Update message on interface
13.
14.           public MyTaskThread(Handler mh)
              // Define a constructor
15.           {
16.                   super();
// Call the parent class builder to create objects
17.                   isEnded = false;
18.                   mainHandler = mh;
19.           }
20.
21.       @Override
22.           public void run()
              // Write run code in thread body run method
23.           {
24.           Message msg ;
25.                   for (int i = 0; !isEnded; i++)
```

```
26.                             {
27.                                 try {
28.                                     Thread.sleep(stepTime);
                                        // designate time for every  step of
                                        the thread to sleep
29.                                     String s = "Complete" + i +"step";
30.                                     msg = new Message();
31.                                     msg.what = MSG_REFRESHINFO;
                                        // Define message type
32.                                     msg.obj = s;
                                        // attach data to message
33.                                     mainHandler.sendMessage(msg);
                                        // send message
34.                                     } catch (InterruptedException e) {
35.                                         e.printStackTrace();
36.                                     }
37.                                 }
38.                             }
39.
40.             public void stopRun()
                // Stop control function for stop thread run
41.                 {
42.                     isEnded = true;
43.                 }
42.         }
```

This is the implementation code of the custom thread class MyTaskThread, which is the key to this application. This application is using the first approach, thread inheritance, to achieve threading. In line 5, let the customized class inherit from Thread, and then from line 14 to line 39, let the threads run code on the rewrite run function. To cope with the work of the thread, in line 6 to line 9 we define the relevant variables. The constant stepTime represents the length of every step of the thread delay time, measured in milliseconds. The mark isEnded controls whether to continue every step in the body of the loop in the run function to continue. Note that the variable is preceded by the volatile modifier: Volatile variables. Each time a thread accesses the variable, it will read the final values in the memory after the variables have been modified. A write request must be written to memory too. This avoids the copy that is in cache or in the register not matching with the value in the memory variable, which causes an error. The mainHandler is the variable that saves the main thread handler. MSG_REFRESHINFO is a constant type that handles custom message.

Line 10 to line 15 is a constructor. In this function body, we initialize the value of the thread-running control variables isEnded and then save mainHandler as the main thread handler object passed as a parameter.

Line 16 to line 33 is the core thread code that rewrites the run function. The code is composed of a loop to determine whether to continue to use the control variable isEnded. Here, we call one loop as a step. Every step of the work is also simple: when the Thread class static function sleep is called in line 28 after a specified time, a message is generated and assembled in line 24 to line 27. Finally, in line 28, the message is sent to the specified (message loop) handler.

Line 34 to line 37 is a custom control function to stop the thread from running. The code is very simple; it changes the run loop control variable value.

Thread Synchronization

A multithreaded process inevitably involves a problem: how to deal with threads' access to shared data, which relates to thread synchronization. Thread data sharing is also known as *critical section*. Access to shared data is also known as the competition for resource access. In general, in operating system textbooks, thread synchronization includes not only the synchronization of this passive selected access to shared data but also the active choice synchronization between threads in order to collaborate to complete a task. Thread synchronization especially focuses on access to shared data. In this section, we discuss synchronization issues on shared data access.

In multithreaded programming, if the access to shared data does not use certain synchronization mechanisms, data consistency and integrity cannot be guaranteed. There are two ways to do the Java thread synchronization: one is called an internal lock data object and the other is just called synchronization. Both of these methods are implemented with the synchronized keyword. Statements modified by the synchronized block can guarantee the exclusivity of the operations between threads, considered unique or *atomic* in the term of the operating system. In Java it is called *synchronization*. A synchronized block is also known as *Genlock*.

In the first method of locking data objects, at any time, only one thread may access the object that is locked. The code framework is shown in Figure 9-36.

```
Object var;    // Object variable
synchronized(var) {
        … …    // Operation of the shared variable
}
```

Figure 9-36. *Method One*

In the above code, *var* must be the variable that each thread can access, so that it becomes a synchronization variable. In practice, the synchronization variable and shared variables can be either the same or different variables. The Object class in the code in the figure can be replaced with the subclass of Object, because besides the simple classes in Java, any class can be the Object offspring class. Object in the code can be replaced by any class.

Note that a primitive type (such as int and float, but not String class) cannot be the synchronization variable, as shown in Figure 9-37.

```
int var;
synchronized(var) {
// compiler error : int is not a valid type's argument for the synchronized statement
}
```

Figure 9-37. Invalid Synchronized Block

When you use the second method, the synchronization method, only one thread visits a code segment at any time, such as in Figure 9-38.

```
class MyClass {
        public synchronized void method1()
        { ... }
}
```

Figure 9-38. Synchronizing a Method

Besides the synchronization for the general class (function) shown in the previous figure, there is also synchronization for the static function of the class, as shown in Figure 9-39.

```
class MyClass {
        public synchronized static void method2()
        { ... }
}
```

Figure 9-39. Synchronizing a Static Method

In the synchronization method, what gets locked is the object that calls the synchronization method. When an object of MyClass: obj1 implements the synchronization method in a different thread, mutual exclusion will be formed to achieve the synchronization result. But another object, obj2, generated by the class MyClass can call this method with the synchronized keyword. As a result, the code in the previous figure can be written in equivalent terms to those in Figure 9-40.

```
class MyClass {
    public void method1()
    {
        synchronized (this)
            { …/* function body */ }
    }
}
```

Figure 9-40. *Synchronizing General Method*

The static synchronization method is shown in Figure 9-41.

```
class MyClass {
    public static void method2()
    {
        synchronized (MyClass.class)
            { …/* function body */ }
    }
}
```

Figure 9-41. *Locking on a Class*

In the second method, the static method, the class literally is treated as a lock. It generates the same result as the synchronized static function. The timing to get a lock is also special; the lock is acquired when calling the class that this object belongs to, and no longer the specific object that this class generates.

The rules that Java uses to implement a lock by the synchronized function are generalized in the following:

- *Rule 1*: When two parallel threads visit the synchronized(this) synchronization code segment of the same object, there is only one thread that can be run at any time. Another thread must wait until the current thread finishes running the code segment to run the same code segment.

- *Rule 2*: When a thread visits a synchronized(this) synchronization code segment of an object, another thread can still visit a non-synchronized(this) synchronization code segment of an object.

- *Rule 3*: When a thread visits a synchronized(this) synchronization code segment of an object, the visit of all other threads to all other synchronized(this) synchronization code segments of the object will be blocked.

- *Rule 4*: When a thread visits a synchronized(this) synchronization code segment of an object, it acquires the object lock of this object. As a result, all visits from other threads to all synchronized(this) synchronization code segments of an object will be temporally locked.

- *Rule 5*: The previously stated rules apply to all other object locks.

Although synchronization can guarantee granularity of the object or block of statements executed, mutual exclusiveness of this granularity degrades the thread concurrency, so that the code, which originally could run in parallel, has to run in serial execution. Therefore, we need to be cautious and limit use the synchronized function to cases where a synchronized lock is needed. On the other hand, we need to make the lock granularity as small as possible in order to both ensure the correctness of the program and improve operational efficiency. This is done by raising the degree of concurrency as high as possible.

Thread Communication

In multithreaded design, with data exchange among threads, setting the signal collaboration to complete a task is a common problem. Generalized threading issues are a large part of the problem, similar to the typical example of the producer-consumer problem. These are the threads that have to cooperate to accomplish a task.

It is generally recommended that a semaphore be used to achieve thread synchronization primitives. Java does not directly provide the semaphore primitives or programming interface but rather achieves the function of the semaphore with a class function such as wait, notify, notifyAll, and so on.

The classes wait, notify, and notifyAll belong to the function of the Object class, and are not part of the Thread class. Every object has a waiting queue (Wait Set) in Java. When an object has just been created, its wait queue is empty.

The wait function can make the objects in the current thread wait until another thread calls the notify or notifyAll method of this object. In other words, when a call waits in the queue of the object, there is a thread where the thread enters a wait state. Only when the notify method is called can we put the thread from the queue out to make this thread become runnable. The notifyAll method waits for all threads in the queue to become runnable. Notify and notifyAll are not much different in function.

The wait, notify, and notifyAll functions need to be used in conjunction with synchronized to establish the synchronization model, which can guarantee the granularity of the former functions. For example, before calling wait, we need to get the object's synchronization lock so that this function can be called. Otherwise the compiler can call the wait function, but it will receive an IllegalMonitorStateException runtime exception.

Following are several examples of code frameworks of wait, notify, and notifyAll. Figure 9-42 shows code to wait for a resource.

```
synchronized(obj) {
      while(!condition)
            try {
                  obj.wait();
            } catch (InterruptedException e) {
            }
   ......Use code of obj
}
```

Figure 9-42. *Locking on an Object*

Figure 9-43 shows the code for using notify and providing resources (an example of which is the complete use of resources and returned to the system).

```
synchronized(obj) {
      condition = true;
      obj.notify();
}
```

Figure 9-43. *Using Notify*

The previous figure is the stand-alone use case of synchronization object obj. We can also write synchronization code in a class. The framework of this code can be written as in Figure 9-44.

```
class MyClass{
        public synchronized void func1 {
                while (!condition)
                        try {
                                wait();
                        } catch (InterruptedException e) {
                        }
                ...... codes for using MyClass resource
        }
        public synchronized void func2 {
                condition = true;
                notifyAll();
        }
}
```

Figure 9-44. *A Class Example of Synchronized*

The thread that is waiting for resources calls the myclass.func1 function, and the thread that provides resources calls myclass.func2 function.

Principles of Multithreaded Optimization for Intel Atom Processors

The multithreaded software design allows program code in different threads to run at the same time. However, blind or excessive use of multithreaded programming may not lead to performance improvement and may even downgrade the software performance. Therefore, we need to look at the principles of multithreaded optimization on Android x86.

First of all, the start, or scheduling, of a thread requires a certain amount of overhead and occupies a certain amount of processor time. For processors that do not support hyperthreading and multicore processing, the system cannot physically let the threads run at the same time. There is significant overhead if we split one physical processor into multiple logical processors with virtualization technologies to have each thread run on a logical core in an attempt to support multithreaded programs. Such a multithreading strategy not only makes it difficult to achieve improvement in performance but may even lead to the multithreaded execution speed being slower than a single-threaded program. Therefore, to achieve multithreaded performance acceleration (a prerequisite to being faster than single-threaded execution speed) using multithreaded design, the processor must support hyperthreading, contain multicores, or have multiple processors.

Second, for processors that support hyperthreading or multicore, it is not always true that more threads will make the software run faster. There is a performance/price ratio that needs to be considered. The physical basis for multithreaded design in performance tuning can be explained as allowing multiple threads to run at the same time in parallel on the physical layer. The maximum number of concurrently running threads supported by the processor is therefore the optimum number of threads for multithreaded optimization.

Intel Hyper-Threading Technology can support two threads running in parallel, and also has multicore support for multiple threads running in parallel. For example, for a dual-core Intel processor that supports Intel Hyper-Threading Technology, the maximum number of threads supported to run in parallel is:

2 core × 2 (Intel HTT) = 4 threads

Therefore, this machine supports multithreaded optimization, and the maximum number of threads (threads running concurrently) is equal to four.

For example, if the target machine is a Lenovo K800 phone, which uses a single-core Intel Atom Z2460 processor, in accordance with the above formula, we can conclude that running two threads can make the machine achieve optimal performance. For a Motorola MT788 target machine, which uses a single-core Intel Atom Z2480 processor, the optimal number of threads is two. If the target machine is a Lenovo K900 with a dual-core processor, the Intel Atom Z2580 processor with Intel HTT, then the optimal number of threads reached will be four.

In general, when we consider multithreaded optimization on the Android platform, it is necessary to carefully look into the processor information to see if it supports hyperthreading or multicore technology.

Case Study: Intel GPA–Assisted Multithreaded Optimization for an Android Application

In the previous section, we explained several optimization techniques and principles. In this section, we use a comprehensive example to explain the knowledge of the optimization. In this case, the multithreaded optimization is combined with optimization assisted by Intel GPA to optimize the application to make it run faster.

The app that we use as an example performs the calculation of Pi (π). We will now introduce the background of this app. We know the mathematical formula to be as follows:

$$\int_0^1 \frac{1}{x^2+1}\,dx = \arctan(1) - \arctan(0) = \frac{\pi}{4}$$

We know that the integration formula can be expressed using the infinitive:

s

In fact, Δx cannot be infinitely small, so we only can make Δx as small as possible. Therefore, the result of the formula is closer to π. If we use *step* to represent Δx, then

$$num\_steps = \frac{1}{step}$$

must be at maximum to get an accurate approximation of Pi. Consider that

$$f(x) = \frac{1}{x^2 + 1}$$

is a raised function. Here, we take a median value to calculate the sum; that is, we use

$$f\left(\frac{i + 0.5}{num\_steps}\right)$$

to replace

$$f\left(\frac{i}{num\_steps}\right)$$

to calculate the sum. The result calculated by this formula will not always be smaller than the actual value of π. So eventually we get the final formula upon which this application is based:

$$\frac{\pi}{4} \approx \sum_{i=0}^{num\_steps} f(x) \times step = \sum_{i=0}^{num\_steps} f\left(\frac{i + 0.5}{num\_steps}\right) \times step = step \times \sum_{i=0}^{num\_steps} f\left[(i + 0.5) \times step\right]$$

Based on this formula, we can derive the equivalent computing source code.

Original Application and Intel GPA Analysis

We can derive the source code for our case study app from the formula we just came up with in the previous section. The source code will not be optimized. We'll refer to it as the original application and name it SerialPi.

The design of this app is the same as the example given in the preceding **Thread Example** section. The task of calculating π is put into a worker thread (here named a *task thread*). A button is set on main application screen to control the running of the thread, and a TextView is used to display the result of the task thread. The interface showing the app's single run is shown in Figure 9-45.

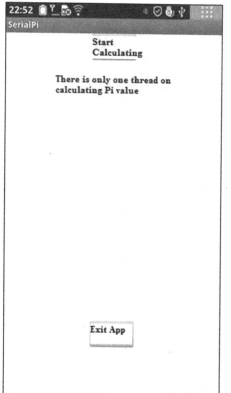

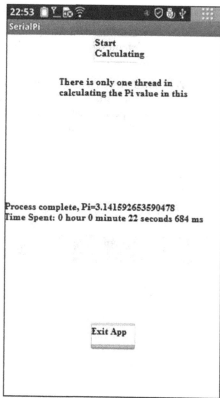

(a). App Start

(b). Calculating PI

Figure 9-45. *App Run Interface of SerialPi*

The interface that comes up after the application starts is shown in Figure 9-45(a). When you click the Start Calculating button, all buttons on the interface gray out until the computing of *πthread* is complete. The interface then displays the computation result of π as well as the total running time of the thread. You can click the Exit App button, as shown in Figure 9-45(b), which allows you to exit the application. From the interface shown, we know it takes about 22 seconds for this app to calculate π. When running this application repeatedly, the calculation time is about the same every time (22 seconds).

The structure of the application steps and key code is as follows:

1. New build SerialPi. The proposed project property is set to use the default value. Note that the [Build SDK] is set to support the x86 API.

2. Edit activity_main.xml; place two Buttons and two TextViews in the layout, the ID attribute of a TextView is set as @+id/ taskOuputInfo, which is used to display the results of the task thread, as shown in Figure 9-46.

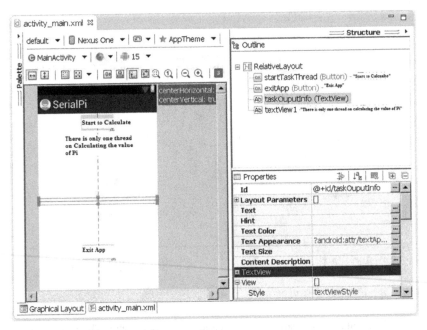

Figure 9-46. *Main Outline of SerialPi App*

3. Create a new thread class MyTaskThread in the new project and use it to calculate the value of π. Edit the source code file MyTaskThread.java as follows:

```
1.    package com.example.serialpi;
2.    import android.os.Handler;
3.    import android.os.Message;

4.    public class MyTaskThread extends Thread {
5.            private Handler mainHandler;
6.            public static final int MSG_FINISHED = 1;
7.    // Defined the message type  for the end of the calculation
```

```
8.          private static final long num_steps = 200000000;
9.    // num_steps variables in Formula, the total number of steps
      private static final double step = 1.0 / num_steps;
10.   // Step variable  in formula, step length
11.         public static double pi = 0.0;

12.   // the calculation of results of π
13.
14.         static String msTimeToDatetime(long msnum){
15.   // The function converts the number of milliseconds into hours:
      minutes: seconds. Milliseconds "format
16.         long hh,mm,ss,ms, tt= msnum;
17.         ms = tt % 1000; tt = tt / 1000;
18.         ss = tt % 60; tt = tt / 60;
19.         mm = tt % 60; tt = tt / 60;
20.         hh = tt % 60;
21.         String s = "" + hh +"hour "+mm+"minute "+ss + "秒 " + ms
            +"Miliseconds";
22.         return s;
23.         }
24.
25.      @Override
26.         public void run()
27.         {
28.         double x, sum = 0.0;
            long i;
            for (i=0; i< num_steps; i++){
29.            x = (i+0.5)*step;
30.            sum = sum + 4.0/(1.0 + x*x);
31.         }
32.         pi = step * sum;

33.         Message msg = new Message();
34.         msg.what = MSG_FINISHED;
            // Define message Type
35.         mainHandler.sendMessage(msg);
            // Send Message
36.         }
37.
38.         public MyTaskThread(Handler mh)         // Constructor
39.         {
40.             super();
41.             mainHandler = mh;
42.         }
43.     }
```

Similar to the framework and the example of code given in the preceding **Thread Example** section, thread inheritance laws are used to achieve thread initialization. Pay close attention to the code segments highlighted in gray. They are the ones most directly related to the calculation of π. In lines 7 and 8, we define variables of the same name in the formula for calculation of π in the form of a static variable. Line 9 defines the variable for saving the results of the π calculation. Note that this variable is public, so that the main thread can access it.

Lines 22 through 28 are the code for calculating π according to the formula. Where the *x* variable is an independent variable *x* of function

$$f(x) = \frac{1}{x^2 + 1}$$

the sum is a cumulative variable of $\sum$. After the cumulative $\sum$, finally in line 28, let π = *step* × $\sum$ to calculate the final results. Refer to the two long sections of code framework in the preceding **Thread Example** section; it should not be difficult to understand the mathematics behind the code.

Note that in the thread's run function, once the calculation is complete, the message is sent to the main thread (interface) in line 29.

4. Edit the source code of the main activity class file: MainActivity.java. The code is allowed to control the run of the thread and displays the calculated results as follows:

```
1.    package com.example.serialpi;
2.    import android.os.Bundle;
3.    import android.app.Activity;
4.    import android.view.Menu;
5.    import android.widget.Button;
6.    import android.view.View;
7.    import android.view.View.OnClickListener;
8.    import android.os.Process;
9.    import android.widget.TextView;
10.   import android.os.Handler;
11.   import android.os.Message;

12.   public class MainActivity extends Activity {
13.          private MyTaskThread myThread = null;
14.      private TextView tv_TaskOutputInfo;
             // Display (Calculated) Task thread output
15.      private Handler mHandler;;
16.          private long end_time;
17.          private long time;
18.          private long start_time;

19.      @Override
20.      public void onCreate(Bundle savedInstanceState) {
21.             super.onCreate(savedInstanceState);
```

```
22.            setContentView(R.layout.activity_main);
23.            tv_TaskOutputInfo = (TextView)findViewById(R.id.taskOuputInfo);
24.            final Button btn_ExitApp = (Button) findViewById(R.id.exitApp);
25.            btn_ExitApp.setOnClickListener(new /*View.*/OnClickListener(){
26.                public void onClick(View v) {
27.                    exitApp();
28.                }
29.            });
30.            final Button btn_StartTaskThread =
               (Button) findViewById(R.id.startTaskThread);
31.            btn_StartTaskThread.setOnClickListener(new
               /*View.*/OnClickListener(){
32.                public void onClick(View v) {
33.                            btn_StartTaskThread.setEnabled(false);
34.                            btn_ExitApp.setEnabled(false);
35.                    startTask();
36.                }
37.            });
38.            mHandler = new Handler() {
39.                public void handleMessage(Message msg) {
40.                    switch (msg.what)
41.                    {
42.                    case MyTaskThread.MSG_FINISHED:
43.                        end_time = System.currentTimeMillis();
44.                        time = end_time - start_time;
45.                        String s = " The end of the run,Pi=
                           "+ MyTaskThread.pi+ "  Time consumed:"
46.                                                              +
47.    MyTaskThread.msTimeToDatetime(time);
48.                        tv_TaskOutputInfo.setText(s);
49.                        btn_ExitApp.setEnabled(true);
50.                        break;
51.                    default:
52.                        break;
53.                    }
54.                }
55.            };
       }
56.
57.        @Override
58.        public boolean onCreateOptionsMenu(Menu menu) {
59.            getMenuInflater().inflate(R.menu.activity_main, menu);
60.            return true;
       }
61.
62.        private void startTask() {
63.            myThread = new MyTaskThread(mHandler);       // Create a thread
```

```
64.                    if (! myThread.isAlive())
65.                    {
66.                            start_time = System.currentTimeMillis();
67.                            myThread.start();
                               // Start thread
68.                    }
      }
69.
70.        private void exitApp() {
71.             try {
72.                   if (myThread!=null)
73.                   {
74.                          myThread.join();
75.                          myThread = null;
76.                   }
77.             } catch (InterruptedException e) {
78.             }
79.                    finish();
                       // Exit the activity
80.             Process.killProcess(Process.myPid());
                // Exit the application process
81.        }
}
```

The code listed here is similar to the code framework of the example MainActivity class in the **Thread Example** section. The lines of code highlighted in gray are added to estimate the running time of the task code. Three variables are first defined in line 16 to line 18: *start_time* as the task's start time, *end_time* as the end time of the task, and *time* as the length of the task's running time. These three variables are parts of the following formula:

```
time = end_time - start_time
```

In line 65, when we start the task threads, the current time of the machine is recorded in the start_time variable. In line 43 to line 44, when the message is received that the task thread has finished running, the machine's time is recorded in end_time. The currentTimeMillis function is a static function provided by the Java System class in the java.lang package. This function returns the current time in milliseconds.

    5.   With reference to the example given in the **Sample Usage of Intel GPA on Android** section, modify the project AndroidManifest.xml file to make it comply with the requirements of Intel GPA monitoring.

After the coding is completed and the app is compiled and generated, we can deploy applications to the actual target device. In this case, we use the Lenovo K800 mobile phone as a test target.

Now we use Intel GPA to analyze our SerialPi application. Specific steps can be found in the **Sample Usage of Intel GPA on Android** section. The first step is to monitor and analyze the case of the two CPU loads. Clicking the Intel GPA Start button will start recording the CPU load. The results of the analysis are shown in Figure 9-47 (a), (b), and (c).

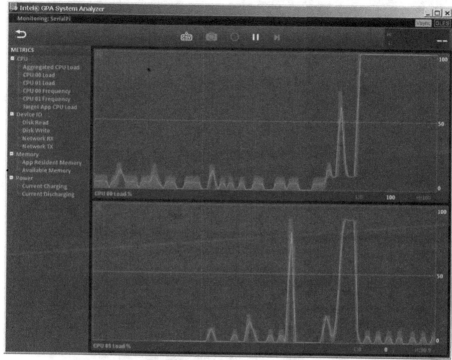

(a). Click Start Calculation button

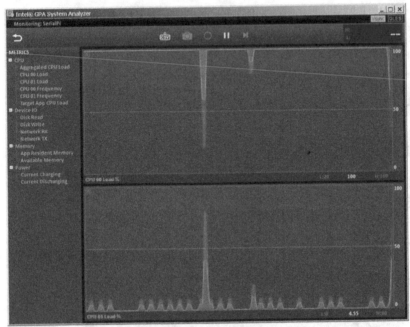

(b). Thread Running on Computation Task

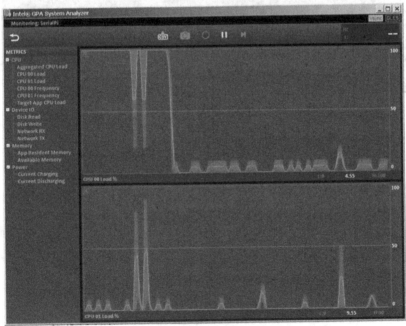

(c). Task Threads at End of Run

Figure 9-47. *Intel GPA Analysis Screen for SerialPi*

Figure 9-47 (a) shows the analysis of clicking on the Start button, with the task thread running at the start. Figure 9-47(b) shows task threads running. Figure 9-47(c) shows task threads at the end of the run. From these three screens, we can see that the load on the CPU is at a low level before the app starts to run or after the end of the run. Once the computing task threads start to run, the load on the CPU sharply rises to 100 percent of the full load level. We can also see that during the running of the task threads, only one of two CPUs is at full capacity, and the other is at a low load level. By analyzing the graph, you will notice that the 100 percent-full load does not always occur on a specific CPU. Instead, the 100 percent-full load is alternatively rotating between two CPUs, which reflects the Java Runtime time support for task scheduling; the processor system itself is transparent to applications. Although a two-CPU load rate is subject to rotation, the load rate is in a "complementary" state: a rising load on one CPU means the load on the other drops. That is, the total load (the sum of loads of two CPUs at any time) does not exceed the 100 percent-full load of a single CPU, which is useful when running more than one application.

Optimized Application and Intel GPA Analysis

The previous example is the code derived directly from the formula for calculating the value of π. In this simple mathematical example, is there any room for optimization? The answer is definitely yes! Optimizing requires us to look into the algorithm of the app and to apply the principles we just learned, making full use of the hardware features of Intel's Atom processors to release the full performance potential.

How do you tap the performance potential of the Intel Atom processor? As we explained earlier, multicore Intel Atom processors with Intel Hyper-Threading Technology have support for multithreading running in parallel on multiple physical cores. For example, the Lenovo K800 phone uses an Intel Atom Z2460 processor and supports two threads running in parallel. This is the entry point of our algorithm optimization in accordance with the previously mentioned strategy to divide and conquer. By carefully analyzing the code of the Run function of the MyTaskThread class, we managed to make computing tasks allocated to multiple threads run (in this case two); the threads running in parallel can make the app run faster. In order to calculate the cumulative value of the integral area for π, in line 24 we calculated the integral area one step at a time and added the cumulative sum. Now we take a different approach and divide the integral area into many blocks and let each thread be responsible for calculating one such block. Finally, we get the π value by adding the cumulative area of blocks calculated by each thread. In this way, we use a "divide and conquer" strategy to complete the task distribution and get the final results. We call this algorithm optimization approach ThreadPi. When ThreadPi is calculating the cumulative value of the integral area (which is the π value), we let the calculation step of each thread accumulate the step size to increase the total number of threads. This allows each of them to be responsible for the cumulating sum of their own area of the block.

The UI of the app ThreadPi when running is shown in Figure 9-48.

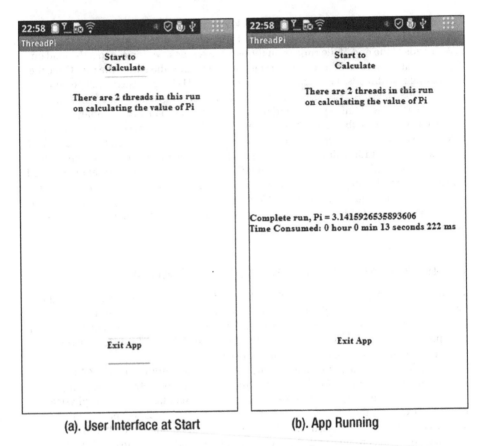

(a). User Interface at Start   **(b). App Running**

Figure 9-48. *User Interface of ThreadPi Running Separately*

The interface of this optimized application (ThreadPi) is the same as in the original application (SerialPi). In Figure 9-48(b), we can see that this application uses thirteen seconds to complete the calculation of the π value. Its time is reduced to almost half of that of the original application (twenty-two seconds). The only difference is that the optimized application uses two threads to calculate π.

This application is based on modifying the original application code; the key changes that were made are as follows:

1. The thread class of the computing tasks' MyTaskThread source code file was modified to MyTaskThread.java as follows:

```
1.    package com.example.threadpi;
2.    import android.os.Handler;
3.    import android.os.Message; .
```

```
4.      public class MyTaskThread extends Thread {
5.              private Handler mainHandler;
6.              public static final int MSG_FINISHED = 1;
7.              private static final long num_steps = 200000000;
8.      // num_steps variable in formula, total steps
9.              private static final double step = 1.0 / num_steps;
10.     // step variable in formula, step length
11.             public static double pi = 0.0;
                //  Calculated result of π
12.             public static final int num_threads = 2;
                // Thread count
13.             private int myNum;                              // Thread #
                private static Object sharedVariable = new Object();
14.     // synchronization lock variable for Pi variable
15.             private static int finishedThreadNum = 0;
16.     // count of threads finishing calculation
17.
18.             static String msTimeToDatetime(long msnum){
19.     // The function to convert the number of milliseconds into hours:
        minutes: seconds. Millis
20.             long hh,mm,ss,ms, tt= msnum;
21.             ms = tt % 1000; tt = tt / 1000;
22.             ss = tt % 60; tt = tt / 60;
        mm = tt % 60; tt = tt / 60;
23.             hh = tt % 60;
24.             String s = "" + hh +"hour "+mm+"minute "+ss + "   " + ms
                +"milliseconds";
25.             return s;
26.             }

27.             public void setStepStartNum(int n)
28.     // set thread # for thread, in response to startting position of i
29.             {
30.                     myNum = n;
31.             }
32.
33.             @Override
34.             public void run()
35.             {
```

```
36.                     double x, partialSum = 0.0;
37.          long i;
38.              for (i = myNum; i < num_steps; i += num_threads) {
39.                  x = (i + 0.5) * step;
40.                      partialSum += 4.0 / (1.0 + x * x);
41.              }
42.              synchronized (sharedVariable) {
43.                  pi += partialSum * step;
44.                  finishedThreadNum++;
45.                  if (finishedThreadNum >= num_threads) {
        //waiting all threads finishing run and send message
46.                      Message msg = new Message();
47.                      msg.what = MSG_FINISHED;
                         //Define message type
48.                      mainHandler.sendMessage(msg);
                         //Send message
49.                  }
50.              }
51.          }

             public MyTaskThread(Handler mh)
             // constructor
             {
                     super();
                     mainHandler = mh;
             }
     }
```

The code segments highlighted in gray in the preceding code represent the main difference between the application (ThreadPi) and the original application (SerialPi). In lines 10 through 13, we define the variables required for multithreaded computing tasks. The variable num_threads computes the number of threads when a computing task starts. In this case, the Lenovo K800 has an Intel Atom processor with two logical CPUs, so the value is set to two. The myNum variable computes the thread number, which is selected in the range of zero to num_threads-1. The variable sharedVariable is introduced by a synchronization lock applied to the variable pi. Since pi is a simple variable, it cannot be directly locked. The finishedThreadNum variable represents the number of threads used to complete calculation. When the value of finishedThreadNum is equal to that of num_threads, we consider all computing threads are at the end of the run.

In lines 23 through 26, there is a function we added specifically for the MyTaskThread. It marks the index number of the thread.

Lines 30 through 44 are the prototype code of the computing thread. Lines 30 through 35 are the direct code to calculate π. Compared with the corresponding code for the original application, we can see that the sum variable of the original application has been replaced with partialSum instead, which reflects the fact that the area of this thread is just part of the total area. The most important difference is in line 32: the step length variable i is not 1, but num_threads, which means that every time the application is run, the thread counter moves forward a number of steps. The initial position of variable i is not 0, but derived from the thread number. This is a little like the track-and-field competition, where each athlete (thread) starts at the beginning of their lane rather than at the same starting point. Following thread computing is like athletes running in their own lanes around the track.

When a thread calculates the cumulating sum and needs to add this data onto the total cumulating sum (which is the pi variable), this is a variable shared by multithreads, and therefore needs to add a synchronization lock. This step corresponds to lines 36 through 44. In line 36, we add a synchronization lock, while in line 37 the result of the thread's own calculations is added to the public results of pi. In line 38, we add 1 to the number of threads at the end of the calculation. In line 39, by comparing the number of threads finishing the calculation to the total number of threads, we determine if all computing threads have run to completion. Only by the end of all threads is the message sent to the main thread.

2. The source code file of the main activity class MainActivity MainActivity.java was modified, as in the following:

```
1.    package com.example.threadpi;
2.    import android.os.Bundle;
3.    import android.app.Activity;
4.    import android.view.Menu;
5.    import android.widget.Button;
6.    import android.view.View;
7.    import android.view.View.OnClickListener;
8.    import android.os.Process;
9.    import android.widget.TextView;
10.   import android.os.Handler;
11.   import android.os.Message;

12.   public class MainActivity extends Activity {
13.       private MyTaskThread thrd[] = null;
14.       private TextView tv_TaskOutputInfo;
15.       private Handler mHandler;;
16.       private long end_time;
17.       private long time;
18.       private long start_time;

19.       @Override
20.       public void onCreate(Bundle savedInstanceState) {
21.           super.onCreate(savedInstanceState);
22.           setContentView(R.layout.activity_main);
23.           tv_TaskOutputInfo = (TextView)findViewById(R.
              id.taskOuputInfo);
24.           TextView tv_Info = (TextView)findViewById(R.id.textView1);
25.           String ts = "This example currently has"+ MyTaskThread.
              num_threads + "threads on calculatingπvalue";
26.           tv_Info.setText(ts);
```

```
27.            final Button btn_ExitApp = (Button) findViewById(R.id.exitApp);
29.            btn_ExitApp.setOnClickListener(new /*View.*/OnClickListener(){
30.               public void onClick(View v) {
31.                  exitApp();
32.               }
33.            });
34.            final Button btn_StartTaskThread =
               (Button) findViewById(R.id.startTaskThread);
35.            btn_StartTaskThread.setOnClickListener(new
               /*View.*/OnClickListener(){
36.               public void onClick(View v) {
37.                  btn_StartTaskThread.setEnabled(false);
38.                  btn_ExitApp.setEnabled(false);
39.                  startTask();
40.               }
41.            });
42.            mHandler = new Handler() {
43.               public void handleMessage(Message msg) {
44.                  switch (msg.what)
45.                  {
46.                  case MyTaskThread.MSG_FINISHED:
47.                     end_time = System.currentTimeMillis();
48.                     time = end_time - start_time;
49.                     String s = "Run End,Pi="+
                        MyTaskThread.pi+ "  Time spent:"
50.                                                    + MyTaskThread.
msTimeToDatetime(time);
51.                     tv_TaskOutputInfo.setText(s);
52.                     btn_ExitApp.setEnabled(true);
53.                     break;
54.                  default:
55.                     break;
56.                  }
57.               }
58.            };
59.         }
60.
61.      @Override
62.      public boolean onCreateOptionsMenu(Menu menu) {
63.         getMenuInflater().inflate(R.menu.activity_main, menu);
         return true;
64.      }
65.
66.      private void startTask() {
67.            thrd = new MyTaskThread[MyTaskThread.num_threads];
68.         start_time = System.currentTimeMillis();
```

```
69.                    for( int i=0; i < MyTaskThread.num_threads; i++){
70.                        thrd[i] = new MyTaskThread(mHandler);
                           // Create a thread
71.                        thrd[i].setStepStartNum(i);
72.                        thrd[i].start();
                       }
73.            }
74.
75.        private void exitApp() {
76.                    for (int i = 0; i < MyTaskThread.num_threads
                       && thrd != null; i++) {
77.                        try {
78.                                thrd[i].join();
                                   // Wait for thread running to end
79.                        } catch (InterruptedException e) {
80.                        }
81.                    }
82.                finish();
83.            Process.killProcess(Process.myPid());
           }
       }
```

The code segments highlighted in gray in the source code represent the main difference between the optimized application and the original application. In line 13, the single thread object variable of the original application changes to an array of threads. In the section on starting computing tasks that goes from line 67 through line 71, starting a single thread in the original application is changed to starting all threads in the array and setting the index number of the thread when starting the app. As for the meaning of the thread number, it has been introduced in the MyTaskThread code description. Other changes include waiting for the end of a single thread in order to wait for the end of the thread array (lines 74 through 79).

After these optimizations are completed, we need to compile, generate, and deploy the application to the target device, the same way as we did with the original application. We can run the application independently and measure the run time of this optimized application. The computing time is reduced to almost half of its original length.

Figure 9-49 shows the results of using Intel GPA to analyze this optimized application (ThreadPi). The analysis process is the same as the process we used for the original application (SerialPi).

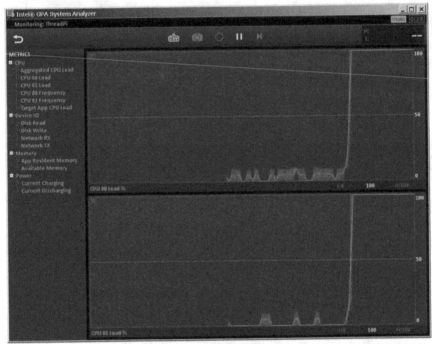

(a). Starting to Calculate

(b). Running of the Thread

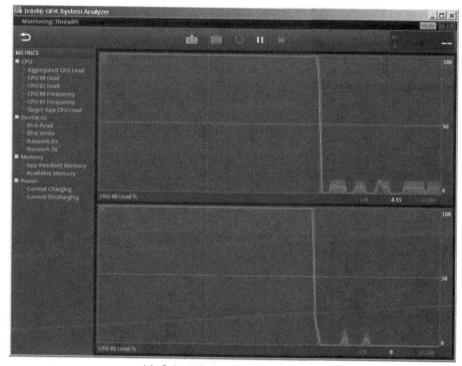

(c). Calculation of the Thread Finish

Figure 9-49. *Screenshots for Intel GPA Analysis of ThreadPi*

As can be seen in the diagram, when the Start button is clicked, the calculation (task) thread starts running. Both CPU loads raise from a low load to 100 percent-full capacity. When the calculation is complete, two CPU loads drop back down to the low-load condition. Unlike the original application (SerialPi), during the time that the computing task is running, both CPUs are 100 percent fully loaded. There is no longer any load rotation. This indicates that the optimized application (ThreadPi) has two parallel CPUs working at full capacity on the calculation task, which makes the application run an order of magnitude faster.

Overview

In this chapter, we have done a deep dive into performance optimizations on the Android x86 platform. Starting with a high-level overview of performance optimization methodologies, we talked about the key points to remember: reducing instructions, reducing frequency of execution, choosing the most efficient instructions, using parallelism correctly, and optimizing the available caching features. We also discussed optimizations that are done for us and common misconceptions with performance.

From here, we looked into Intel VTune, a performance-profiling tool for Android and x86, with an in-depth installation and setup guide. Next, we covered Android-specific multithreading and design and looked at how it is implemented from an in-depth, code-centric point of view. Finally, we connected all of the dots and used Intel GPA to observe our Android application and then performed a small case study on how a correct parallel implementation should look.

■ ■ ■

CHAPTER 10

x86 NDK and C/C++ Optimizations

Technological progress has merely provided us with more efficient means for going backwards.

—Aldous Leonard Huxley

In the previous chapter we introduced the basic principles of performance optimization, optimization methodologies, and related tools for Android application development. Since Java is the primary application development language for Android developers, optimization tools presented in the previous chapter were mainly for Java. We know that the Java application is running in a virtual machine, and its speed is inherently slower than C/C++ applications, which are directly compiled and run on the hardware instruction. In addition, due to the underlying and fundamental nature of C/C++, developers for C/C++ applications have created more optimization tools.

Vectorization

The Intel compiler supports advanced code generation, including *auto-vectorization*. For the Intel C/C++ compiler, vectorization is loop unrolling with the generation of single instruction, multiple data (SIMD) instructions operating on several elements at the same time. The developer can unroll loops manually and insert appropriate function calls corresponding to SIMD instructions. This approach is not forward-scalable and incurs high development costs. The work has to be redone when the new microprocessor with advanced instruction support is released. For example, early Intel Atom microprocessors did not benefit from vectorization of loops processing double-precision floating point while single-precision was processed by SIMD instruction effectively.

Auto-vectorization simplifies programming tasks because the programmer doesn't have to learn the instruction sets for each particular microprocessor. For example, the Intel compiler always supports the latest generations of Intel microprocessors.

The -vec options turn on vectorization at the default optimization level for microprocessors supporting IA32 architecture—both Intel and non-Intel. To improve the quality of vectorization, you need to specify the target microprocessor on which the code will execute. For optimal performance on Android smartphones based on Intel architecture, it's best to use the -xSSSE3_ATOM option. Vectorization is enabled with the Intel C++ compiler at optimization levels of -O2 and higher.

Many loops are vectorized automatically and most of the time the compiler generates optimal code on its own. However, sometimes it may require guidance from the programmer. The biggest problem with efficient vectorization is making the compiler estimate data dependencies as precisely as possible.

To take full advantage of Intel compiler vectorization, the following techniques are useful:

- Generate and understand a vectorization report

- Improve performance by pointer disambiguation

- Improve performance using inter-procedural optimization

- Use compiler pragmas

Vectorization Report

This section starts with the implementation of memory copying. The loop takes the structure commonly used in Android source code:

Listing 10-1. Memory Copying Implementation

```
// It is assumed that the memory pointed to by dst
// does not intersect with the memory pointed to by src

void copy_int(int* dst, int* src, int num)
{
int left = num;
if ( left <= 0 ) return;
do {
    left--;
    *dst++ = *src++;
} while ( left > 0 );
}
```

For experiments with vectorization, you'll reuse the hello-jni project. To do so, add the function to the new file called jni/copy_cpp.cpp. Add this file to the list of source files in jni/Android.mk as follows:

Listing 10-2. Vectorization Failure

```
LOCAL_SRC_FILES := hello-jni.c copy_int.cpp
```

To enable a detailed vectorization report, add the –vec-report3 option to the APP_
CFLAGS variable in jni/Application.mk:

```
APP_CFLAGS := -O3 -xSSSE3_ATOM  -vec-report3
```

If you rebuild libhello-jni.so, you will notice that several remarks are generated:

```
jni/copy_int.cpp(6): (col. 5) remark: loop was not vectorized: existence of
vector dependence.
jni/copy_int.cpp(9): (col. 10) remark: vector dependence: assumed ANTI
dependence between src line 9 and dst line 9.
jni/copy_int.cpp(9): (col. 10) remark: vector dependence: assumed FLOW
dependence between dst line 9 and src line 9.
...
```

Unfortunately auto-vectorization failed, because too little information was
available to the compiler. If the vectorization were successful, the assignment would be
replaced as follows:

```
*dst++ = *src++;
//The previous statement would be replaced with
*dst = *src;
*(dst + 1) = *(src + 1);
*(dst + 2) = *(src + 2);
*(dst + 3) = *(src + 3);
dst += 4; src += 4;
```

The first four assignments would be performed in parallel by SIMD instructions.
But parallel execution of assignments is invalid if the memory accessed on the left sides
is also accessed on the right sides of assignment. Consider, for example, the case when
dst+1 is equal to src+2. In this case the final value at dst+2 would be incorrect.

The remarks indicate which types of dependencies are conservatively assumed by
the compiler preventing vectorization:

- *Flow* dependence is a dependence between the earlier store and
  the later load from the same memory location.

- *Anti* dependence is a dependence between an earlier load and
  a later store to the same memory location.

- *Output* dependence is between two stores to the same memory
  location.

From the code comment, it is safe to assume that the author required that the
memory pointed to by dst and src not overlap. To communicate information to the
compiler, it is sufficient to add restrict qualifiers to the dst and src arguments:

```
void copy_int(int * __restrict__ dst, int * __restrict__ src, int num)
```

The restrict qualifier was added to the C standard published in 1999. To enable support of C99, you need to add -std=c99 to options. Alternatively, you may use the -restrict option to enable it for C++ and other C dialects. In the previous code, the __restrict__ keyword has been inserted and is always recognized as a synonym for the restrict keyword.

If you rebuild the library again, you will notice that the loops are vectorized:

```
jni/copy_int.cpp(6): (col. 5) remark: LOOP WAS VECTORIZED.
```

In this example, vectorization failed due to compiler conservative analysis. There are other cases when the loop is not vectorized, including when:

- The instruction set does not allow for efficient vectorization. The following remarks indicate this type of issue:

  - "Non-unit stride used"

  - "Mixed data types"

  - "Operator unsuited for vectorization"

  - "Contains unvectorizable statement at line XX"

  - "Condition may protect exception"

- Compiler heuristics prevent vectorization. Vectorization is possible but may actually lead to a slow down. If this is the case, the diagnostics will contain:

  - "Vectorization possible but seems inefficient"

  - "Low trip count"

  - "Not inner loop"

- Vectorizer's shortcomings:

  - "Condition too complex"

  - "Subscript too complex"

  - "Unsupported loop structure"

The amount of information produced by vectorizer is controlled by -vec-reportN. You may find additional details in the compiler documentation.

Pragmas

As you saw, you can use the restrict pointer qualifier to avoid conservative assumptions about data dependencies. But sometimes it's tricky to insert restrict keywords. If many arrays are accessed in the loop, it might also be too laborious to annotate all pointers. To simplify vectorization in these cases, you can use the Intel-specific pragma simd. You can use it to vectorize inner loops, assuming there are no dependencies between iterations.

Pragma simd applies only to for loops operating on native integer and floating-point types:

- The for loop should be countable with the number of iterations known before the loop starts.

- The loop should be innermost.

- All memory references in the loop should not fault (it is important for masked indirect references).

To vectorize the loop with a pragma, you need to rewrite the code into a for loop, as shown in Listing 10-3.

Listing 10-3. Memory Copying Implementation that Can Be Vectorized

```
void copy_int(int* dst, int* src, int num)
{
#pragma simd
for ( int i = 0; i < num; i++ ) {
*dst++ = *src++;
}
}
```

Rebuild the example and note that the loop is vectorized. Simple loop restructuring for pragma simd and insertions of #pragma simd in Android OS sources allow you to improve the performance of the Softweg benchmark by 1.4x without modifying the benchmark itself.

Auto-Vectorization and Limits

The previous sections' examples were based on the assumption that you had a good understanding of the code before starting your optimization efforts. If you are not familiar with the code, you can help the compiler to analyze it by extending the scope of the analysis. In the example with copying, the compiler should make conservative assumptions because it knows nothing about the copy_int routine's parameters. If call sites are available for analysis, the compiler can try to prove that the parameters are safe for vectorization.

To extend the scope of the analysis, you need to enable *interprocedural optimizations.* A few of these optimizations are enabled by default during single file compilation. Interprocedural optimizations are described in a separate section.

Vectorization cannot be used to speed up the Linux kernel code, because SIMD instructions are disabled in kernel mode with the -mno-sse option. This was done intentionally by kernel developers.

Interprocedural Optimizations

The compiler can perform additional optimizations if it can optimize across function boundaries. For example, if the compiler knows that some function call argument is constant, then it can create a special version of the function specifically tailored to that constant argument. This special version later can be optimized with knowledge of the parameter value.

To enable optimization within a single file, specify the -ip option. When this option is specified, the compiler generates a final object file that can be processed by the system linker. The disadvantage of generating an object file is almost complete information loss; the compiler does not even attempt to extract information from the object files.

Single file scope may be insufficient for the analysis due to the information loss. In this case, you need to add the -ipo option. When you use this option, the compiler compiles files into an intermediate representation that is later processed by special Intel tools: xiar and xild.

You use the xiar tool for creating static libraries instead of the GNU archiver ar, and you use xild instead of the GNU linker ld. It is only required when the linker and archiver are called directly. A better approach is to use the compiler drivers icc or icpc for final linking. The downside of the extended scope is that the advantage of separate compilation is lost—each modification of the source requires relinking and relinking causes complete recompilation.

There is an extensive list of advanced optimization techniques that benefit from global analysis. **Chapter 9: Performance Optimizations for Android Applications on x86** introduced some of these techniques, and others will be discussed later this chapter. Note that some optimizations are Intel-specific and are enabled with -x* options.

Unfortunately, things are slightly more complicated in Android with respect to shared libraries. By default, all global symbols are preemptable. Preemptability is easy to explain by example. Consider the instance where the following libraries are linked into the same executable:

Listing 10-4. libone.so, a Linked Library Example

```
int id(void) {
    return 1;
}
```

Listing 10-4 is the first library linked, and the second is described in Listing 10-5.

Listing 10-5. libtwo.so, a Second Linked Library Example

```
int id( void ) {
    return 2;
}
int foo( void ) {
    return id();
}
```

Assume that the libraries were created simply by executing icc –fpic –shared –o <libname>.so <libname>.c. Only the strictly required options, –fpic and –shared, are given.

If the system dynamic linker loads the library libone.so before the library libtwo.so, the call to the function id() from the function foo() is resolved in the libone.so library.

When the compiler optimizes the function foo(), it cannot use its knowledge about id() from the libtwo.so library. For example, it cannot inline the id() function. If the compiler inlined the id() function, it would break the scenario involving libone.so and libtwo.so.

As a consequence, when you write shared libraries you should carefully specify which functions can be preempted. By default all global functions and variables are visible outside a shared library and can be preempted. The default setup is not convenient when you implement few native methods. In this case, you need to export only symbols that are called directly by the Dalvik Java virtual machine.

A symbol's visibility attribute specifies whether a symbol is visible outside the module and whether it can be preempted:

- "Default" visibility makes a global symbol visible outside the shared library and able to be preempted.

- "Protected" visibility makes a symbol visible outside the shared library, but the symbol cannot be preempted.

- "Hidden" visibility makes a global symbol visible only within the shared library and forbids preemption.

Returning to the hello-jni application, it is necessary to specify that the default visibility is hidden and that the functions exported for JVM have protected visibility.

To set default visibility to hidden, add -fvisibility=hidden to the APP_CFLAGS variable in jni/Application.mk:

```
APP_CFLAGS := -O3 -xSSSE3_ATOM  -vec-report3 -fvisibility=hidden -ipo
```

To override the visibility of Java_com_example_hellojni_HelloJni_stringFromJNI, add the attribute to the function definition:

```
Jstring __attribute__((visibility("protected")))
  Java_com_example_hellojni_HelloJni_stringFromJNI(JNIEnv* env, jobject thiz)
```

With this flag set, the default visibility is hidden. This is the extent of the interprocedural optimizations that exist for the Intel NDK applications.

Optimization with Intel IPP

You know from Chapter 7 that Android applications can bypass NDK development tools and use existing .so shared libraries developed by third parties. We use the Intel IPP libraries as an example in this chapter. Typical applications that use this library include multimedia and streaming applications, but any application where any time performance is an issue would benefit from this tool.

Intel IPP (Integrated Performance Primitives) is one of the high-performance libraries that Intel provides. It is a powerful function library for Intel processors and chipsets, and it covers math, signal processing, multimedia, image and graphics processing, vector computing, and other areas. A prominent feature of Intel IPP is that its code has been extensively optimized based on the features of any Intel processor, using a variety of methods. It can be said that it is a highly optimized, high-performance service library associated with Intel processors. Intel IPP has cross-platform features; it provides a set of cross-platform and operating system general APIs, which can be used for Windows, Linux, and other operating systems, and supports embedded, desktop, server, and other processor-scale systems.

In fact, Intel IPP is a set of libraries, each with different function areas within the corresponding library, and the libraries within Intel IPP differ slightly by the number of functions supported in different processor architectures. For example, Intel IPP 5.X image processing functions can support 2,570 functions in the Intel Architecture, while it supports only 1,574 functions in the IXP processor architecture.

The services provided by a variety of high-performance libraries, including Intel IPP, are multifaceted and multilayered. Applications can use Intel IPP directly or indirectly. Intel IPP provides support for applications, as well as for other components and libraries.

Applications using Intel IPP can be at two levels—they use the Intel IPP function interface directly, or use sample code to indirectly use Intel IPP. In addition, using the OpenCV library (a cross-platform Open Source Computer Vision Library) is equivalent to indirectly using the Intel IPP library. Both the Intel IPP and Intel MKL libraries eventually run on high-performance Intel processors on various architectures.

Taking into account the power of Intel IPP, and in accordance with the characteristics of optimized features of the Intel processor, you could use the Intel IPP library to replace some key source code that runs often and consumes a lot of time. You can obtain much higher performance acceleration than with general code. This is simply a "standing on the shoulders of giants" practical optimization method. Users can achieve optimization without manually writing code in critical areas.

Intel recently released Intel Android development environment code named Beacon Mountain. It provides both Intel IPP and Intel Threaded Building Blocks (TBB) for Android application developers. The average user can easily use Intel IPP, Intel TBB, Intel GPA, and other tools for Android application development. Examples of the Intel IPP can be found at `http://software.intel.com/en-us/articles/intel-integrated-performance-primitives-intel-ipp-intel-ipp-sample-code`.

NDK Integrated Optimization Examples

We have introduced optimization based on the knowledge and basic theory of NDK-based optimization. This section uses a case study to demonstrate comprehensive optimization techniques by integrating NDK with C/C++.

The case is divided into two steps. The first step demonstrates a technique used on a local function compiled from C/C++ code to accelerate the computing tasks in a traditional Java-based program. The second step demonstrates the use of NDK compiler optimizations to achieve the C/C++ optimization task itself. We introduce each step in the following two sections of the chapter, which are closely linked.

C/C++: The Original Application Acceleration

In the previous chapter, we introduced the use of Java code examples (SerialPi) to calculate π. In this section, we will change the computing tasks from Java to C code, using NDK to turn it into a local library. We then compare it with the original Java code tasks and you'll get some first-hand experience using C/C++ native library functions to achieve the traditional Java-based tasks acceleration.

The application used for this case study is named NDKExp, and we are using the Lenovo K800 as the target cell phone, which runs the interface shown in Figure 10-1.

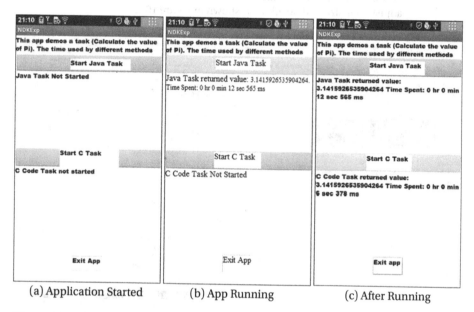

(a) Application Started   (b) App Running   (c) After Running

Figure 10-1. Original Version of NDKExp Running Interface

Figure 10-1 (a) shows the application's main interface, including three buttons—Start Java Task, Start C Task, and Exit App. Clicking the Start Java Task button will start a traditional Java task (as shown in the source code of SerialPi written in Java, which calculates π). When the task is completed, the calculated results will be displayed below the button with the time spent, as shown in Figure 10-1 (b). Clicking the Start C Task button will start a computing task written in C using the same math formula to calculate π. When the task is completed, the calculated results will be displayed below the button with the time spent, as shown in Figure 10-1 (c).

As seen in Figure 10-1, for the same task, the application written in traditional Java takes 12.565 seconds to complete; the application written in C and compiled by the NDK development tool takes 6.378 seconds to complete. This example allows you to visually experience the power of using the NDK to achieve performance optimization.

This example is implemented as follows.

Step 1: Create a New Android Application Project

1. Generate the project in Eclipse, name the project NDKExp, and choose the Build SDK option to support the x86 version of the API (in this case, the Android 4.0.3). Others are using the default values. After you have completed all these steps, generate the project.

2. Modify the main layout file. Put three text views and three buttons in the layout, set their Text and ID attributes, and adjust their size and position, as shown in Figure 10-2.

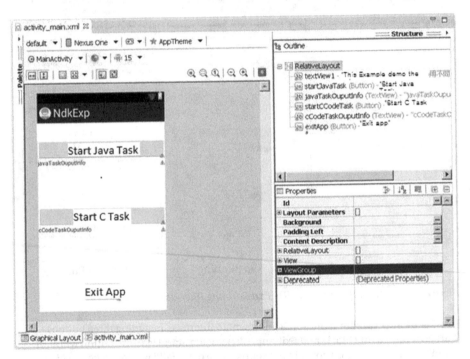

Figure 10-2. *Layout of the Original Version NDKExp*

3. Modify the main layout of the class source code file MainActivity.java. It reads as follows:

```
1. package com.example.ndkexp;
2. import android.os.Bundle;
3. import android.app.Activity;
4. import android.view.Menu;
5. import android.widget.Button;
6. import android.view.View;
7. import android.view.View.OnClickListener;
```

```
8.  import android.os.Process;
9.  import android.widget.TextView;
10. import android.os.Handler;
11. import android.os.Message;
12.
13. public class MainActivity extends Activity {
14.     private JavaTaskThread javaTaskThread = null;
15.     private CCodeTaskThread cCodeTaskThread = null;
16.      private TextView tv_JavaTaskOuputInfo;
17.      private TextView tv_CCodeTaskOuputInfo;
18.      private Handler mHandler;;
19.     private long end_time;
20.     private long time;
21.     private long start_time;
22.      @Override
23.      public void onCreate(Bundle savedInstanceState) {
24.          super.onCreate(savedInstanceState);
25.          setContentView(R.layout.activity_main);
26.          tv_JavaTaskOuputInfo = (TextView)findViewById
    (R.id.javaTaskOuputInfo);
27.          tv_JavaTaskOuputInfo.setText("Java the task is not
    started ");
28.          tv_CCodeTaskOuputInfo = (TextView)findViewById
    (R.id.cCodeTaskOuputInfo);
29.          tv_CCodeTaskOuputInfo.setText("C  code task is not
    start ");
30.          final Button btn_ExitApp = (Button) findViewById
    (R.id.exitApp);
31.          btn_ExitApp.setOnClickListener(new /*View.*/
    OnClickListener(){
32.              public void onClick(View v) {
33.                  exitApp();
34.              }
35.          });
36.          final Button btn_StartJavaTask = (Button)
    findViewById(R.id.startJavaTask);
37.          final Button btn_StartCCodeTask = (Button)
    findViewById(R.id.startCCodeTask);
38.          btn_StartJavaTask.setOnClickListener(new /*View.*/
    OnClickListener(){
39.              public void onClick(View v) {
40.                  btn_StartJavaTask.setEnabled(false);
41.                  btn_StartCCodeTask.setEnabled(false);
42.                  btn_ExitApp.setEnabled(false);
43.                  startJavaTask();
44.              }
45.          });
```

```
46.              btn_StartCCodeTask.setOnClickListener(new /*View.*/
        OnClickListener(){
47.                  public void onClick(View v) {
48.                      btn_StartJavaTask.setEnabled(false);
49.                      btn_StartCCodeTask.setEnabled(false);
50.                      btn_ExitApp.setEnabled(false);
51.                      startCCodeTask();
52.                  }
53.              });
54.          mHandler = new Handler() {
55.              public void handleMessage(Message msg) {
56.              String s;
57.              switch (msg.what)
58.              {
59.              case JavaTaskThread.MSG_FINISHED:
60.                  end_time = System.currentTimeMillis();
61.                  time = end_time - start_time;
62.                  s = " The return value of the Java task "+
        (Double)(msg.obj) +"  Time consumed:"
63.                      + JavaTaskThread.msTimeToDatetime(time);
64.                      tv_JavaTaskOuputInfo.setText(s);
65.                      btn_StartCCodeTask.setEnabled(true);
66.                  btn_ExitApp.setEnabled(true);
67.              break;
68.              case CCodeTaskThread.MSG_FINISHED:
69.                  end_time = System.currentTimeMillis();
70.                  time = end_time - start_time;
71.                  s = " The return value of the C code
        task"+ (Double)(msg.obj) +"  time consumed:"
72.                      + JavaTaskThread.msTimeToDatetime(time);
73.                      tv_CCodeTaskOuputInfo.setText(s);
74.                      btn_StartJavaTask.setEnabled(true);
75.                  btn_ExitApp.setEnabled(true);
76.              break;
77.              default:
78.                  break;
79.              }
80.              }
81.          };
82.      }
83.
84.      @Override
85.      public boolean onCreateOptionsMenu(Menu menu) {
86.          getMenuInflater().inflate(R.menu.activity_main, menu);
87.          return true;
88.      }
89.
```

```
90.     private void startJavaTask() {
91.       if (javaTaskThread == null)
92.         javaTaskThread = new JavaTaskThread(mHandler);
93.       if (! javaTaskThread.isAlive())
94.       {
95.             start_time = System.currentTimeMillis();
96.             javaTaskThread.start();
97.             tv_JavaTaskOuputInfo.setText("The Java task is
     running...");
98.       }
99.     }
100.
101.    private void startCCodeTask() {
102.      if (cCodeTaskThread == null)
103.        cCodeTaskThread = new CCodeTaskThread(mHandler);
104.      if (! cCodeTaskThread.isAlive())
105.      {
106.            start_time = System.currentTimeMillis();
107.            cCodeTaskThread.start();
108.            tv_CCodeTaskOuputInfo.setText("C codes task is
     running...");
109.      }
110.    }
111.    private void exitApp() {
112.      try {
113.        if (javaTaskThread !=null)
114.        {
115.          javaTaskThread.join();
116.          javaTaskThread = null;
117.        }
118.      } catch (InterruptedException e) {
119.      }
120.      try {
121.        if (cCodeTaskThread  !=null)
122.        {
123.          cCodeTaskThread.join();
124.          cCodeTaskThread = null;
125.        }
126.      } catch (InterruptedException e) {
127.      }
128.      finish();
129.        Process.killProcess(Process.myPid());
130.    }
131.
132.   static {
133.     System.loadLibrary("ndkexp_extern_lib");
134.   }
135. }
```

The preceding code is basically the same as the example code for SerialPi. The code in lines 123 through 134 is the only new part. This code requires that the libndkexp_extern_lib.so shared library file be loaded before the application is running. The application needs to use local functions in this library.

4. The new threads task class JavaTaskThread in the project is used to calculate π. The code is similar to the MyTaskThread class code in the SerialPi example and is omitted here.

5. The thread task class CCodeTaskThread in the new project calls the local function to calculate π; its source code files CCodeTaskThread.java read as follows:

```
1.  package com.example.ndkexp;
2.  import android.os.Handler;
3.  import android.os.Message;

4.  public class CCodeTaskThread extends Thread {
5.      private Handler mainHandler;
6.      public static final int MSG_FINISHED = 2;
            // The message after the end of the task
7.      private native double cCodeTask();
            // Calling external C functions to accomplish computing
        tasks
8.      static String msTimeToDatetime(long msnum){
9.      long hh,mm,ss,ms, tt= msnum;
10.        ms = tt % 1000; tt = tt / 1000;
11.        ss = tt % 60; tt = tt / 60;
12.        mm = tt % 60; tt = tt / 60;
13.        hh = tt % 60;
14.        String s = "" + hh +" Hour "+mm+" Minute "+ss + " Second
        " + ms +" Millisecond ";
15.        return s;
16.      }
17.      @Override
18.      public void run()
19.      {
20.        double pi = cCodeTask();
        // Calling external C function to complete the calculation
21.        Message msg = new Message();
22.        msg.what = MSG_FINISHED;
23.        Double dPi = Double.valueOf(pi);
24.          msg.obj = dPi;
25.          mainHandler.sendMessage(msg);
26.      }
```

```
27.    public CCodeTaskThread(Handler mh)
28.    {
29.       super();
30.       mainHandler = mh;
31.    }
32. }
```

The previous code is similar to the code framework of the MyTaskThread class of the SerialPi example. The main difference is at line 20. The original Java code for calculating π is replaced by calling a local function cCodeTask. To state that the cCodeTask function is a local function, you must add the local declaration of the function in line 7.

6.   Build the project in Eclipse. Similarly here we have just a build, rather than run.

7.   Create the jni subdirectory in the project's root directory.

Step 2: Write the C Implementation Code of the cCodeTask Function

According to the method described in the **NDK Examples** section of **Chapter 7: Creating and Porting NDK-based Android Applications,** you need to compile the file into a .so library file. The main steps are as follows:

1.   Create a C interface file. Since the case is a CCodeTaskThread class using a local function, you need to generate the class header file according to the class file of this class. At the command line, go to the project directory and then run the following command:

```
E:\temp\Android Dev\workspace\NdkExp> javah -classpath "D:\
Android\android-sdk\platforms\android-15\android.jar";bin/classes
com.example.ndkexp.CCodeTaskThread
```

This command will generate a file in the project directory named com_example_ndkexp_CCodeTaskThread.h. The main content of the document is as follows:

```
...
23.  JNIEXPORT jdouble JNICALL Java_com_example_ndkexp_
     CCodeTaskThread_cCodeTask
24.  (JNIEnv *, jobject);
     ...
```

In lines 23-24, the prototype of local function cCodeTask is defined.

2. Based on the previous header files, you create corresponding C code files in the jni directory of the project. In this case, we named it mycomputetask.c, which reads as follows:

```
1.   #include <jni.h>
2.   jdouble Java_com_example_ndkexp_CCodeTaskThread_cCodeTask
     (JNIEnv* env, jobject thiz )
3.   {
4.     const long num_steps = 100000000;  // The total step length
5.     const double step = 1.0 / num_steps;
6.       double x, sum = 0.0;
7.       long i;
8.     double pi = 0;
9.
10.    for (i=0; i< num_steps; i++){
11.          x = (i+0.5)*step;
12.          sum = sum + 4.0/(1.0 + x*x);
13.      }
14.      pi = step * sum;
15.
16.    return (pi);
17.  }
```

Lines 4 through 16 are the body of the function—the code calculating π, which is the code that corresponds to the MyTaskThread class in the SerialPi example. Note that in line 4, the value of the variable num_steps (the total step length) must be the same as the value of the same step size that the JavaTaskThread class represents. Otherwise, there is no significance in comparing.

The first line of each jni file must contain the headers. Line 2 is the cCodeTask function prototype and is based on a slightly modified header files obtained in the previous step.

Line 16 shows the return results. With the double type of Java, which corresponds to the jdouble type of C, C can have a pi variable in type double returned directly to it. This is something we discussed in the introduction to this chapter.

3. In the project jni directory, you must create the Android.mk and Application.mk files. The content of Android.mk reads as follows:

```
1.  LOCAL_PATH := $(call my-dir)
2.  include $(CLEAR_VARS)
3.  LOCAL_MODULE     := ndkexp_extern_lib
4.  LOCAL_SRC_FILES  := mycomputetask.c
5.  include $(BUILD_SHARED_LIBRARY)
```

Line 4 specifies the C code in the case file. Line 3 indicates the filename of the generated library, and its name must be consistent with the parameters of the System. loadLibrary function in line 133 of the project file MainActivity.java.

4. According to the method described in **Chapter 7**'s section on **NDK Examples**, you compile the C code into the .so library file under the lib directory of the project.

5. Deployment: run the project.

The application running interface is shown in the Figure 10-3.

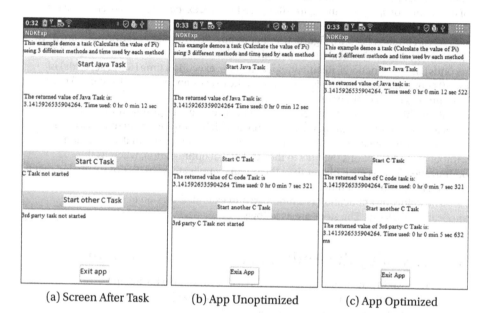

| (a) Screen After Task | (b) App Unoptimized | (c) App Optimized |

Figure 10-3. *Extended Version of the NDKExp Running Interface*

Compiler Optimization Extension Application

In the previous example, you witnessed the capabilities of NDK for application acceleration. However, this application implemented only one local function and can't provide you with information to compare the effects of compiler optimizations. For this purpose, you need to rebuild the application and use it to experiment with the effects of compiler optimizations.

The application running the interface is shown in Figure 10-3.

The application has four buttons. When you click on the Start Java Task button, the response code does not change.

When you click the Start C Task or Start Other C Task button, the application will start a local function to run.

The code (the function body) of the two functions is the same. It calculates the values of π, but with a different name. The first one calls the cCodeTask function, while the second one calls the anotherCCodeTask function. These two functions are located in the mycomputetask.c and anothertask.c files and they correspond to the library files libndkexp_extern_lib.so and libndkexp_another_lib.so, respectively, after being compiled. In this case, you compile libndkexp_extern_lib.so using the -O0 option and compile libndkexp_another_lib.so using the -O3 option, so one is compiled non-optimized and the other is compiled optimized.

Therefore, clicking Start C Task will run the unoptimized version of the C function, as shown in Figure 10-3 (b), and clicking Start Other C Task will run the optimized version of the C functions, such as in Figure 10-3 (c). After task execution, the system displays the calculated results for the consumption of time.

As can be seen from the figure, whether or not the compiler optimizations are used, the running time of the local function is always shorter than the running time (12.522 seconds) of Java functions. Relatively speaking, the execution time (5.632 seconds) of the -O3 optimization function is shorter than the execution time (7.321 seconds) of the unoptimized (-O0 compiler option) function.

From this comparison, you can see that using compiler optimizations actually reduces application execution time. Not only that, it is even shorter than the original application running time (6.378 seconds). This is because the original application without compiler options defaults to the -O1 level of optimization, whereas the -O3 optimization level is even higher than the original application, so it's not surprising that it has the shortest running time.

The following application is a modified and extended version of the original application NDKExp. The steps are as follows.

Step 1: Modify the Android Part of the Application

1. Modify the main layout file. Add a text view and a button in a layout. Set their Text and ID properties, and adjust their size and position, as shown in Figure 10-4.

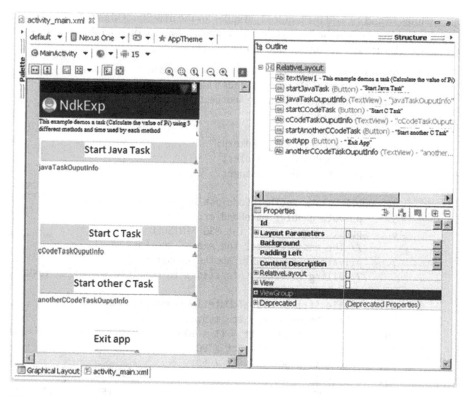

Figure 10-4. *Extended Version NDKExp Layout*

2. Modify the class source code file MainActivity.java of the main layout. The main changes are as follows:

```
   ...
13.  public class MainActivity extends Activity {
14.    private JavaTaskThread javaTaskThread = null;
15.    private CCodeTaskThread cCodeTaskThread = null;
16.    private AnotherCCodeTaskThread anotherCCodeTaskThread = null;
17.    private TextView tv_JavaTaskOuputInfo;
18.    private TextView tv_CCodeTaskOuputInfo;
19.    private TextView tv_AnotherCCodeTaskOuputInfo;
     ...
182.   static {
183.     System.loadLibrary("ndkexp_extern_lib");
184.     System.loadLibrary("ndkexp_another_lib");
185.   }
186. }
```

In lines 16 and 19, add the required variables for the new Start Other C Task button. The key change is in the line 184. In addition to loading the original shared library files, those files are also added into another library file.

3. In the project, add a thread task class with the name AnotherCCodeTaskThread that calls a local function to calculate π. Its source code file AnotherCCodeTaskThread. java reads as follows:

```
1.   package com.example.ndkexp;
2.   import android.os.Handler;
3.   import android.os.Message;

4.   public class AnotherCCodeTaskThread extends Thread {
5.     private Handler mainHandler;
6.     public static final int MSG_FINISHED = 3;
       // The message after the end of the task
7.     private native double anotherCCodeTask();
       // Calling external C functions to complete computing tasks

8.     static String msTimeToDatetime(long msnum){
9.       long hh,mm,ss,ms, tt= msnum;
10.      ms = tt % 1000; tt = tt / 1000;
11.      ss = tt % 60; tt = tt / 60;
12.      mm = tt % 60; tt = tt / 60;
13.      hh = tt % 60;
14.      String s = "" + hh +"Hour "+mm+"Minute "+ss + "Second " +
    ms +"Millisecond";
15.      return s;
16.    }

17.    @Override
18.    public void run()
19.    {
20.    double pi = anotherCCodeTask();
       // Calling external C function to complete the calculation
21.      Message msg = new Message();
22.      msg.what = MSG_FINISHED;
23.      Double dPi = Double.valueOf(pi);
24.      msg.obj = dPi;
25.      mainHandler.sendMessage(msg);
26.    }

27.    public CCodeTaskThread(Handler mh)
28.    {
29.    super();
30.    mainHandler = mh;
31.    }
32. }
```

The previous code is almost transcribing the code of the CCodeTaskThread class. It only does a little processing by calling another external C function called anotherCCodeTask to complete computing tasks in line 20. In line 7 it provides appropriate instructions for local functions and changes the value of the message type in line 6. In this way it distinguishes itself with a completed message by the previous C function. Line 4 shows that the task class is inherited from the thread class.

4. Build the project in Eclipse. Similarly here, you have just a build, rather than a run.

Step 2: Modify the Makefile File of mycomputetask.c and Rebuild the Library Files

1. Modify the Android.mk file under the jni directory of the project, which reads as follows:

```
1.  LOCAL_PATH := $(call my-dir)
2.  include $(CLEAR_VARS)
3.  LOCAL_MODULE    := ndkexp_extern_lib
4.  LOCAL_SRC_FILES := mycomputetask.c
5.  LOCAL_CFLAGS    := -OO
6.  include $(BUILD_SHARED_LIBRARY)
```

Unlike the original application, in line 5 you add the parameters of the command LOCAL_CFLAGS passed to gcc. The value -OO means no optimization.

2. Compile the C code file into the .so library file in the lib directory of the project.

3. Save the .so library files in the lib directory of the project (in this example, the file is libndkexp_extern_lib.so) to some other directory in the disk somewhere. The following operations will delete this .so library file.

Step 2: Write the C Implementation Code for the anotherCCodeTask Function

Copy the processing steps for the cCodeTask function from the previous section. Then compile the file into the .so library file. The main steps are as follows:

1. Create a C interface file. At the command line, go to the project directory, and then run the following command:

```
E:\temp\Android Dev\workspace\NdkExp> javah -classpath
"D:\Android\android-sdk\platforms\android-15\android.jar";bin/
classes  com.example.ndkexp.AnotherCCodeTaskThread
```

This command will generate a directory named project com_example_ndkexp_ AnotherCCodeTaskThread.h file. The main contents of the file are:

```
    ...
23.  JNIEXPORT jdouble JNICALL Java_com_example_ndkexp_
AnotherCCodeTaskThread_anotherCCodeTask
24.  (JNIEnv *, jobject);
    ...
```

Lines 23–24 define the local function anotherCCodeTask prototype.

2. According to the previously mentioned header files in the project jni directory, establish corresponding C code files, in this case named anothertask.c, the content of which is based on the mycomputetask.c modification. The modification as follows:

```
1.  #include <jni.h>
2.  jdouble Java_com_example_ndkexp_AnotherCCodeTaskThread_
anotherCCodeTask (JNIEnv* env,  jobject thiz )
3.  {
    ...
17. }
```

The second line of mycomputetask.c is replaced by the prototype of the anotherCCodeTask function. This is the same function prototype copied from the description about the function prototype of the .h file, which was created in the previous step with minor revisions. The final form can be seen in code line 2.

3. Modify the Android.mk file under the jni directory in the project, as follows:

```
1.  LOCAL_PATH := $(call my-dir)
2.  include $(CLEAR_VARS)
3.  LOCAL_MODULE      := ndkexp_another_lib
4.  LOCAL_SRC_FILES   := anothertask.c
5.  LOCAL_CFLAGS      := -O3
6.  include $(BUILD_SHARED_LIBRARY)
```

In line 4, the value is replaced with the new C code file anothertask.c. In line 3, the value is replaced with new library filename, which is consistent with the parameters of the System.loadLibrary function (which is in line 184 of the MainActivity.java file in the project). In line 5, the value of the LOCAL_CFLAGS parameter for the passed gcc command is replaced with -O3, which represents the highest level of optimization.

4. Compile the C code file into the .so library file under the lib directory of the project. Then you can see that the libndkexp_extern_lib.so documents under the lib directory in the project disappeared and were replaced by a newly generated libndkexp_another_lib.so file. It is very important to save library files.

5. Put the previously saved libndkexp_extern_lib.so library file back into the libs directory in the project.

There are now two files in the directory. You can use the dir command to verify:

```
E:\temp\Android Dev\workspace\NdkExp>dir libs\x86
2013-02-28  00:31          5,208 libndkexp_another_lib.so
2013-02-28  00:23          5,208 libndkexp_extern_lib.so
```

6. You redeploy, and run the project.

The application running the interface is shown in Figure 10-3, earlier in this chapter.

Multiple Situations Comparison of Compiler Optimization Extensions

Through the case studies in this chapter, you have first-hand experience about the effects of compiler optimization. Task execution time was shortened from 7.321 seconds before optimization to 5.632 seconds after optimization. We only compared the difference of the gcc -O3 and -O0 command. You can extend this configuration by modifying the Android. mk file when compiling the two files—mycomputetask.c and anothertask.c—and then continue to compare the differences in the optimizing effects when using different compiler command options. To modify the Android.mk file, you only need to modify the value of the LOCAL_CFLAGS item. You can select many options of the gcc command to compare. Here are a few examples to illustrate this process.

Example: Compare the Optimization Results by Using SSE Instructions

You can have the Start C Task button correspond to the Android.mk file of mycomputetask.c compile:

```
LOCAL_CFLAGS      := -mno-sse
```

and have the Start Other C Task button correspond to the Android.mk file of the anothertask.c compile:

```
LOCAL_CFLAGS      := -msse3
```

The former tells the compiler not to compile SSE instructions; the latter allows the compiler to program into SSE3 instructions. The reason to choose SSE3 instructions is that SSE3 is the highest level of instructions that the Intel Atom processor supports.

The results of running the application are shown in Figure 10-5.

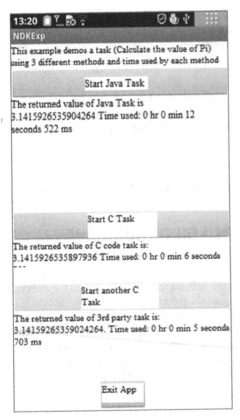

Figure 10-5. *Optimization Comparison of Compiler SSE Instructions for Application NDKExp*

Seen from Figure 10-5, the same task using an SSE instruction execution time is shorter than not using an SSE instruction. The execution time is shortened from the original 6.759 seconds to 5.703 seconds.

It needs to be noted that, in this example, we finished modifying Android.mk files and reran ndk-build to generate the .so library file. We immediately deployed and ran the NDKExp project, but found out that we could not reach the desired effect. The reason is because only the .so library files are updated. The project manager of Eclipse does not detect that that the project needs to rebuild. As a result, the apk did not get updates, and NDKExp application on the target machine code would not update the original code. Considering this situation, you can use the following methods to avoid this problem:

1. Uninstall the application from the phone.

2. Delete the classes.dex, jarlist.cache, and NdkExp.apk documents from the bin subdirectory of host project directory.

3. Delete the project in Eclipse.

4. In Eclipse, re-import the project.

5. Finally, redeploy and run projects, so you can have the desired effect.

This example only compares the effect of the SSE instructions. Interested readers can try other gcc compiler options and compare their operating results.

In addition, in the previous examples, what we are concerned with is the NDK effect only, so the C functions still use single-threaded code. Interested readers could combine the NDK optimization knowledge they learned from this chapter with the multithreading optimization in the previous chapter and change the C function to multithreading to implement along with the compiler optimization. Such a written set of optimization techniques in a variety of applications will certainly allow the application to run faster.

Overview

Similar to Chapter 9, this chapter focused heavily on the code and technical aspects of the Android NDK on Intel's x86 architecture. We walked through creating a simple Android NDK application to show off how all of these pieces connect and ran it on an x86 emulator. The chapter also provided a high-level look at the optimizations that the Android NDK compiler can provide its developers. We then looked at Intel's Integrated Performance Primitives library (IPP), a high-performance library provided to x86 developers. Finally, we wrapped the chapter up with some examples of how to use all of the tools and tricks discussed.

▓▓ ▓

CHAPTER 11

Using Intel Hardware Accelerated Execution Manager on Windows, Mac OS, and Linux to Speed Up Android on x86 Emulation

I do not fear computers. I fear the lack of them.

—Isaac Asimov

Once the Android SDK is installed, the Android emulator is running, and your development environment is set up to your liking, there is still one frustration ahead: the Android emulator can be extremely slow. Especially when testing and debugging larger applications, the emulator's speed is a noticeable bottleneck in development. The best solution to this is the Intel Hardware Accelerated Execution Manager (Intel HAXM) with Intel Virtualization Technology (Intel VT). If your development system uses one of the supported Intel processors, this hardware-assisted virtualization engine, or hypervisor, will enable lightning-fast Android emulation.

Introduction

This software:

- Uses Intel VT, available on select Intel processors.

- Provides hardware-accelerated emulation of Intel x86 Android virtual devices.

- Integrates with the Android SDK.

- Intel HAXM requires the Android SDK to be installed (version 17 or higher). For best performance, using SDK version 2.0 or higher is recommended.

- Recent Windows or Mac OS X (32/64-bit).

As an important note, Intel HAXM cannot be used on systems without an Intel processor nor an Intel processor without the required hardware features. To determine the capabilities of your Intel processor, please visit `http://ark.intel.com/`. Additionally, Intel HAXM can only accelerate Android x86 system images for emulator x86. HAXM has been validated with x86 system images provided by Intel at `http://www.intel.com/software/android`.

Downloading Intel HAXM

Intel HAXM can be installed either through the Android SDK Manager (recommended), or manually, by downloading the installer from Intel's web site.

■ **Note** Intel HAXM does not automatically check for updates. To get the latest version, download the Intel HAXM package using the Android SDK Manager (recommended) or from the Intel Software Network Android developer site.

Downloading Through Android SDK Manager

1. Start the Android SDK Manager.

2. Under Extras, check the box next to Intel x86 Emulator Accelerator (HAXM), as seen in Figure 11-1.

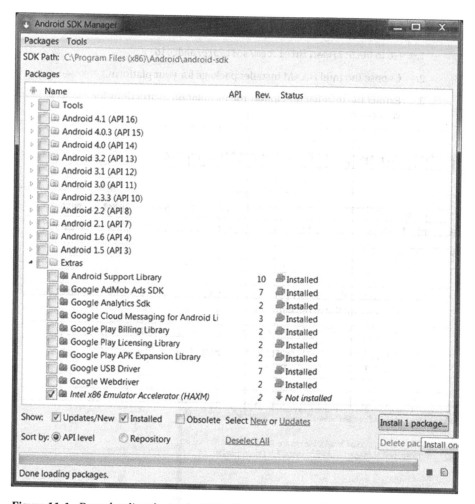

Figure 11-1. *Downloading the Intel x86 Emulator Accelerator (HAXM)*

3. Click the Install Package button.

4. Review the Intel Corporation license agreement. If you accept the terms, select Accept and click Install.

5. The SDK Manager will download the installer to the Tools directory, under the main SDK directory.

6. Extract the installer inside the Tools directory and follow the installation instructions for your platform.

Downloading Manually

1. Go to http://www.intel.com/software/android.

2. Choose the Intel HAXM installer package for your platform.

3. Extract the installer and follow the installation instructions for your platform.

Installing Intel HAXM on Windows

■ **Warning** Intel HAXM installation will fail if your system does not meet the system requirements, including support for Intel processor features, such as Intel Virtualization Technology (Intel VT).

---

1. Download the installer package from http://www.intel.com/software/android or by using the SDK manager.

2. Run the installer (and accept the UAC prompt, if applicable).

3. If an older version Intel HAXM is installed, you will see something like Figure 11-2.

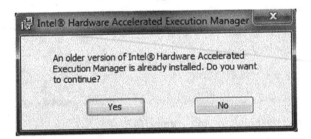

Figure 11-2. Notification Dialog

4. Click Yes to upgrade Intel HAXM, or click No to exit the installation and keep the currently installed version of Intel HAXM.

5. You will see a screen like Figure 11-3.

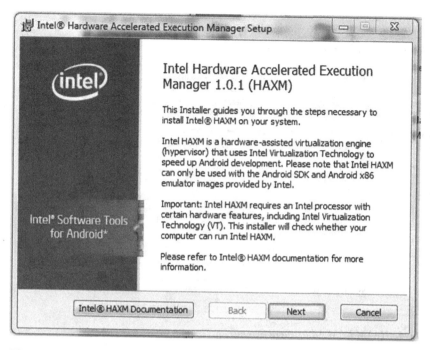

Figure 11-3. HAXM Installation Screen

■ **Note** You can access the documentation at any time by clicking Intel HAXM documentation.

---

6. Click Next.

7. Read the Intel HAXM End-User License Agreement (EULA) and, if you agree, accept the EULA and continue installing Intel HAXM.

8. You will be prompted to adjust the amount of RAM allocated to Intel HAXM, as shown in Figure 11-4.

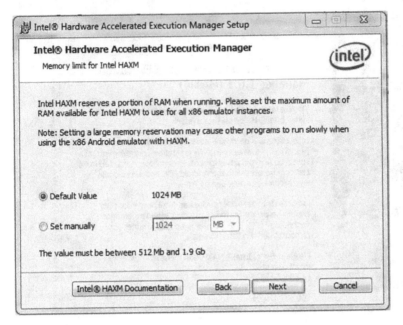

Figure 11-4. HAXM RAM Adjustment Screen

■ **Note**   The installer also functions as a configuration tool for Intel HAXM. To change your
memory settings, run the installer again.

---

9.   Figure 11-5 confirms your Intel HAXM memory allocation
     settings.

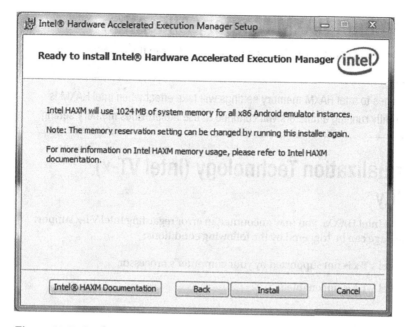

Figure 11-5. *Intel HAXM Ready to Install*

10. When the Intel HAXM installation is finished, click Finish to exit the installer.

Intel HAXM is now installed and ready to use. To verify that Intel HAXM is running, open
a command prompt window and execute the following command:

```
sc query
intelhaxm
```

If Intel HAXM is working, the command will show a status message indicating that
the state is **4 RUNNING**.

To stop Intel HAXM, use these commands:

```
sc stop
intelhaxm
```

To start Intel HAXM, use these commands:

```
sc start
intelhaxm
```

Adjusting Intel HAXM Memory Allocation

To change the amount of memory allocated to Intel HAXM, run the installer again.

■ **Note**   Changes to Intel HAXM memory settings will take effect when Intel HAXM is restarted. Currently running emulators will continue to use the previous memory setting.

Intel Virtualization Technology (Intel VT-x) Capability

When installing Intel HAXM, you may encounter an error regarding Intel VT-x support. This error message can be triggered by the following conditions:

- Intel VT-x is not supported by your computer's processor.

- Intel VT-x is not enabled.

Intel VT-x Is Not Supported

Intel HAXM requires an Intel processor with Intel VT-x functionality and cannot be used on systems lacking this hardware feature. To determine the capabilities of your Intel processor, visit http://ark.intel.com/.

Intel VT-x Is Not Enabled

In some cases, Intel VT-x may be disabled in the system BIOS and must be enabled within the BIOS setup utility. To access the BIOS setup utility, you press a certain key during the computer's boot sequence. This key is dependent on which BIOS is used, but it is typically F2, Delete, or the Esc key. Within the BIOS setup utility, Intel VT may be identified by the terms "VT," "Virtualization Technology," or "VT-d." Make sure to enable all of the virtualization features. For specific information on entering BIOS setup and enabling Intel VT, contact your hardware manufacturer.

Tips and Tricks

The following list contains some recommendations to get the best experience out of the Android emulator using the Intel HAXM driver:

- Enable the GPU acceleration in the AVD Manager for your image. The HAXM driver executes most CPU instructions natively through Intel Virtualization Technology in the processor and the GPU acceleration offloads the OpenGL calls to the host GPU. As of SDK release 19, the GPU acceleration is considered "experimental" by Google.

- Launch the emulator from the command line to get more verbose output.

- Use the following command to launch the emulator:

```
emulator-x86 –avd <avd name> -partition-size 1024 –gpu on –verbose
```

- A partition size of 1024 allows 1GB of apps to be installed. This is different from the SDCard size option in the AVD manager, which specifies how much storage for storing media files is allotted inside of the emulator. Setting the GPU to **on** will provide better graphics performance.

- Make sure the **Path** environment variable to the GPU emulation libraries is set in Control Panel ➤ System ➤ Advanced System Settings ➤ Environment Variables. You can also set it manually each time a new command prompt is launched. Setting it manually is recommended if you are using multiple SDK installs. The following **<sdk install location>** typically refers to:

```
"c:\Users\<your username>\android-sdk" set PATH=%PATH%;<sdk install location>\tools\lib
```

- When installing Intel HAXM, set the driver to use half of the available RAM in the system. For example, if your system has 6GB of installed memory, then use 3GB for the Intel HAXM driver. This allows for a good balance of memory for the HAXM driver as compared to the system memory.

- When creating the image, don't set the Device RAM Size option larger than the amount of RAM allocated to the Intel HAXM driver. In the previous example, the Device RAM Size should not be larger than 3GB since only 3GB were allocated to Intel HAXM.

- The maximum memory for the Intel HAXM driver that can be chosen for a 32-bit system is 1.6 GB. For a 64-bit system, the maximum is 8GB.

Sometimes, when booting an image for the first time, it will appear to be hung at the boot screen. The boot process is completed, but the home screen doesn't appear. Click on the Home button on the emulator to show the home screen.

Mac OS

1. Download the installer package from http://www.intel.com/software/android or by using the SDK Manager.

2. Open the DMG fil e, then run the installer contained inside.

3. If an older version Intel HAXM is installed, you will see a notification dialog. Click OK to dismiss the dialog. Then you can either exit the installer, to keep your current version of Intel HAXM, or continue with the installation and upgrade your version of Intel HAXM.

4. You will see a welcome screen, like Figure 11-6.

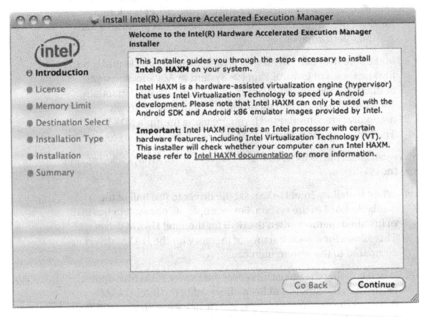

Figure 11-6. *Intel HAXM Welcome Screen on Mac OS*

5. Click Continue.

6. Read the Intel HAXM End-User License Agreement (EULA) and, if you agree, accept the EULA and continue installing Intel HAXM.

7. You will be prompted to adjust the amount of RAM that will be allocated to Intel HAXM, as shown in Figure 11-7.

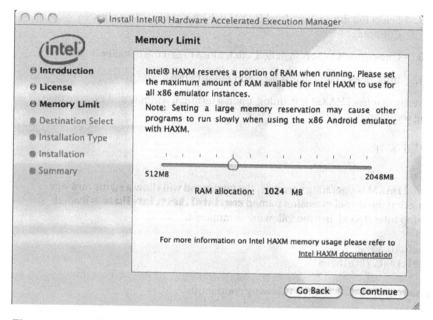

Figure 11-7. Intel HAXM RAM Adjustment Screen on Mac OS

8. Figure 11-8 confirms your Intel HAXM memory allocation settings.

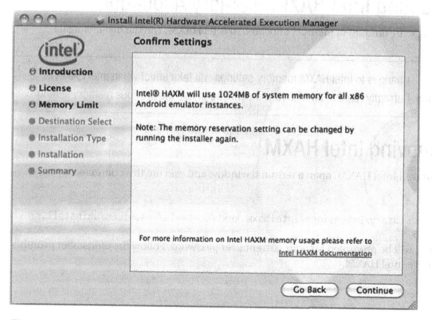

Figure 11-8. Intel HAXM Finish Screen on Mac OS

9. Select the drive where Intel HAXM will be installed, then click Continue.

10. Once Intel HAXM is installed, click Close to exit the installer.

11. Intel H AXM is now installed and ready to use.

To verify that Intel HAXM is running, open a terminal window and execute the following command:

```
kextstat | grep
intel
```

If Intel HAXM is operating correctly, the command will show a status message indicating that the kernel extension named **com.intel.kext.intelhaxm** is loaded.

To stop Intel HAXM, use the following commands:

```
sudo kextunload -b
com.intel.kext.intelhaxm
```

To start Intel HAXM, use the following commands:

```
sudo kextload -b
com.intel.kext.intelhaxm
```

Adjusting Intel HAXM Memory Allocation

To change the amount of memory allocated to Intel HAXM, run the installer again.

■ **Note** Changes to Intel HAXM memory settings will take effect when Intel HAXM is restarted. Currently running emulators will continue to use the previous memory setting.

Removing Intel HAXM

To uninstall Intel HAXM, open a terminal window and execute this command:

```
sudo
/System/Library/Extensions/intelhaxm.kext/Contents/Resources/uninstall.sh
```

You will be prompted for your current user password. Follow the uninstaller prompts to remove Intel HAXM.

■ **Important**   Removing Intel HAXM will disable acceleration of all Intel x86 Android emulators. Existing Android virtual devices will continue to function, but will no longer be accelerated. Installing Intel HAXM again will re-enable Android emulator acceleration.

Troubleshooting

Intel HAXM requires an Android x86 system image provided by Intel. You can download these images through the Android SDK manager or manually from the Intel Developer Zone web site.

Intel Execute Disable (XD) Bit Capability Error

When installing Intel HAXM, you may encounter an error regarding Intel XD support. This error message can be triggered by the following conditions:

- Intel XD is not supported by your computer's processor.
- Intel XD is not enabled.

Intel XD Is Not Supported

Intel HAXM requires an Intel processor with Execute Disable (XD) bit functionality and cannot be used on systems lacking this hardware feature. To determine the capabilities of your Intel processor, visit http://ark.intel.com/.

Intel XD Is Not Enabled

■ **Note**   Apple computers have Intel XD permanently enabled if supported by the processor.

If you receive an error message indicating that Intel XD is not enabled, your computer does not meet the minimum system requirements to use Intel HAXM. To determine the capabilities of your Intel processor, visit http://ark.intel.com/.

Intel Virtualization Technology (VT-x) Capability

When installing Intel HAXM, you may encounter an error regarding Intel VT-x support.

This error message can be triggered by the following conditions:

- Intel VT-x is not supported by your computer's processor.
- Intel VT-x is not enabled.

Intel VT-x Is Not Supported

Intel HAXM requires an Intel processor with Intel VT-x functionality and cannot be used on systems lacking this hardware feature. To determine the capabilities of your Intel processor, visit http://ark.intel.com/.

Intel VT-x Is Not Enabled

■ **Note** Apple computers have Intel VT-x permanently enabled if supported by the processor.

If you receive an error message indicating that Intel VT is not enabled, your computer does not meet the minimum system requirements to use Intel HAXM. To determine the capabilities of your Intel processor, visit http://ark.intel.com/.

Tips and Tricks

The following list contains recommendations to get the best experience out of the Android emulator using the Intel HAXM driver:

- Enable the GPU acceleration in the AVD manager for your image. The Intel HAXM driver executes most CPU instructions natively through the Intel Virtualization Technology in the processor and the GPU acceleration offloads the OpenGL calls to the host GPU.

- Use the following command in the terminal to launch the emulator:

```
./emulator-x86 –avd <avd name> -partition-size 1024 –gpu on
```

- A partition-size of 1024 allows 1GB of apps to be installed. This is different from the SDCard size option in the AVD manager, which specifies how much storage for storing media files is allotted inside of the emulator. Setting the GPU to **on** will provide better graphics performance.

- Make sure that the environment variables for the GL libraries are set correctly. Set the **LD_LIBRARY_PATH** variable by using the following command in the terminal. Modify the command to point to your SDK installation.

```
export LD_LIBRARY_PATH=<sdk install location>/tools/lib
```

- To automatically run this command whenever a new terminal is started, you can add this command to your **~/.bash_profile** script.

- When installing Intel HAXM, set the driver to use half of the available RAM in the system. For example, if your system has 6GB of installed memory, then use 3GB for the Intel HAXM driver. This allows a good balance of memory for the Intel HAXM driver as compared to the system memory.

- When creating the image, don't set the Device RAM Size option larger than the amount of RAM allocated to the Intel HAXM driver. In the previous example, the device RAM size should not be larger than 3GB since only 3GB were allocated to Intel HAXM.

- The maximum memory for the Intel HAXM driver on a 32-bit system is 1.6GB. For a 64-bit system, the maximum is 8GB.

- Sometimes, when booting an image for the first time, it will appear to be hung at the boot screen. The boot process is completed but the home screen doesn't appear. Click on the Home button on the emulator to show the home screen.

Linux

Since Google mainly supports Android builds on the Linux platform, and a lot of Android developers are using AVD on Eclipse hosted by a Linux system, it is critical that Android developers take advantage of Intel hardware-assisted KVM virtualization for Linux just like Intel HAXM for Windows and IOS. To enable KVM on the Ubuntu host platform and to begin using the Intel Android x86 emulator with Intel hardware-assisted virtualization (hypervisor), use the following steps.

KVM Installation

The first step is to install the required KVM by following the instructions from the Ubuntu community page (https://help.ubuntu.com/community/KVM/Installation). To check if your system's processor supports hardware virtualization, use this command:

```
$ egrep -c '(vmx|svm)' /proc/cpuinfo
```

If the output is **0**, it means that your CPU doesn't support hardware virtualization. The next step is to install the CPU checker:

```
$ sudo apt-get install cpu-checker
```

Now you can check if your CPU supports KVM by issuing the following command:

```
$kvm-ok
```

If you see this message:

```
"INFO: Your CPU supports KVM extensions
INFO: /dev/kvm exists
KVM acceleration can be used"
```

It means you can run your virtual machine faster with the KVM extensions. However, if you see this:

```
"INFO: KVM is disabled by your BIOS
HINT: Enter your BIOS setup and enable Virtualization Technology (VT),
and then hard poweroff/poweron your system
KVM acceleration can NOT be used"
```

You need to go to the BIOS setup and enable Intel VT.

Install KVM

For Ubuntu Lucid (10.04) or later, use the following command:

```
$ sudo apt-get install qemu-kvm libvirt-bin ubuntu-vm-builder bridge-utils
```

Next, add your **<username>** account to the **kvm** and **libvirtd** groups:

```
$ sudo adduser your_user_name kvm
$ sudo adduser your_user_name libvirtd
```

After the installation, you need to log in again so that your user account becomes an effective member of the **kvm** and **libvirtd** user groups. The members of these groups can run virtual machines. You can verify that your installation has been successful with the following command:

```
$ sudo virsh -c qemu:///system list
```

Your screen will paint the following if the installation was successful:

```
Id Name                           State
```

Start the AVD from Android SDK Directly from Terminal

Now start the Android for x86 Intel emulator, shown in Figure 11-9, using the following command:

```
$ <SDK directory>/tools/emulator-x86 -avd Your_AVD_Name -qemu -m 2047
-enable-kvm
```

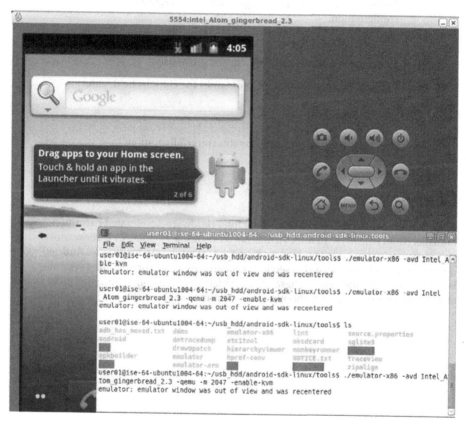

Figure 11-9. *Intel HAXM on Linux*

Only a 64-bit Ubuntu can allow you to run allocated memory of 2GB or more. My 64-bit Ubuntu has 6GB of memory, so I used one third of it for Android AVD. My AVD named **Intel_Atom_gingerbread_2.3.** '**-qemu**' provides the options to **qemu**, and the **-m** specifies the amount of memory for the emulated Android (that is, guest). If you use too small a value for that, it's possible that performance will suffer because of frequent swapping activities. Add **-show-kernel** to see the message from the kernel.

Start the AVD by AVD Manager in Eclipse

The following procedures are recommended by Google. If you are running the emulator
from Eclipse, run your Android application with an x86-based AVD and include the KVM
options:

1. In Eclipse, click your Android project folder and then select Run ➤ Run
   Configurations.

2. In the left panel of the Run Configurations dialog, select your
   Android project to run a configuration or to create a new
   configuration.

3. Click the Target tab.

4. Select the x86-based AVD you created previously.

5. In the Additional Emulator Command-Line Options field, enter:

```
-qemu -m 2047 -enable-kvm
```

6. Run your Android project using this run configuration.

Overview

This chapter covered the installation of the Intel Hardware Accelerated Execution
Manager (Intel HAXM) with Intel Virtualization Technology (Intel VT). These tools
provide you with the fastest and most efficient all-around experience as an Android x86
developer. This chapter included sections specific to each major operating system—
Windows, Mac OS, and Linux. These sections highlighted not only the install process, but
also tips and tricks for troubleshooting some common problems.

CHAPTER 12

∎ ∎ ∎

Performance Testing and Profiling Apps with Platform Tuning

I have not failed. I've just found 10,000 ways that won't work.

— Thomas Edison

In computing, hardware acceleration involves using computer hardware to perform functions faster than would be possible with software running on the general-purpose CPU. Normally, processors are sequential and instructions are executed one-by-one. Various techniques are used to improve processing performance, and hardware acceleration, as discussed in **Chapter 11**, is one of them. The main difference between hardware and software optimization is arguably the level of abstraction. Due to the nature of hardware optimization, they potentially provide much greater speed improvements than software optimizations. Hardware accelerators are designed for computationally intensive software code.

More and more developers use FFmpeg to develop Android video applications and OpenCV to develop image processing software, which all have NDK adaptations. Multimedia applications usually have high-performance requirements, and this chapter describes some common optimization technology on x86 Android.

Start with Your First x86 Full Format Video Player

The built-in codec program on Android is very limited, so developers use the FFmpeg free open source media framework to support full-format decoding. The FFmpeg project includes libraries of audio/video codecs and a command-line program for transcoding multimedia files, and enables cross-platform audio and video streaming using either an LGPL or GPL license according to your choice of components. It provides recording, conversion, and streaming audio and video functions. FFmpeg is the most popular open source framework used for multimedia Android development; it's a good starting point for researching Intel architecture performance software tuning. For more information about the FFmpeg project, visit http://www.ffmpeg.org/.

We'll start by making a new, full-format x86 player. The open source `tewilove_faplayer` is recommended for this project. It's based on the VLC player, but `tewilove_faplayer` includes all needed components, whereas the VLC player must first do a bootstrap to download all components. The VLC player's compiling script is also more complicated than `tewilove_faplayer`. The project URL is `https://github.com/shaobin0604/faplayer`, where project notes can be read and the ZIP file can be downloaded. The `tewilove_faplayer` can be easily used as is on ARM platforms; for x86, there are some necessary modifications:

1. Modify `vlc_fixups.h`. Delete `__cplusplus`, as it will otherwise lead to a compiling problem.

2. Modify `\jni\vlc\config.h`. Add the macro as defined here:

```
#define CAN_COMPILE_MMX   1
#define CAN_COMPILE_MMXEXT 1
#define CAN_COMPILE_SSE 1
#define CAN_COMPILE_SSE2 1
#define asm __asm__
#define MODULE_NAME_IS_i422_yuy2_sse2
#define MODULE_NAME_IS_i420_yuy2_sse2
#define MODULE_NAME_IS_i420_rgb_sse2
```

3. Modify `libvlcjni.h`. Delete `yuv2rgb`; it is ARM NEON code, not x86 code.

4. Modify `Application.mk` as follows:

```
APP_ABI := x86
BUILD_WITH_NEON := 0
OPT_CPPFLAGS += -frtti –fexceptions
```

5. Delete `Android.mk` in `ext\ffmpeg`; you must replace it with the x86 FFmpeg version.

Compile x86 FFmpeg: Cross-Compile

Broadly speaking, open source programs often support cross-compiling. FFmpeg is no exception. Here is a script file that you can use to build FFmpeg on Linux and Android:

```
#!/bin/bash
NDK=$ANDROID_NDK_ROOT  #your ndk root path
PLATFORM=$NDK/platforms/android-14/arch-x86
#PREBUILT=$NDK/toolchains/arm-linux-androideabi-4.4.3/prebuilt/linux-x86
PREBUILT=$NDK/toolchains/x86-4.4.3/prebuilt/linux-x86
function build_one
{
./configure --target-os=linux \
    --prefix=$PREFIX \
```

```
    --enable-cross-compile \
    --extra-libs="-lgcc" \
    --arch=x86 \
    --cc=$PREBUILT/bin/i686-android-linux-gcc \
    --cross-prefix=$PREBUILT/bin/i686-android-linux- \
    --nm=$PREBUILT/bin/i686-android-linux-nm \
    --sysroot=$PLATFORM \
    --extra-cflags=" -O3 -fpic -DANDROID -DHAVE_SYS_UIO_H=1 -Dipv6mr_
interface=ipv6mr_ifindex -fasm -Wno-psabi -fno-short-enums -fno-strict-
aliasing -finline-limit=300 $OPTIMIZE_CFLAGS " \
    --disable-shared --enable-static \
    --extra-ldflags="-Wl,-rpath-link=$PLATFORM/usr/lib -L$PLATFORM/usr/lib
-nostdlib -lc -lm" \
    --disable-ffplay --disable-avfilter --disable-avdevice --disable-ffprobe \
--disable-yasm \
    $ADDITIONAL_CONFIGURE_FLAG

make clean
make -j4 install
}

#x86
CPU=x86
OPTIMIZE_CFLAGS="-march=atom -ffast-math -msse3 -mfpmath=sse"
PREFIX=./android/$CPU
ADDITIONAL_CONFIGURE_FLAG=
build_one
```

After running this script, you can use libavcode.a, libavformat.a, libavutil.a, and libswscale.a; link these libraries to your project as prelink static libraries.

Compile x86 FFmpeg: Android.mk

It's best to cross-compile FFmpeg; it's simple and quick. But if FFmpeg is needed to compile the Android.mk, this can still be done. *Havlenapetr* FFmpeg can be used to build this script.

Havlenapetr is an early Android FFmpeg project and therefore has relatively simple audio and video synchronization features. It is suitable for beginners to learn how to transplant FFmpeg on Android. Its project URL is https://github.com/havlenapetr.

When you have all of the tools downloaded and the preparation completed, it's time to make *faplayer x86*, which is a full format x86 player. You must first play a 1080p MP4 on the device—this will use the Android default player. For software tuning, modify the selectMediaPlayer function in PlayerActivity.java and set useDefault to false. Play the 1080p MP4 again on Android 2.3. As expected, the performance is suboptimal. Luckily, with software tuning, you can improve the performance. (If you cannot display an image on Android 4.0, see the section titled **How to Display an Image Using the Android 4.0 NDK** later in this chapter.)

How to Determine CPU Usage and Find Hotspots

Intel's Graphics Performance Analyzers (GPA) and VTune amplifier are strongly recommended as tuning tools, but if GPU usage is not the target, there are other tuning tool options, such as OProfile (which will require building a system image).

Show CPU Usage Dynamically Onscreen

CPU usage can be inquired by /proc/stat, using the command cat /proc/stat on Linux (and thus Android). The command will produce some strings like these:

```
cpu   4884 440 2841 75755 1681 320 121 0 0 0
cpu0  2211 212 1639 38296  462 223  90 0 0 0
cpu1  2673 228 1202 37459 1219  97  31 0 0 0
```

Here are some CPU usage functions written in Java. You can use them to show CPU usage onscreen:

```
/sys/devices/system/cpu/cpu0/cpufreq/cpuinfo_max_freq
/sys/devices/system/cpu/cpu0/cpufreq/cpuinfo_min_freq
/sys/devices/system/cpu/cpu0/cpufreq/scaling_cur_freq
/proc/stat
    public static long getCurCpuFreq() {
        String result = "N/A";
        try {
            FileReader fr = new FileReader(
                        /sys/devices/system/cpu/cpu0/cpufreq/scaling_cur_
freq");
            BufferedReader br = new BufferedReader(fr);
            String text = br.readLine();
            br.close();
            fr.close();
            result = text.trim();
        } catch (FileNotFoundException e) {
            e.printStackTrace();
        } catch (IOException e) {
            e.printStackTrace();
        }
        return Long.parseLong(result)/1000;
    }
}
```

```java
public static long getCurUsage() {
    try
    {
        BufferedReader reader = new BufferedReader( new
InputStreamReader( new FileInputStream( "/proc/stat" ) ), 1000);
        String load = reader.readLine();
        reader.close();
        String[] toks = load.split(" ");
        long currTotal = Long.parseLong(toks[2]) +
Long.parseLong(toks[3]) + Long.parseLong(toks[4])+Long.parseLong(toks[6])
+Long.parseLong(toks[7])+Long.parseLong(toks[8]);
        long currIdle =
Long.parseLong(toks[5]);

        usage =(long) ((currTotal - total) * 100.0f / (currTotal -
total + currIdle - idle));
        total = currTotal;
        idle = currIdle;
    }
    catch( IOException ex )
    {
        ex.printStackTrace();
    }
    return usage;
}
```

Get Function Running Time

1. Use function clock() (you must include time.h).

2. Use register rdtsc.

```c
static inline uint64_t read_time(void)
{
    uint32_t a, d;
    __asm__ volatile("rdtsc" : "=a" (a), "=d" (d));
    return ((uint64_t)d << 32) + a;
}
```

These two functions return the runtime of a function.

Use Yasm to Get the Best-Performing x86 Library

Yasm is an x86 ASM assembler. In the case of FFmpeg porting, it is generally
recommended that you add the -disable-yasm option, when you're compiling the ARM
version. But if you're compiling an x86 version, disable-yasm will discard a large amount
of optimization code, which will significantly reduce performance.

Yasm is a complete rewrite of the NASM assembler under the "new" BSD license (some portions are under other licenses; see the Yasm site at http://yasm.tortall.net/ for details). Yasm currently supports the x86 and AMD64 instruction sets; accepts NASM and GAS assembler syntax; outputs binary, ELF32, ELF64, 32- and 64-bit Mach-O, RDOFF2, COFF, Win32, and Win64 object formats; and generates source debugging information in STABS, DWARF 2, and CodeView 8 formats.

How to Use Yasm

If Yasm is cross-compiled, it is quite simple. After the Yasm source is downloaded on Linux, and the make is installed, it is as simple as running configure, make, and make install.

```
./configure --enable-shared --prefix=/usr/local
make
make install
```

Then you run delete -disable-yasm and run the build script again. But if you're using Android.mk directly, note that the Google NDK build script does not support .asm. The following link is an improvement of the Google NDK build script. You can visit http://software.intel.com/en-us/articles/using-yasm-compiler-on-android-ndkbuild for more details.

The Result of Using Yasm

For 1080p mp4 software decoding, Figure 12-1 compares three configurations.

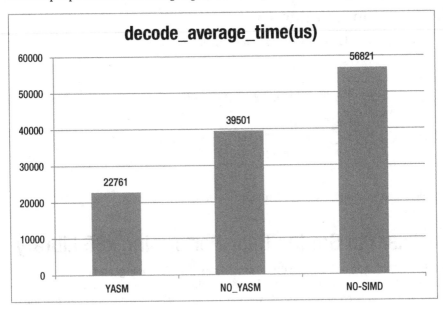

Figure 12-1. *YASM Comparisons, in Nanoseconds*

```
YASM: -enable yasm -enable asm
NO-YASM: -disable yasm -enable asm
NO-SIMD: -disable yasm -disable asm
```

Enabling Yasm can create significant performance improvements. In the previous example, the average time drops by 57.6% just by enabling Yasm. (The average time drops by 150% with both Yasm and ASM enabled; see the next section of this chapter for more information about SIMD and ASM.) Downloading and installing Yasm can be a valuable step for many kinds of open source optimization projects, including those on x264, Vp8, and manifestly x86.

Use SSE (Intel's Streaming SIMD Extensions) to Optimize Color Space Transformation

The *color space* of an image represents the color in a machine-readable format. Just as different people might describe Vincent van Gogh's *Irises* as "purple" or "indigo," a plasma television represents the color in RGB format[1] whereas the print file for a poster of the painting uses the CMYK code.[2] To translate the images between these different color space formats, a color space transformation must occur. Video is generally YUV format; LCD screens are RGB format; and camera output is generally nv21 format. FFmpeg provides the swscale function to perform this transformation. For large image files, color space transformation will consume much more CPU power, as you can see in Table 12-1. Using Intel's Streaming SIMD Extensions (SSE) instruction set can produce a 6-16 time performance improvement.

Table 12-1. *SSE Optimizations*

3040*1824 NV21-RGB888	SWS_BILINEAR	SWS_FAST_BILINEAR
Not Using Yasm	425 ms	158 ms
Using Yasm	179 ms	155 ms
Using SSE NV21-RGB888	27 ms	27 ms

SSE (SIMD technology) is the most important optimization technology on x86 Android (ARM has NEON—which is also a SIMD technology), especially for multimedia apps. This is due to the performance optimization that it provides across the board.

---

[1]The red, green, blue (RGB) code is an additive color model based on the three primary colors of light. The color of the irises is represented as 69, 102, 137.

[2]The subtractive color model known as CMYK represents the four ink colors used in most commercial printing systems: cyan, magenta, yellow, and key or black. The CMYK values for the irises are 50, 26, 0, 46.

What Is SIMD?

Single instruction, multiple data (SIMD) devices have multiple processing elements that perform the same operation on multiple data points simultaneously. Most modern CPU designs include SIMD instructions in order to improve multimedia performance. Intel's Medfield CPUs support MMX, MMX2, SSE, SSE2, SSE3, an SSSE3, but SSE4 and AVX are not supported. SIMD support can also be checked dynamically at runtime (see cpuid on FFmpeg 1.0—function ff_get_cpu_flags_x86 on cpu.c).

There are three ways to implement SIMD code.

- C/C++ language-level intrinsic functions, defined with emmintrin.h. Until now, few open source libraries have used it except for WEBP. If SIMD code is implemented in this way, it's easy to adapt to all hardware platforms. (It becomes interchangeable with NEON code for the ARM platform, for example.)

- Inline assembler (the most widely used). It doesn't require separate assembly and link steps and is more convenient than a separate assembler.

- Separate assembler. It has many styles (NASM, TASM, MASM, and so on), and the file extension .s, .asm. (An assembler with the file extension .asm cannot be compiled normally by the Android NDK; you must use the patch that is provided in the earlier section, "How to Use Yasm.")

How SIMD Works

To add two 8-bit integer arrays, the generic C code looks like this:

```
Int s[16];
for(int i=0;i<16;i++){
    S[i]=data1[i]+data2[i];  //ensure s[i] is 0~255
}
```

But if you use SSE, you just need:

```
movups data1,xmm1
movups data2,xmm2
paddusb xmm1,xmm2
movntq xmm2,S
```

With the one instruction paddusb, you can perform 16 add operations at the same time. This sounds fantastic, but it actually has limitations. All the data must be well organized, and the algorithm can be vectorized. However, this indeed improves performance, especially for multimedia apps.

SIMD has five types of instructions:

- Data movement, such as movd, movq, and movups
- Boolean logic: psllw and psrlw
- Math: paddb and pmulhw
- Comparisons: pcmpeqb
- Data packing: packssdw, punpcklbw, and pshufb

Data packing (see Figures 12-2 and 12-3) is the most difficult part for SIMD. In the following two figures you can see two different operations, their organization and structure, and how they perform the data packing procedure.

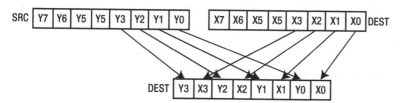

Figure 12-2. Data Packing with Punpcklbw

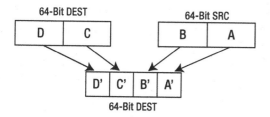

Figure 12-3. Data Packing with Packssdw

Packed shuffle bytes (pshufb) takes registers of bytes R = [R0 R1 R2 ... R15] and M = [M0 M1 M2 ... M15] and replaces R with $[R_{M0} R_{M1} R_{M2} ... R_{M15}]$; except that it replaces the ith entry with 0 if the top bit of M_i is set. This is shown in the following code:

R0	R1	R2	R3	R4	R5	R6	R7	R8	R9	R10	R11	R12	R13	R14	R15
M0	M1	M2	M3	M4	M5	M6	M7	M8	M9	M10	M11	M12	M13	M14	M15

```
R0  := (mask0 & 0x80) ? 0 : SELECT(a, mask0 & 0x07)
R1  := (mask1 & 0x80) ? 0 : SELECT(a, mask1 & 0x07)
...
R15 := (mask15 & 0x80) ? 0 : SELECT(a, mask15 & 0x0f)
```

The pshufb instruction can put any 8-bit data to any place according to a 128-bit mask.

Implement NV21-RGB SSE Code

FFmpeg yuv2rgb is MMX2 code, so you must first modify it to SSE code, because MMX is 8-bit aligned and SSE is 16-bit aligned. You must enlarge the data to 16 bits:

1. Modify swscale_internal.h and yuv2rgb_mmx.c:

```
DECLARE_ALIGNED(8, uint64_t, redDither);
==>
DECLARE_ALIGNED(16, uint64_t, redDither);
DECLARE_ALIGNED(8, uint64_t, redDither1);

DECLARE_ASM_CONST(16, uint64_t, mmx_redmask) = 0xf8f8f8f8f8f8f8f8ULL;
==>
DECLARE_ASM_CONST(8, uint64_t, mmx_redmask1) = 0xf8f8f8f8f8f8f8f8ULL;
DECLARE_ASM_CONST(16, uint64_t, mmx_redmask) = 0xf8f8f8f8f8f8f8f8ULL;
```

Now redDither and mmx_redmask can be used as 8-bit data or 16-bit data.

2. Change the mov and mm instructions:

```
#if HAVE_SSE2
        #define MM1 "%xmm"
        #define MM "%%xmm"
        #define MOVD "movq"
        #define MOVQ "movups"
        #define MOVNTQ "movntps"
        #define SFENCE "sfence"
        #define SIMD8    "16"
#else
#if HAVE_MMX2
        #define MM1 "%mm"
        #define MM "%%mm"
        #define MOVD "movd"
        #define MOVQ "movq"
        #define MOVNTQ "movntq"
        #define SFENCE "sfence"
        #define SIMD8 "8"
#endif
```

MMX uses a mm register while SSE uses an xmm register. Because SSE has 128-bit data length (16 bytes), the data offset is 16 when using SSE (SIMD 8 is 16).

3. RGB_PACK24 must be rewritten due to fact that the data length of MMX and SSE are different.

```
DECLARE_ASM_CONST(16, uint8_t, rmask1[16]) = {0x00,0x80,0x80,0x01,
0x80,0x80,0x02,0x80,0x80,0x03,0x80,0x80,0x04,0x80,0x80,0x05};
...
```

```
MOVQ"      "MM""red",            "MM"5 \n"\
"pshufb    "MANGLE(rmask1)",     "MM"5 \n"\
MOVNTQ"    "MM"5,                (%1) \n"\
```

Here, pshufb is used. The key idea is to use pshufb to put each R, G, B value into the right place and use it to get RGB888 data. The following code shows what each RGB segment is composed of. For example RGB0 is R0, G0, and B0.

R0	R1	R2	R3	R4	R5
G0	G1	G2	G3	G4	
B0	B1	B2	B3	B4	
RGB0	RGB1	RGB2	RGB3	RGB4	
R6	R7	R8	R9	R10	
G5	G6	G7	G8	G9	G10
B5	B6	B7	B8	B9	
RGB5	RGB6	RGB7	RGB8	RGB9	RGB10
R11	R12	R13	R14	R15	
G11	G12	G13	G14	G15	
B10	B11	B12	B13	B14	B15
RGB11	RGB12	RGB13	RGB14	RGB15	

4. Add ff_nv2rgb_init_mmx, and add ff_nv2rgb_get_func_ptr in the function ff_get_unscaled_swscale:

```
/* yuv2bgr */
if ((srcFormat==PIX_FMT_YUV420P || srcFormat==PIX_FMT_YUV422P
|| srcFormat==PIX_FMT_YUVA420P) && isAnyRGB(dstFormat)
    && !(flags & SWS_ACCURATE_RND) && !(dstH&1)) {
    c->swScale= ff_yuv2rgb_get_func_ptr(c);
}
/* nv2bgr */
if (srcFormat==PIX_FMT_NV21 && isAnyRGB(dstFormat)&& !(flags
& SWS_ACCURATE_RND) && !(dstH&1)) {
    c->swScale= ff_nv2rgb_get_func_ptr(c);
}
```

How to Display an Image Using the Android 4.0 NDK

Surface_lock and Surface_unlockAndPost can be used on the NDK layer to display an image on a device. These two functions move from libsurfaceflinger_client.so to libgui.so, and to libui.so on Android 4.0.

Using nm (Windows is nm.exe), you can perform analysis on libui.so. For example, on Windows, you can use nm.exe libui.so >>1.txt, and open 1.txt to find Surface_lock. You can find the string "_ZN7android7Surface4lockEPNS0_11SurfaceInfoEPNS_6RegionE", use it with dlsym, and then get the function handle from libui.so.

```
clz = (*env)->GetObjectClass(env, s);
f_Surface_mSurface = (*env)->GetFieldID(env, clz, "mSurface", "I");
if (f_Surface_mSurface == 0)
{
    jthrowable e = (*env)->ExceptionOccurred(env);
    if (e)
    {
        (*env)->DeleteLocalRef(env, e);
        (*env)->ExceptionClear(env);
    }
    f_Surface_mSurface = (*env)->GetFieldID(env, clz, "mNativeSurface",
"I");
}
(*env)->DeleteLocalRef(env, clz);
surface = (*env)->GetIntField(env, s, f_Surface_mSurface);
```

With this, the code above the jni function can be added; it receives the Java layer surface object and gets the surface handle from the object. The f_Surface_mSurface and Surface_lock and Surface_unlockAndPost functions can be used to show an image on the NDK layer.

The Common Cross-Compile Script

Open source configuration files can generally be used to cross-compile for Android. The following is a common script for the x86 platform. It uses SSE to optimize JPEG encoding and decoding.

```
#!/bin/bash

HOSTCONF=x86
BUILDCONF=i686-pc-linux-gnu
NDK=$ANDROID_NDK_ROOT
```

```
TOOLCHAIN=$NDK/toolchains/x86-4.4.3/prebuilt/linux-x86
PLATFORM=$NDK/platforms/android-14/arch-x86
PREFIX=/home/lym/libjpeg-turbo-1.2.1/android/x86
ELF=$TOOLCHAIN/i686-android-linux/lib/ldscripts/elf_i386.x

export ARCH=x86
export SYSROOT=$PLATFORM
export PATH=$PATH:$TOOLCHAIN/bin:$SYSROOT
export CROSS_COMPILE=i686-android-linux
export CC=${CROSS_COMPILE}-gcc
export CXX=${CROSS_COMPILE}-g++
export AR=${CROSS_COMPILE}-ar
export AS=${CROSS_COMPILE}-as
export LD=${CROSS_COMPILE}-ld
export RANLIB=${CROSS_COMPILE}-ranlib
export NM=${CROSS_COMPILE}-nm
export STRIP=${CROSS_COMPILE}-strip
export CFLAGS="-I$PLATFORM/usr/include -O3 -nostdlib -fpic -DANDROID -fasm
-Wno-psabi -fno-short-enums -fno-strict-aliasing -finline-limit=300 -fomit-
frame-pointer -march=i686 -msse3 -mfpmath=sse"
export CXXFLAGS=$CFLAGS
export LDFLAGS="-Wl,-T,$ELF -Wl,-rpath-link=$PLATFORM/usr/lib -L$PLATFORM/
usr/lib -nostdlib -lc -lm"

./configure --enable-shared --host=$HOSTCONF --build=$BUILDCONF --with-
sysroot=$SYSROOT --prefix=$PREFIX
make clean
make -j4 install
```

Benefitting from the long history of the x86 platform, nearly all open source projects have done optimizations on the x86 platform, especially in the multimedia category. A large number of arithmetic functions have been written to SIMD code (FFmpeg), vp8, x264, and OpenCV). Generally, you need to choose the right source and use the right compiling script. When necessary, debugging the NDK assembly code is possible on Linux.

Testing and Profiling with Hardware Acceleration

With the Android 4.0 NDK, video and audio decoding are based on OpenMAX AL 1.0.1, which permits both software and hardware decoding. OpenMAX (Open Media Acceleration), developed by the Khronos Group, is a royalty-free, cross-platform API. Its set of C-language programming interfaces provides object abstractions for audio, video, and still images. It allows these resources to be easily ported across a wide range of platforms. It's intended for devices that process or consume large amounts of multimedia data, particularly embedded and mobile devices such as smartphones and tablets. OpenMAX has three layers of interfaces, as shown in Figure 12-4—the Application layer (AL), the Integration layer (IL), and the Development layer (DL).

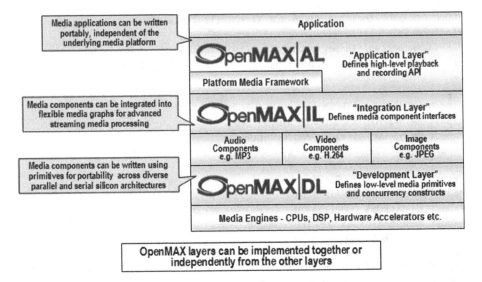

Figure 12-4. *The OpenMAX Layers*

Using the Integration Layer (IL) for Hardware Encoding

Before Android 4.1, Google did not expose any hardware codec interfaces to developers, so a large number of multimedia apps had to use FFmpeg, x264, and VP8 as the video codec. Especially when video encoding, software encoding will use most of the CPU resources (640×480 H.264 encoding will occupy nearly 90% of CPU resources for an ARM v9 1.2-GHz dual-core). This is an enormous drain on the Android device's performance. So up until version 4.1, no wonderful video recording apps had been developed for Android. Developer and user interest was certainly present, but such applications just weren't feasible. Now developers can use the OpenMAX Integration Layer (IL) to get a hardware encoder interface. (To clarify, both ARM and Intel architecture can use this method for hardware encoding, but ARM architectures will meet compatibility issues.) The OpenMAX IL is implemented by various vendors and Google does not guarantee its compatibility, so it's not guaranteed to work well on all Android-enabled hardware systems. But for Android on Intel architecture, specifically, the compatibility issues have been resolved.

How to Get the OMX-IL Interface on Android for Intel Architecture

Libwrs_omxil_core_pvwrapped.so is the OMX-IL interface layer on the Medfield Intel architecture platform. Developers can load this as follows to access the OMX-IL interface.

```
pf_init = dlsym( dll_handle, "OMX_Init" );
pf_deinit = dlsym( dll_handle, "OMX_Deinit" );
pf_get_handle = dlsym( dll_handle, "OMX_GetHandle" );
pf_free_handle = dlsym( dll_handle, "OMX_FreeHandle" );
pf_component_enum = dlsym( dll_handle, "OMX_ComponentNameEnum" );
pf_get_roles_of_component = dlsym( dll_handle, "OMX_GetRolesOfComponent" );
```

After getting these handles, you can call pf_component_enum and pf_get_roles_of_component to get the right hardware encoding interface. All of the video codec interfaces are listed here:

```
component OMX.Intel.VideoDecoder.AVC
  - role: video_decoder.avc
component OMX.Intel.VideoDecoder.H263
  - role: video_decoder.h263
component OMX.Intel.VideoDecoder.WMV
  - role: video_decoder.wmv
component OMX.Intel.VideoDecoder.MPEG4
  - role: video_decoder.mpeg4
component OMX.Intel.VideoDecoder.PAVC
  - role: video_decoder.pavc
component OMX.Intel.VideoDecoder.AVC.secure
  - role: video_decoder.avc
component OMX.Intel.VideoEncoder.AVC
  - role: video_encoder.avc
component OMX.Intel.VideoEncoder.H263
  - role: video_encoder.h263
component OMX.Intel.VideoEncoder.MPEG4
  - role: video_encoder.mpeg4
```

You can choose the right component according to your needs. For example, if you want to do MP4 encoding, you can choose OMX.Intel.VideoEncoder.MPEG4, and call pf_get_handle to get the hardware MP4 encoding handle.

How Does the OMX-IL Work?

In order to create or configure and connect the OpenMAX components, the application is written as an Integration Layer (IL) client. This IL client is used to invoke OpenMAX APIs for different components, as represented in Figure 12-5. In this application, components allocate the video buffers in response to OMX APIs on the IL client. The IL client is responsible for taking the buffers from one component and passing them to other components. The functions OMX_GetParameter and OMX_SetParameter are used as a parameter/configuration set and get. OMX_SendCommand is used to send commands to a component, including an enable/disable port command and a state change command. OMX_EmptyThisBuffer and OMX_FillThisBuffer pass the buffers to components. OmxEventHandler, OmxEmptyBufferDone, and OmxFillBufferDone (OMX_CALLBACKTYPE) must be registered when calling pf_get_handle.

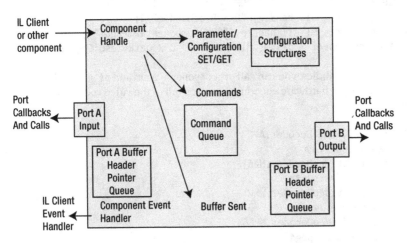

Figure 12-5. *The OpenMAX components and the Integration Layer Client*

After allocating the OMX buffer and calling OMX_SendCommand to set the OMX_StateExecuting state, you can use FillThisBuffer and EmptyThisBuffer and their callback functions to do hardware encoding. Figure 12-6 shows the call sequence.

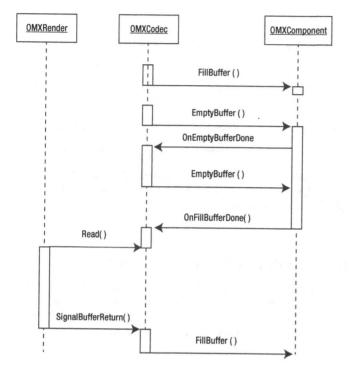

Figure 12-6. *The OMX-IL Rendering Pipeline*

Call FillThisBuffer to fill one raw picture into the OMX local buffer and call EmptyThisBuffer to make the OMX component do the hardware encoding; when you're finished encoding or when the local output buffer is full, the OMX component will call OnEmptyThisBufferDone to tell the client to do EmptyThisBuffer again. So one FillThisBuffer may make several instances of OnEmptyThisBufferDone. If the OMX component finds that the input buffer is empty, it will call OnFillThisBufferDone to tell the client to fill more buffer space.

Demo: Special Effects Video Recorder

In this section, you use a hardware video encoder to implement a special effects video recorder. The idea is to get data from the camera and add a mark to the camera preview image. When recoding, the mark should be recorded into the video file. It sounds like a simple design, but before Android 4.1, the only choice was a software encoder (FFmpeg or x264), which would waste lots of CPU resources. Starting with Android 4.1, a new class MediaCodec has been introduced; it's the same as OMX-IL, but implemented by Google, and Google guarantees its compatibility.

Table 12-2 represents a demonstration of the CPU usage for three video recorders. The recorder file format is .MP4, which uses an MPEG-4 encoder. Generally, VP8 video encoding requires the least CPU usage, followed by MPEG-4 encoding, while H.264 encoding will cost the most CPU resources).

319

Table 12-2. *Hardware vs. Software Encoders*

Video Recorder	Frequency	CPU Usage	Total Resource
1024x576 preview	600 MHz	35%	35% x 600/1600 = 13.125%
Hardware Encoder Without Sound	600 MHz	45%	45% x 600/1600 = 16.875%
Software Encoder Without Sound	1600 MHz	50%	50% x 1600/1600 = 50%

If you're using a hardware encoder, total CPU resources needed are just 3.7% (hardware encoding – preview), whereas a software encoder will need 46.9%. The resolution used in this example is 1024×576. If you want 1080P video recording, the software solution is impossible!

Packaging a Hardware Video Encoder Library

The following code shows a dynamic library named libomx.so. It provides three simple functions—EncInit, EncVideo, and EncRelease. The usage is also simple—you call EncInit to initialize the hardware encoder, call EncVideo to do the hardware encoding, and call EncRelease to release the hardware encoder. The two main structures are stEncConfig and stEncPic:

- stEncConfig (use in EncInit)
-     stcfg.id = ENC_MPEG4;   //choose the encoder
-     stcfg.type = ENC_DEFAULT; //for feature use, now must this value
-     stcfg.w=1080;   //encoding size
-     stcfg.h=1920;
-     stcfg.framerate = 15;   //encoding framerate
-     stcfg.controlrate = enum OMX_VIDEO_CONTROLRATETYPE;
-     stcfg.bitrate = xxxx;   //your bitrate

- stEncPic(use in EncVideo)
-     pic.w=1080;   //picture size
-     pic.h=1920;
-     pic.stride = 1080;   //picture stride
-     pic.pbuf[0]=pmem;   //yuv420 image data
-     pic.pbuf[1]=pmem+1920*1080;
-     pic.pbuf[2]=pmem+1920*1080/4;

Implement Camera Preview

Because you cannot use the common Google Android API to develop this demo, you must implement camera preview. I recommend using setPreviewCallbackWithBuffer to get the camera preview data. Although setPreviewCallbackWithBuffer and setPreviewCallback can both get the preview data, the first is more efficient and will avoid Java garbage collection.

Guideline: Hold enough memory for frequent use. Doing so will avoid dummy Java garbage collection.

In the preview callback, you should pass image data to the NDK layer; do not add unnecessary code. I have added `camera.getParameters().getPreviewSize().width` as an example to show that it costs a significant amount of CPU usage.

Guideline: Call any object function as seldom as possible. Assign its value to a variable and use the variable instead.

In the NDK layer, transform the preview data from NV21 to RGB565 (or RGB88, according to your screen configuration) and then display the data to the screen (use `Surface_lock` and `Surface_unlockAndPost`).

Profiling Java Code with Traceview

You can use Traceview to analyze the performance of Java code. Traceview has been integrated into Eclipse through a new plug-in. The plug-in integrates with the DDMS plug-in so that using the start/stop profiling button will open traces in Eclipse directly instead of launching the standalone tool. Additionally, if you Ctrl-click (Command-click on a Mac) on a method it will open the source file in the editor (you must add `android:debuggable="true"`).

Choose the right package name, which is `com.Filters`, and Press Start Method Profiling, as shown in Figure 12-7. Wait for a while and then stop the profiling: you can see the trace result in Figure 12-8.

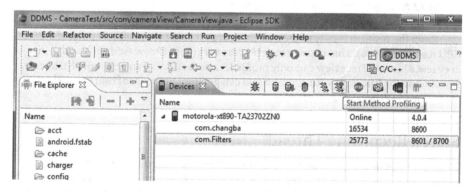

Figure 12-7. *Using Filters in Eclipse*

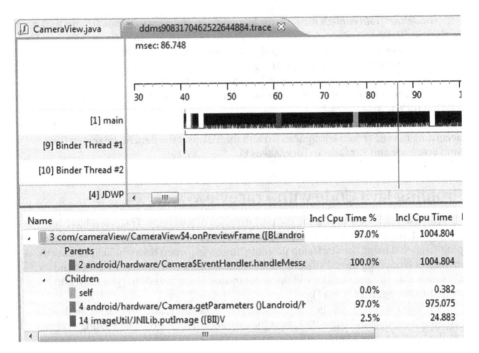

Figure 12-8. *Profiling the Camera Application*

From the result, it is easy to see that `Camera.getParameters` will cost most of the CPU resources (97%). That is `camera.getParameters().getPreviewSize().width` in `PreviewCallback`. Traceview can only profile Java code. If you want to profile NDK code, you can use the Intel tool VTune, which you can get from `http://software.intel.com/en-us/intel-vtune-amplifier-xe`.

Start a Recording Thread

To reference output from `-example.c` in FFmpeg, you can use this as a base version. The remaining work is determining how to get the video and sound data in a recording thread. The general idea is that once you get one frame of video (or audio), you can lock the buffer and invoke a recording thread to start working. However, this is very inefficient. The parallelism of the camera preview thread, the audio thread, and the hardware recording thread has been destroyed, and most of time, the CPU is just waiting. This is where the `CircleBuffer` class comes in; the producer (camera preview thread, audio thread) will cautiously fill the buffer into `CircleBuffer` (if the buffer is full, just overlap the last buffer, so that the data will always refresh even when the recording thread is slow), and the consumer will cautiously get the buffer from it (if the buffer is null, you can choose getting the previous buffer or waiting).

Guideline: Keep the parallelism for all threads as much as possible. `CircleBuffer` *is generally a good choice.*

Adding Special Effects

Now, video raw data has been processed on the NDK layer, so you can easily add special effects such as a video mark. Simply alpha-blend your mark image (Y data, discard UV data) into video raw data. This work can be done by the CPU and also by the GPU. In fact, Google video recording also supports limited (very limited) video effects. It uses the GPU instead of the CPU to decrease CPU load. GPU rendering (OpenGL-ES) is very complicated and hard to understand. Even though the code is simple, developers should have an in-depth understanding of OpenGL. Here I just explain a basic work flow for GPU rendering.

1. Get and initialize the default EGL display.

    ```
    EGLDisplay eglDisplay = eglGetDisplay(EGL_DEFAULT_DISPLAY);
    eglInitialize(mEglDisplay, &majorVersion, &minorVersion);
    ```

2. Create an integer array with one element. It will hold the return value that indicates the number of EGL configurations that matched the attributes specified by the configAttributes array. Create an EGLConfig array with one element to store the first EGL configuration that matches the attributes. Invoke eglChooseConfig() and provide, as arguments, the EGLDisplay object that you initialized in Step 1, the array that specifies the configuration attributes to match, a placeholder for the first matching EGLConfig object, the size of the EGLConfig placeholder, and the num_configs array to store the number of configurations that matched. Store the single configuration from the eglConfigs array in the EGLConfig variable eglConfig.

    ```
    EGLint configAttribs[] = {
        EGL_SURFACE_TYPE, EGL_WINDOW_BIT,
        EGL_RENDERABLE_TYPE, EGL_OPENGL_ES2_BIT,
        EGL_RED_SIZE, 8,
        EGL_GREEN_SIZE, 8,
        EGL_BLUE_SIZE, 8,
        EGL_NONE
    };
    eglChooseConfig(mEglDisplay, configAttribs, &config, 1, &numConfigs);
    ```

3. Invoke eglCreateWindowSurface() to create an EGL surface and provide, as arguments, eglDisplay and eglConfig, which are the instances of EGLDisplay and EGLConfig that you set up in Steps 1 and 2. In the following code sample, eglCreateWindowSurface() is invoked from a class that is derived from the Screen class, and this argument binds the EGLSurface object to the current screen.

```
eglCreateWindowSurface(mEglDisplay, config,mNativeWindow.get(), NULL);
```

4. Invoke `eglCreateContext()` to create an EGL context.

```
eglCreateContext(mEglDisplay, config, EGL_NO_
CONTEXT,contextAttribs);
```

5. Invoke `eglMakeCurrent()` to bind the EGL context to the EGL surface and EGL display.

```
eglMakeCurrent(mEglDisplay, mEglSurface, mEglSurface,
mEglContext);
```

6. Create the programs and load shader into EGL. Your special effect function needs to be implemented as a shader.

```
loadShader(GL_FRAGMENT_SHADER, fSrc[i], &fShader);
createProgram(vShader, fShader, &mProgram[i]);
```

7. Do the rendering.

```
glTexSubImage2D(GL_TEXTURE_2D, 0, 0, 0, mFrameWidth,
mFrameHeight, GL_RGB, GL_UNSIGNED_SHORT_5_6_5, pixels);
glDrawElements(GL_TRIANGLES, 6, GL_UNSIGNED_BYTE, 0);
```

8. If you want to read an image from EGL, you can call `glReadPixels`.

Actually, you can also use `GLSurfaceView`. A `GLSurfaceView` provides the following features:

- Manages a surface, which is a special piece of memory that can be composited into the Android view system.

- Manages an EGL display, which enables OpenGL to render into a surface.

- Accepts a user-provided Renderer object that does the actual rendering.

- Renders on a dedicated thread to decouple rendering performance from the UI thread.

- Supports both on-demand and continuous rendering.

- Optionally wraps, traces, and/or error-checks the renderer's OpenGL calls.

For more information about `GLSurfaceView`, check `http://developer.android.com/reference/android/opengl/GLSurfaceView.html`. You can find a sample of it at `http://www.learnopengles.com/how-to-use-opengl-es-2-in-an-android-live-wallpaper`.

Use OpenMAX AL on Android 4.0

The OpenMAX AL API provides application-level multimedia solutions with portability across an array of platforms by providing a common abstraction for a system's media playback and recording functionality. The API organizes this abstraction around a set of high-level objects. An application acquires all objects from one "engine" object, which encapsulates an OpenMAX AL session and serves as an umbrella for all other objects.

The Advantage of Using Native Multimedia API (OpenMAX AL)

Starting with Android 4.0, Google included the Android native multimedia APIs based on the Khronos group OpenMAX AL 1.0.1 standard, as of Android API level 14 (Android platform version 4.0) and higher. It provides a direct, efficient path for low-level streaming multimedia. The new path is ideal for applications that need to maintain complete control over media data before passing it to the platform for presentation.

For example, media applications can now retrieve data from any source, apply proprietary encryption/decryption, and then send the data to the platform for display. Applications can also now send processed data to the platform as a multiplexed stream of audio/video content in MPEG-2 transport stream format. The platform demuxes, decodes, and renders the content. The audio track is rendered to the active audio device, while the video track is rendered to either a Surface or a SurfaceTexture. When rendering to a SurfaceTexture stream format, the application can apply subsequent graphics effects to each frame using OpenGL.

■ **Note**   Although it's based on OpenMAX AL, the Android native multimedia API is not a conforming implementation of either OpenMAX AL 1.0.1 profile (media player or media player/recorder). This is because Android does not implement all of the features required by either of the profiles. Any known cases where Android behaves differently than the specification are described in the section "Android Extensions" that follows. The Android OpenMAX AL implementation has limited features and is intended primarily for certain performance-sensitive native streaming multimedia applications, such as video players. Table 12-3 indicates objects and interfaces supported by Android's OpenMAX AL implementation. A shaded cell means the feature is supported.

Table 12-3. Objects and Interfaces Supported by Android's OpenMAX AL Implementation

Objects and Interfaces	Engine	Media Player	Output Mix
Dynamic interface management			
Engine			
Object			
Play			
Prefetch status			
Stream information			
Video decoder capabilities			
Volume			
Native display data locator		Video sink	
Output mix data locator		Audio sink	
MIME data format		source	

Demo: Streaming Media Player

Google has provided a sample for a streaming media player. You can check the sample in samples\native-media\jni \native-media-jni.c in your android-sdk folder. The function Java_com_example_nativemedia_NativeMedia_createStreamingMediaPlayer will create a native streaming media player.

The usage is very simple, but you should note two points:

- The video source must be a NativeWindow. You can call ANativeWindow_fromSurface to get the native window from Surface, which passes from the Java layer. And the Surface must be a GLSurfaceView to ensure hardware rendering.

- Register XA_ANDROIDBUFFERQUEUEEVENT_PROCESSED callback for filling the streaming buffer. The demo is reading the buffer from a file, but you can also read the buffer from the Internet, so that you can implement a P2P streaming media player.

Use a Powerful Media API: MediaCodec on Android 4.1

Android has a great media library that allows all sorts of powerful actions. Until recently, there was no way to encode and decode audio/video, which gives developers the ability to do almost anything. Fortunately, the Jelly Bean release introduced the android. media.MediaCodec API. It is designed following the same principles and architecture of OpenMAX (a well-known standard in the media industry), transitioning from a pure high-level media player to the encoder/decoder level.

Sample Code: Audio Decoder

This sample code shows how to implement a decoder. It uses two classes—MediaCodec and MediaExtractor. MediaExtractor facilitates extraction of demuxed, typically encoded, media data from a data source. MediaCodec, of course, is used as a low-level codec.

First you should use MediaExtractor to get the media format:

```
MediaExtractor extractor = new MediaExtractor();
extractor.setDataSource(sampleFD.getFileDescriptor(),sampleFD.
getStartOffset(), sampleFD.getLength());
MediaFormat format = extractor.getTrackFormat(0);
```

Secondly, you can create MediaCodec and configure it.

```
MediaCodec codec;
ByteBuffer[] codecInputBuffers;
ByteBuffer[] codecOutputBuffers;

MediaCodec codec = MediaCodec.createByCodecName(name);
codec.configure(format, null,null,0);  //no display, so surface is null
codec.start();
```

Finally, you do the decoding. Like OMX-IL, it has two ports. You should call dequeueInputBuffer to send the decoding buffer to MediaCodec, and call dequeueOutputBuffer to receive the outside buffer.

```
int inputBufIndex = codec.dequeueInputBuffer(TIMEOUT_US);
if (inputBufIndex >= 0) {
    ByteBuffer dstBuf = codecInputBuffers[inputBufIndex];
    int sampleSize = extractor.readSampleData(dstBuf, 0);
    long presentationTimeUs = 0;
    if (sampleSize < 0) {
        sawInputEOS = true;  sampleSize = 0;
    } else {
        presentationTimeUs = extractor.getSampleTime();
    }
    codec.queueInputBuffer(inputBufIndex, 0, sampleSize,
                presentationTimeUs,
                sawInputEOS ? MediaCodec.BUFFER_FLAG_END_OF_STREAM : 0);
    if(!sawInputEOS){
        extractor.advance();
    }
}
final int res = codec.dequeueOutputBuffer(info, TIMEOUT_US);
if(res >= 0){
        int outputBufIndex = res;
        ByteBuffer buf = codecOutputBuffers[outputBufIndex];
```

```
        final byte[] chunk = new byte[info.size];
        buf.get(chunk);
        buf.clear();
        if(chunk.length > 0){
                audioTrack.write(chunk,0,chunk.length);
        }
        codec.releaseOutputBuffer(outputBufIndex, false);
        if((info.flags && MediaCodec.BUFFER_FLAG_END_OF_STREAM) != 0){
                sawOutputEOS = true;
        }
} else if(res == MediaCodec.INFO_OUTPUT_BUFFERS_CHANGED){
        codecOutputBuffers = codec.getOutputBuffers();

} else if(res == MediaCodec.INFO_OUTPUT_FORMAT_CHANGED){
        final MediaFormat offormat = codec.getOutputFormat();

mAudioTrack.setPlaybackRate(oformat.getInteger(MediaFormat.KEY_SAMPLE_
RATE));
}
```

Use MediaCodec in NDK

MediaCodec is a Java layer class, but you must do the decoding (or encoding) in C code, which is in the NDK layer. Therefore, it is important to call the Java class in the NDK. This can be done by using the jni function FindClass.

Sample code for FindClass is shown here:

```
jclass audio_record_class = jni_env->FindClass("android/media/AudioRecord");
int size = jni_env->CallStaticIntMethod(audio_record_class
,jni_env->GetStaticMethodID(audio_record_class,"getMinBufferSize", "(III)I")
                ,prefered_rate
                ,2/*CHANNEL_CONFIGURATION_MONO*/
                ,2/*  ENCODING_PCM_16BIT */);
```

Configuring MediaCodec with a surface will provide the best performance, as it can use hardware rendering. You can reference native media (for example, OpenMAX AL) to add the surface (or GLSurfaceView). If you're using a normal surface, you can use a textview for subtitles, and an imageview for the play bar. If you're using GLSurfaceView, you can extend this class and implement your own renderer.

Overview

There are currently only two hardware acceleration technologies that can be used on the Android app layer: OpenGL and OpenMAX. OpenGL includes GLSurfaceView and OpenGL-ES 1.0 and 2.0 in the NDK, and it is generally used as a renderer or for multimedia effects processing. OpenMAX includes OpenMAX AL in NDK, MediaCodec, and OMX-IL (which is not Google code, but must be implemented by the author). Each technology has a usage scenario and applicable Android version. Up until now, the popular Android versions were 2.3 and 4.0, so this chapter has only covered the versions from Android 2.3 through Android 4.1. Table 12-4 indicates which hardware accelerators can be used with which version of Android.

Table 12-4. *Hardware Accelerators Compatibility with Android Versions*

	OMX-IL	OMX-AL	MediaCodec
2.3 audio			
2.3 video decode			
2.3 video encode	Codec (Intel architecture only)		
4.0 audio		Player (NDK only)	
4.0 video decode		Player (NDK only)	
4.0 video encode	Codec (Intel architecture only)		
4.1 audio			Codec
4.1 video decode			Codec
4.1 video encode	Codec (Intel architecture only)		Codec

OpenGL is complex but the usage scenario is relatively fixed (video effect and image processing), so the table lists only the usage of OpenMAX.

The Android 4.1 MediaCodec is an important update for multimedia apps. It gives apps the ability to process images before encoding or after decoding. Using Android on Intel architecture grants this ability even before Android 4.1, and after 4.1, hardware acceleration can still give better and better effects.

APPENDIX A

References

Chapter 1: History and Evolution of the Android OS

Origins

http://www.webcitation.org/5wk7sIvVb
http://en.wikipedia.org/wiki/Andy_Rubin

First Android Distribution in 2007

http://www.openhandsetalliance.com/press_110507.html
http://www.cbsnews.com/2100-500395_162-6209772.html
http://oxrep.oxfordjournals.org/content/17/2/248.short
http://www.google.com/intl/en/policies/terms/

What is Android?

http://en.wikipedia.org/wiki/Android_(operating_system)#cite_note-AndroidInc-6
http://books.google.com/books?hl=en&lr=&id=hOlltXyJ8aIC&oi=fnd&pg=PT7&dq=linux&ots=gN3lF-b7OW&sig=ticDFAxOzLF3ocyAyAZUtk8oink#v=onepage&q=linux&f=false
http://developer.android.com/guide/basics/what-is-android.html
http://kebomix.wordpress.com/2010/08/17/android-system-architecture/
http://os.ibds.kit.edu/downloads/sa_2010_braehler-stefan_android-architecture.pdf
http://www.scandevconf.se/db/Marakana-Android-Internals.pdf
http://en.wikipedia.org/wiki/WebKit
http://developer.android.com/about/versions/index.html

The Open Handset Alliance (OHA)

http://en.wikipedia.org/wiki/Open_Handset_Alliance
http://www.openhandsetalliance.com/oha_faq.html
http://www.openhandsetalliance.com/oha_overview.html
http://www.openhandsetalliance.com/oha_members.html
http://www.acronyms.net/terms/o/Open-Handset-Alliance/index.pdf

The Android Open Source Project (AOSP)

http://www.springerlink.com/content/m0136q318k2p4361/
http://source.android.com/about/index.html
http://source.android.com/about/philosophy.html
http://developer.android.com/about/dashboards/index.html

Android Versions

http://en.wikipedia.org/wiki/Astro_(operating_system)#Android_1.0
http://news.cnet.com/8301-30686_3-10385806-266.html
http://reviews.cnet.com/8301-19736_7-20016542-251/a-brief-history-of-android-phones/
http://developer.android.com/about/dashboards/index.html

Chapter 2: The Mobile Device and Operating System Landscape

Competition in Mobile Space

http://www.mobiledevicemanager.com/mobile-device-statistics/250-million-android-devices-in-use/
http://www.engadget.com/2012/07/02/comscore-may-2012-smartphone/

iOS

http://en.wikipedia.org/wiki/IOS
http://downloadsquad.switched.com/2010/08/12/camera-out-of-app-store-after-revealing-volume-button-snap-tric
http://www.iphonehacks.com/2010/12/quick-snap-camera-plus-app-pulled-from-app-store-for-using-volume-buttons-to-activate-camera-shutter.html
http://en.wikipedia.org/wiki/IPod_Touch
http://en.wikipedia.org/wiki/IPhone
http://en.wikipedia.org/wiki/IPad

Meego

    http://en.wikipedia.org/wiki/MeeGo
    http://en.wikipedia.org/wiki/Tizen

BlackBerry

    http://en.wikipedia.org/wiki/BlackBerry

Windows Phone

    http://en.wikipedia.org/wiki/Windows_Phone
    http://en.wikipedia.org/wiki/Windows_Mobile

Symbian

    http://en.wikipedia.org/wiki/Symbian

Before Android

    http://www.hongkiat.com/blog/evolution-of-mobile-phones/
    http://en.wikipedia.org/wiki/Smartphone
    http://en.wikipedia.org/wiki/IBM_Simon
    http://en.wikipedia.org/wiki/Nokia_9000
    http://en.wikipedia.org/wiki/Kyocera_6035
    http://www.bitrebels.com/technology/the-evolution-of-smartphones-infographic/
    http://researchinmotion.wikia.com/wiki/BlackBerry_5810

The Mobile Market

    http://www.eweek.com/c/a/Mobile-and-Wireless/10-Smartphones-That-Failed-to-Inspire-Buyers-In-2010-696525/
    http://blog.pricesbolo.com/index.php/tag/10-smartphones-that-failed-in-2010/
    http://timesofindia.indiatimes.com/tech/itslideshow/7010501.cms
    http://timesofindia.indiatimes.com/tech/itslideshow/7010503.cms
    http://timesofindia.indiatimes.com/tech/itslideshow/6519089.cms
    http://en.wikipedia.org/wiki/List_of_best-selling_mobile_phones#2010

Motorola i1

http://www.intomobile.com/2010/08/02/review-boost-mobile-motorola-i1-does-prepaid-android-work-well/

http://en.wikipedia.org/wiki/Motorola_i1

http://reviews.cnet.com/smartphones/motorola-i1-boost-mobile/4505-6452_7-34117412-2.html

http://www.slashgear.com/motorola-i1-set-to-crash-onto-sprint-on-july-25th-1994629/

http://www.engadget.com/2010/01/20/motorola-launching-20-30-android-phones-in-2010/

Droid X

http://sparxoo.com/2010/06/21/motorola-droid-x-heats-up-competition-with-apple/

http://en.wikipedia.org/wiki/Droid_X

http://www.pcworld.com/article/201259/Droid_X_Sells_Out_Despite_Verizon_Preparation.html

http://www.androidcentral.com/verizon-stores-selling-out-droid-xs

BlackBerry Torch

http://dvice.com/archives/2011/01/why-the-blackbe.php

http://gizmodo.com/5614843/the-blackberry-torchs-biggest-failure-rims-ridiculous-expectations

http://www.ixibo.com/balckberry-torch-a-failure-against-iphone-and-android/

http://www.zdnet.com/blog/btl/blackberry-torch-best-blackberry-ever-fails-to-generate-buzz/37573

http://business.financialpost.com/2010/08/17/rim-slides-on-sluggish-blackberry-torch-sales/

http://www.thestar.com/business/companies/rim/article/862297--torch-ignites-research-in-motion

iPhone

http://www.slideshare.net/bkiprin/apples-iphone-launch-marketing-strategy-analysis-2858373

http://www.scribd.com/doc/21275028/Apple-iPhone-Marketing-Plan

http://ezinearticles.com/?iPhone-Marketing-Strategy&id=4718557

http://en.wikipedia.org/wiki/IPhone

http://www.techiewww.com/marketing/apple-iphone-marketing-strategy

The Mobile Market: Trends

http://socialmediatoday.com/gonzogonzo/495583/great-trends-mobile-infographic
http://smallbiztrends.com/2012/05/mobile-trend-key-things.html
http://mashable.com/2012/04/30/mobile-trends-brands-marketing/
http://mashable.com/2012/08/22/mobile-trends-ecommerce/
http://www.clickz.com/clickz/column/2168103/mobile-trends-watch
http://memeburn.com/2011/12/five-mobile-trends-to-look-out-for-in-2012/

Location

http://blogs.jpost.com/content/2012-mobile-trends-commerce-product-ecosystems-location-integration
https://discussions.apple.com/thread/3374979?start=0&tstart=0
http://www.itbusinessedge.com/slideshows/show.aspx?c=87261&slide=2

Average Use

http://thenextweb.com/us/2010/05/04/twitter-facebook-soar-myspace-sags-market-share/

Commerce

http://mashable.com/2012/08/22/mobile-trends-ecommerce/
http://www.itbusinessedge.com/slideshows/show.aspx?c=87261&slide=5
http://www.oracle.com/us/products/applications/web-commerce/ecommerce-trends-2012-1504949.pdf
http://www.fortune3.com/blog/2012/01/us-m-commerce-sales-2010-2015-statistics/

Chapter 3: Beyond the Mobile App—A Technology Foundation

Connected Devices

http://www.intel.com/p/en_US/embedded/innovation/connectivity/johnson-article-connectivity
http://www.intel.com/content/www/us/en/home-users/get-more-from-your-devices-with-connecting-apps-from-intel.html
http://newsroom.intel.com/community/intel_newsroom/blog/2012/03/06/new-intel-server-technology-powering-the-cloud-to-handle-15-billion-connected-devices
http://venturebeat.com/2011/10/17/intel-execs-predicts-15b-devices-will-be-connected-to-the-internet/

Home Computing

http://www.apartmenttherapy.com/how-many-americans-have-multip-143096

Automotive

http://www.wired.com/autopia/2012/06/gps-devices-are-dead/
http://lifehacker.com/5626711/the-best-android-apps-for-your-car

Special Requirements
Ruggedized

http://en.wikipedia.org/wiki/Rugged_computer
http://en.wikipedia.org/wiki/IP_Code

Medical

http://medicalconnectivity.com/2011/04/03/emr-integration-for-medical-devices-the-basics/
http://en.wikipedia.org/wiki/Electronic_medical_record

Secure Communications

http://en.wikipedia.org/wiki/Type_1_product
http://en.wikipedia.org/wiki/Federal_Information_Processing_Standard

The Cyber-Fiber of our Connected World
Cellular Networks

http://en.wikipedia.org/wiki/Cellular_network
http://en.wikipedia.org/wiki/GSM
http://en.wikipedia.org/wiki/Code_division_multiple_access
http://en.wikipedia.org/wiki/Multimedia_Messaging_Service
http://en.wikipedia.org/wiki/Short_Message_Service

Open Mobile Alliance

http://en.wikipedia.org/wiki/Open_Mobile_Alliance

Wireless

http://en.wikipedia.org/wiki/Wi-Fi
http://en.wikipedia.org/wiki/Bluetooth#Pairing_and_bonding

Mobile Interfaces
Touch Screens

http://www.knowyourmobile.com/features/392511/touchscreen_lowdown_
capacitive_vs_resistive.html
http://www.goodgearguide.com.au/article/355922/capacitive_vs_resistive_
touchscreens/
http://www.knowyourcell.com/features/687370/touchscreen_lowdown_
capacitive_vs_resistive.html
http://en.wikipedia.org/wiki/Touchscreen

Resistive

http://en.wikipedia.org/wiki/Resistive_touchscreen

Vibration Sensors (Haptics)

http://en.wikipedia.org/wiki/Haptic_technology
http://en.wikipedia.org/wiki/Vibrating_alert

Accelerometer

http://en.wikipedia.org/wiki/Accelerometer

Tilt Sensor

http://en.wikipedia.org/wiki/Tilt_sensor

Hardware Buttons

Chapter 4: Android Development—Business Overview and Considerations
Market Share

http://techcrunch.com/2012/11/02/idc-android-market-share-reached-
75-worldwide-in-q3-2012/
http://www.businessinsider.com/android-market-share-2012-11

http://www.huffingtonpost.com/2012/09/18/android-market-share-q3-2012_n_1893292.html

http://www.huffingtonpost.com/2012/11/02/android-market-share_n_2066986.html

http://www.t-gaap.com/2012/5/24/can-google-make-money-with-android?site_locale=en

http://www.wired.com/business/2012/10/profit-or-no-profit/?pid=707

http://venturebeat.com/2012/11/01/as-android-grabs-75-market-share-can-anyone-tell-me-why-this-is-not-mac-vs-pc-all-over-again/

http://film.wapka.mobi/site_342.xhtml

http://en.wikipedia.org/wiki/International_Data_Corporation

http://androidandme.com/2012/04/opinions/the-future-of-android-in-2012/

http://www.tapscape.com/smartphone-war-android-market-share-hits-75-share/

http://openceo.blogspot.com/2012/11/android-75-market-share-future-is-open.html

http://www.forbes.com/sites/darcytravlos/2012/08/22/five-reasons-why-google-android-versus-apple-ios-market-share-numbers-dont-matter/

http://techpinions.com/android-v-ios-part-6-the-future/9687

http://www.wired.com/business/2012/10/google-ad-prices/

http://www.splatf.com/2011/10/google-revenue/

http://hellboundbloggers.com/2012/04/28/why-android-is-popular/

http://www.nascentstuff.com/why-android-os-is-getting-so-popular/

http://forum.xda-developers.com/showthread.php?t=865371

http://artinandroid.blogspot.com/2011/11/why-android-is-so-successful.html

http://techcrunch.com/2012/05/15/3997-models-android-fragmentation-as-seen-by-the-developers-of-opensignalmaps/

https://play.google.com/store/apps

http://authors.library.caltech.edu/11284/1/MCAaer04.pdf

http://nick.typepad.com/blog/2012/01/androids-legacy-nonsense.html

http://www.phonearena.com/news/The-Update-Battle-Innovation-vs-legacy-support_id23282

Security

http://www.cs.rice.edu/~sc40/pubs/enck-sec11.pdf

Licensing

http://pandodaily.com/2012/01/28/how-google-can-save-android-close-it-license-it-swim-in-the-profits/

http://www.unwiredview.com/2011/07/13/the-real-cost-of-android-potentially-60-per-device-in-patent-fees/

http://www.quora.com/Mobile-Software-Development/What-is-the-licensing-royalty-cost-of-Android-OS

http://www.techrepublic.com/blog/app-builder/app-store-fees-percentages-and-payouts-what-developers-need-to-know/1205

http://developer.android.com/distribute/googleplay/publish/register.html

Chapter 5: The Intel Mobile Processor
Clash of the Mobile Titans: ARM versus Intel

http://beta.fool.com/iamgreatness/2012/07/25/mobile-vs-desktop-intel-ready-crush-arm/7757/

http://seekingalpha.com/article/874181-arm-s-david-vs-intel-s-goliath-outcome-uncertain

http://techland.time.com/2012/07/16/arm-vs-intel-how-the-processor-wars-will-benefit-consumers-most/

http://en.wikipedia.org/wiki/Acorn_Computers

http://www.ot1.com/arm/armchap1.html

http://www.techulator.com/resources/7489-The-All-time-Processor-War-ARM-Intel.aspx

http://en.wikipedia.org/wiki/ARM_architecture

http://media.corporate-ir.net/media_files/irol/19/197211/reports/ar06.pdf

"ARM Holdings PLC Reports Results For The Second Quarter And Half Year Ended 30 June 201." http://www.arm.com/about/newsroom/arm-holdings-plc-reports-results-for-the-second-quarter-and-half-year-ended-30-june-2013.php

http://it.bentley.edu/dommara_prud/arm/index.html

http://www.zdnet.com/amd-arms-power-advantages-could-wane-in-the-coming-years-7000006597/

Intel

http://www.intel.com/content/www/us/en/history/historic-timeline.html

http://en.wikipedia.org/wiki/Semiconductor_sales_leaders_by_year#Ranking_for_year_2011

http://www.intel.com/support/motherboards/desktop/sb/CS-033869.htm

http://en.wikipedia.org/wiki/Handheld_game_console

http://www.extremetech.com/wp-content/uploads/2011/11/Chart_USportableGameRevenue_MarketShare_2009-2011-resized-600.png

http://appleinsider.com/articles/10/03/22/iphone_ipod_touch_carve_19_gaming_share_from_sony_nintendo

Android Atom Platforms

http://www.pcworld.com/article/259737/intel_porting_android_41_to_work_on_atom_tablets_smartphones.html

http://www.phonearena.com/news/Android-Intel-Atom-powered-Phones-Hands-on-Reviews-Lenovo-K800-Orange-Santa-Clara-Lava-Xolo-X900_id27528

http://www.tomshardware.com/news/intel-tablet-medfield-soc-cpu,14389.html

Chapter 6: Installing the Android SDK for Intel Application Development

Installation and Setup

Java Development Kit

```
http://www.oracle.com/technetwork/java/javase/downloads/index.html
```

Eclipse

```
http://www.eclipse.org/downloads/
```

Apache Ant

```
http://ant.apache.org/
```

Software Development Kit

```
http://developer.android.com/sdk/index.html
```

Emulation

```
http://developer.android.com/guide/developing/devices/index.html
http://developer.android.com/tools/devices/emulator.html
```

Ice Cream Sandwich Emulation

```
http://software.intel.com/en-us/articles/android-43-jelly-bean-x86-
emulator-system-image
http://www.computerworld.com/s/article/9230152/Android_4.0_The_ultimate_
guide_plus_cheat_sheet_
http://source.android.com/source/initializing.html
```

Gingerbread Emulation

```
http://blogs.computerworld.com/17479/android_gingerbread_faq
```

KVM

```
https://help.ubuntu.com/community/KVM/Installation
https://help.ubuntu.com/community/KVM
http://android-er.blogspot.com/2010/09/how-to-set-battery-status-of-
android.html
```

Intel Tools

http://www.intel.com/software/android
http://int-software.intel.com/en-us/android
http://software.intel.com/en-us/articles/android-virtual-device-emulation-for-intel-architecture

Chapter 7: Creating and Porting NDK-Based Android Applications

http://www.cygwin.com/
http://developer.android.com/sdk/ndk/index.html
http://www.eclipse.org/cdt/downloads.php
http://download.eclipse.org/tools/cdt/releases/galileo/

Chapter 8: Debugging Android

http://www.intel.com/software/android
http://developer.android.com/sdk/installing.html
http://developer.android.com/guide/developing/device.html
http://developer.android.com/tools/extras/oem-usb.html
http://developer.android.com/tools/device.html#VendorIds.
http://developer.android.com/guide/developing/tools/adb.html
http://developer.android.com/sdk/eclipse-adt.html#installing
http://source.android.com/source/downloading.html
http://www.windriver.com/products/JTAG-debugging/
http://www.lauterbach.com
http://software.intel.com/en-us/articles/embedded-using-intel-tools
http://developer.android.com/guide/developing/device.html
http://www.eclipse.org/downloads/
http://developer.android.com/sdk/index.html

Johnson, Randy and Stewart Christie. "JTAG 101: IEEE 1149.x and Software Debug." http://www.intel.com/content/www/us/en/intelligent-systems/jtag-101-ieee-1149x-paper.html

Chapter 9: Performance Optimizations for Android Applications on x86

http://intel.com/software/gpa
http://software.intel.com/en-us/vcsource/tools/intel-gpa

Chapter 10: x86 NDK and C/C++ Optimizations

http://software.intel.com/en-us/articles/intel-integrated-performance-primitives-intel-ipp-intel-ipp-sample-code

http://www.princeton.edu/~achaney/tmve/wiki100k/docs/Locality_of_reference.html

Chapter 11: Using Intel Hardware Accelerated Execution Manager on Windows, Mac OS, and Linux to Speed Up Android on x86 Emulation

"Installation Instructions for Intel® Hardware Accelerated Execution Manager - Microsoft Windows." http://software.intel.com/en-us/articles/installation-instructions-for-intel-hardware-accelerated-execution-manager-windows

"Installation Instructions for Intel® Hardware Accelerated Execution Manager - Mac OS X." http://software.intel.com/en-us/articles/installation-instructions-for-intel-hardware-accelerated-execution-manager-macosx

"How to Start Intel Hardware-assisted Virtualization (hypervisor) on Linux to Speed-up Intel Android x86 Gingerbread Emulator." http://software.intel.com/en-us/blogs/2012/03/12/how-to-start-intel-hardware-assisted-virtualization-hypervisor-on-linux-to-speed-up-intel-android-x86-gingerbread-emulator

Chapter 12: Performance Testing and Profiling Apps with Platform Tuning

http://elinux.org/images/e/e0/The_OpenMAX_Integration_Layer_standard.pdf

http://www.ffmpeg.org/.

https://github.com/shaobin0604/faplayer

https://github.com/havlenapetr

http://yasm.tortall.net/

http://software.intel.com/en-us/articles/using-yasm-compiler-on-android-ndkbuild

http://software.intel.com/en-us/intel-vtune-amplifier-xe

http://developer.android.com/reference/android/opengl/GLSurfaceView.html

http://www.learnopengles.com/how-to-use-opengl-es-2-in-an-android-live-wallpaper

Index

■ **D**

■ R

■ S

T

U

V

W

X

Get the eBook for only $10!

Now you can take the weightless companion with you anywhere, anytime. Your purchase of this book entitles you to 3 electronic versions for only $10.

This Apress title will prove so indispensible that you'll want to carry it with you everywhere, which is why we are offering the eBook in 3 formats for only $10 if you have already purchased the print book.

Convenient and fully searchable, the PDF version enables you to easily find and copy code—or perform examples by quickly toggling between instructions and   applications. The MOBI format is ideal for your Kindle, while the ePUB can be utilized on a variety of mobile devices.

Go to www.apress.com/promo/tendollars to purchase your companion eBook.

All Apress eBooks are subject to copyright. All rights are reserved by the Publisher, whether the whole or part of the material is concerned, specifically the rights of translation, reprinting, reuse of illustrations, recitation, broadcasting, reproduction on microfilms or in any other physical way, and transmission or information storage and retrieval, electronic adaptation, computer software, or by similar or dissimilar methodology now known or hereafter developed. Exempted from this legal reservation are brief excerpts in connection with reviews or scholarly analysis or material supplied specifically for the purpose of being entered and executed on a computer system, for exclusive use by the purchaser of the work. Duplication of this publication or parts thereof is permitted only under the provisions of the Copyright Law of the Publisher's location, in its current version, and permission for use must always be obtained from Springer. Permissions for use may be obtained through RightsLink at the Copyright Clearance Center. Violations are liable to prosecution under the respective Copyright Law.